THE *Wisdom* of *Solomon*

by
Barbara Condron

Infinite Possibilities in Finite Experiences
Book IV *Infinite Being*

SOM Publishing
Windyville, Missouri 65783 U.S.A.

By the same author

Spiritual Renaissance:

Elevating Your Consciousness for the Common Good

First Opinion: Wholistic Health Care in the 21st Century

The Work of the Soul

The Dreamer's Dictionary

The Bible Interpreted in Dream Symbols

Uncommon Knowledge

Kundalini Rising

Remembering Atlantis: History of the World Vol. 1

How to Raise an Indigo Child

Peacemaking: 9 Lessons for Changing Yourself,

Your Relationships, and Your World

Every Dream is about the Dreamer

Front Cover angel from a painting by Carrie Collins. Design by Barbara Condron. Back cover art by Capucine Chapman

ISBN: 0-944386-33-4

Library of Congress Control Number 2004095295

PRINTED IN THE UNITED STATES OF AMERICA

If you desire to learn more about the research and teachings in this book, write to School of Metaphysics World Headquarters, Windyville, Missouri 65783.
Or call us at 417-345-8411.
Visit us on the Internet at www.som.org
or www.dreamschool.org

"That night the Lord appeared to Solomon in a vision and said to him, Ask what I shall give you.

And Solomon said to the Lord, Thou hast shown great mercy to David my father, and has made me to reign in his stead. Now, O Lord my God, let thy promise to David my father be established; for thou hast made me king over this people, like the dust of the earth in multitude. So give thy servant a hearing heart, that I may go out and come I before this people; for who can judge this thy people that is so great?

And the Lord said to Solomon, Because this was in your mind and you have not asked riches, honor, nor the life of your enemies, neither have you asked for long life; behold, I give you a wise and discerning heart because you have asked for yourself discernment to understand justice. Behold, I have done according to your words.

I have given you a wise and discerning heart, wealth, riches, and honor, such as none of the kings have had that have been before you, neither shall there any after you have the like."

–II Chronicles 1:7-12

In Greek mythology, Zeus became the Lord of the Universe. He took as his first wife Metis, goddess of prudence. Zeus depended upon her for wise counsel but feared that she would produce a son who might overthrow him, as Zeus himself had dethroned his father, Uranus.

Zeus' answer to this dilemma was to trick Metis through a game of shape shifting. When Metis turned herself into a fly, Zeus swallowed her! Thereafter, she sat in his head and guided him from there.

Metis was already pregnant, so she hammered a helmet and wove a splended robe for the coming child. This caused Zeus to suffer from agonizing headaches.

All the gods rushed to help him. Hephaestus, the god of fire and Zeus' son with Hera, split open his father's skull. Out sprang Athena, fully grown and wearing the robe and helmet her mother had made.

Thus Athena, the goddess of wisdom, was born.

–retold from *D'Aulaires' Book of Greek Myths*

King Solomon's story is about having heart.

Athena's story is about keeping your head on straight.

This book is about both. This book teaches the art and science of whole consciousness, the marriage of heart and head for a greater purpose.

Every person is born with the power. Self counsel unlocks it. To know the Self beyond the constraints of the physical body is to free consciousness. You experience this each night when you dream. While the outer mind sleeps, the inner mind is free to explore, discover, and enjoy other worlds, other realities. It is the inner mind that sees the infinite possibilities. Dreams are the most common means of communication for the inner mind, and so heeding the messages in your dreams is a powerful counseling tool. So is the still mind.

Since it is attached to the physical body, the mind easily becomes restless. The head fills with thoughts that cloud our judgement and poison our peace. The heart becomes burdened by future-worries or it bleeds from past-regrets. Cultivating the still mind produces the state of consciousness needed for "setting your head on something" and "mending a broken heart", for calming the "bullheaded" and the "hardhearted", for opening both to higher states of reason and intuition. The still mind clears the head and cleans the heart so we can experience ourselves as superconscious beings. This reality is the purpose for Psi counseling.

Within each of us is a seed of greatness, the potential to be like our mental Creator. Yogic teachings describe this seed as infinite intelligence, infinite energy, and infinite manifestation. This book is about what happens as we endeavor to unite, then transcend, the three.

It may well be that the transitory nature of physical life is the great grasp of Universal Truth we all seek. Being able to receive with equanimity that which is wanted and unwanted, is a measure of one who is mastering the Self. Certainly such wisdom is within our grasp.

This I know for sure, I have changed from living this book, and it is my hope that by writing about my multidimensional experiences you will come to understand more keenly your own.

–Barbara Condron

July 2004

Experiences with Infinite Being

Dreams

Reconciliation

THE *Wisdom* of *Solomon*

The legend goes that a bee strayed into the palace of the great King Solomon. Angry servants tried to kill it, but the bee escaped them, flying to the King for safety.

"Please, O King," pleaded the bee, "spare me today so I may live to serve you tomorrow."

King Solomon smiled to think that this tiny creature could ever hope to serve a mighty monarch. Yet, being merciful he released the bee saying, "Go in peace. I require no service from you in return."

In time a beautiful queen heard of Solomon's reputation and she traveled far to pay him homage. Although she had heard of his wealth, when the Queen of Sheba entered his court, she was amazed at its splendor.

"May the King live forever," she said. "I come to offer the true friendship of my country." Being a ruler herself, she bore the responsibility of her people in tendering such an offer. "I hope that during my stay we may come to know one another."

Word of Solomon's wisdom had traveled far, and this was what most intrigued the queen. The loyalty of his people, the love of his wives and children, were greatly desired. For this reason she hoped to learn from him.

On the first day of her visit, the queen gave Solomon a diamond with a curved and twisted opening that penetrated the large stone. "Is it within your power to draw a thread through a winding hole?' she asked him.

King Solomon smiled and sent for a silkworm. The worm crawled through the hole, drawing a thread of silk right through it. The queen noted the ease of his ingenuity.

The next test the Queen of Sheba arranged for King Solomon involved dozens of boys and girls. The young children, all dressed alike, entered the court. "Can you, your majesty, tell from your throne which are the boys and which are the girls?" she asked.

King Solomon commanded his servants to bring a basin of water before each child and bid them wash their faces. The boys splashed water on their faces while the girls daintily dabbed the water with their fingertips. Thus the king easily told them apart. The Queen of Sheba acknowledged Solomon's grasp of human nature.

On one of their outings, the queen witnessed King Solomon's wisdom in the moment. A small dog had fallen into a deep pool. The water was so low the dog could not be reached. King Solomon tossed a branch into the water for the dog to cling to.

The queen was puzzled saying, "I would not have done so for it is better to drown quickly than to starve slowly."

She watched as King Solomon showed his men how to block the nearby stream with rocks. This caused the stream to overflow into the pool which in turn caused the water to rise higher and higher. Soon the branch floated up to within reach and the dog was safely lifted out. The queen was convinced of Solomon's reasoning power and revered his motivation of compassion for all God's creatures.

The queen's advisors were not convinced of King Solomon's good intention toward their queen and her country. Although King Solomon had won the queen's trust, they were not as forthcoming. They believed if the king was not humbled he would deal with their queen unfairly. Doubt began to rise in the queen's mind. "Tomorrow is our last opportunity to test the king's integrity," they counseled her. "Leave this to us and we will insure his reliability at tomorrow's farewell banquet."

The advisors chose one flower from the king's garden. They then ordered their craftsmen to make ninety-nine false flowers exactly like it. They then placed the one fresh flower among the ninety-nine false ones. The copies were so perfect that the queen could not identify the real one.

"I do not see how anyone can choose the real flower," she remarked.

One of King Solomon's gardeners heard this and reported it to the king.

The King had become proud, and being confident was not concerned. "It suits me that they should prove my wisdom before the multitude. I fear not what they may do."

That night the palace gleamed with light as hundreds of guests came to honor King Solomon and the Queen of Sheba. At just the right moment the queen said, "Your majesty, our craftsmen beg that you judge their work. Among these flowers only one came from your garden. The remainders have been created by servants in your honor.

Won't you select your own flower and let my servants know how theirs compare?"

At first the king was confident in his ability to choose. He sniffed the flowers. They were all equally fragrant. He touched them, and they were all petal smooth. In beautiful color and appearance, the flowers were identical!

As King Solomon stood there, perplexed, the guests began to whisper amongst themselves. "What was wrong? Couldn't the king pick the flower from his own garden? Was this a trick? Perhaps this foreign queen had bested their ruler!" Even Solomon's most loyal servants became nervous. Why didn't the king make his choice and quell this foolish conjecturing by the guests?

As he moved among the flowers, King Solomon felt something tickle his hand. A bee had landed there. "I am at your service, your majesty," whispered the bee. It circled low over the flowers, unseen by any other, and crawled into the one flower which had honey inside.

King Solomon leaned over and plucked the one flower with the bee in it. Here was the flower that had bloomed in his garden!

"Your craftsmen are indeed skilled," he said, presenting the flower to the queen. "I have been admiring their work, but the false cannot be true. A queen deserves life."

The queen bowed, humbled by King Solomon's gift. "Your wisdom is beyond compare, your majesty," she admitted, "Sheba will be honored by your friendship."

The next day, the queen left for home, bearing many rich gifts from the wise king.

Later, in the quiet of his rooms, King Solomon thought gratefully of the bee which had served him so well. He humbly bowed his head. "I have been too proud," he thought. "No one is so great that he needs no help, and none is so small that he cannot give it."

Surely wisdom is given to all living things, and the tiniest creatures are teachers of kings.

As I child I learned the Biblical story of a man named Solomon. He was the son of David, the shepherd boy who slew the giant Goliath and became a king. Solomon was such a righteous man he found favor with God in every way. Never before had the people of his lineage known such wealth and prosperity. Whatever Solomon wanted, the Lord God provided.

I learned early that the Lord promised Solomon anything he asked for, and as a child I wondered why he asked for so much. I particularly wondered what he did with so many wives and children! Somewhere along the line I learned that Solomon actually only asked for one thing: wisdom to guide God's people. How unselfish! I thought. I was intrigued by the simplicity of it, the faith and the devotion.

I was taught that because Solomon prayed for wisdom, the Lord granted him wisom, *and* gave him abundance in everything!

In the School of Metaphysics we teach a practice designed to bring the mind into harmony with the Universal Law of Proper Perspective. That practice is called the Ten Most Wanted List. On the first list I created, love was number one, meaning it was desired more than anything else. Wisdom was number two.

Within a month I received the first lesson in meditation and following my first week of practice, wisdom moved to its place as number one on my Ten Most Wanted List. There it has remained since 1975.

Every day I am in awe and gratitude for the way my life is unfolding. In every area I have more than I have ever wanted or imagined. I attribute this to my commitment to wisdom, to the maturing of my soul through every choice I make.

Understanding Self as infinite is easier than you might think. In some ways, it is so simple that we miss it. We overlook the opportunity. We discount its importance.

It is said there was once a famous Chinese poet who wanted to study the wisdom of the Buddha. He traveled for days to reach a famed teacher. He thought often of the first question he would ask.

Upon arrival the question he chose was: "What is the most important thing in the Buddha's teachings?"

"Don't harm anyone and only do good," replied the teacher.

"How simple!" exclaimed the poet in ridicule. "You are supposed to be a great teacher. This is why I traveled so far to find you. Any child might answer the question in this way!"

The teacher smiled, "Yes, a three-year-old can say it. To know it in your heart requires putting into practice the idea."

Infinite Being, like wisdom, is the fruit of practicing such lofty and noble ideals.

Human man is in the process of separating emotions from heart energy. Most people confuse the two. When I asked V about how she had been since her most recent intuitive breathing session she told me she was learning about her emotions. "I was emotional last night," she confided, "frustrated because I don't seem to be changing."

For months, V has repeatedly said she wants maturity, to take more responsibility for herself. She had spoken to her teacher about this and he had encouraged her to express her emotions more frequently and fully – without harming another.

In V's mind she was beginning to awaken to her state of being. In words she described this as "when I am emotional I remember my experiences more easily."

Remembering a time when I came upon this same awareness, I offered, "Emotional attachment is the indicator of a lesson to learn."

V was making a significant discovery in Self awareness. She was confusing a level of consciousness, the emotional level, with a way the whole mind functions. At that moment, V was attributing a state of mind – which is the recall of information and experience – with the content of her mind – in this case frustration.

"What is the key to memory?" I asked her.

Having studied and practiced essential living skills for almost two years, she reviewed her own knowledge. "Memory is a product of attention being directed in an experience," V replied.

"Right," I affirmed. "So the quality of attention given determines the depth of the experience and its recall at a later time."

We had had many conversations about V's past. Memories of abuse during her childhood haunt her even though the experiences occurred over two decades ago. These memories have ruled her thinking – largely unconscious – for years. Through strengthening the power of her mind she is step-by-step freeing herself from past hurts.

With this experience, it was time for V to update her definitions of memory and emotions. "Undivided attention gives the complete reception of the moment. It unites intelligence, energy, and substance in the mind." V is an excellent writer. I draw upon the example of an article about building the Peace Dome that she wrote recently. V writes by describing the scene, theme, and characters as sensory experiences. Her words paint a picture in the mind of the reader. You can see the Peace Dome, feel its energy, smell the orchard air and taste the newly mown grass. You are there. Completely. This is the power of the mind through undivided attention.

Today V can take this understanding and apply it to herself in a new way.

"Undivided attention causes the subconscious and conscious minds to work in harmony, in sync," I suggested. V has heard the concept before. She has received it with her intelligence. She comprehends the nature of undivided attention and can see it working through goals and ideas. She has experienced the energy of it, through visions and through emotional outbursts. As a teacher of elementary children and of adults from varied backgrounds, she has experienced the manifestation of undivided attention repeatedly.

In the present, V has an opportunity to unify and elevate her comprehension of undivided attention. She is perched to birth a new depth of understanding in the power of her own mind. "Emotion is what glues the two minds together," I begin. "You experience the *effect* of your attention as emotion. When emotion is present and you are aware of it, you have a greater depth of attention involved in your experiencing. Thus greater learning is yours, deeper awareness, which translates into growing understanding and memory recall."

V thought about this for a moment. Brain activity is very easy for this student and soon she asked, "So what about people who are emotional and are scattered with their attention?"

I considered her question, then replied, "Attention guides the interpretation of the mind's experiences. Attention is to the mind what the senses are to the body, receptors of experience. When you are present-minded, with attention in the now, you are more aware of the inner and outer minds – and therefore the emotions – functioning.

"It is very possible for someone who is scatter-brained to be fully present at will." V is on her way to understanding the difference between emotional attachment and heart-centered understanding. Where she directs her attention will be the determining factor in the outcome.

Later that same day, I was talking with another student (I'll identify as Y) about what her Intuitive Health Analysis had identified as "emotional sensitivity". The report described Y's judgement of this ability as a weakness and suggested she reevaluate this, viewing it as the strength it is. She shared that since receiving the report she had begun to realize just how many emotions she absorbed from others. These emotions weren't even hers, but someone else's! Yet she would suck them right in, and they often would overload her system, expressing as skin rashes.

Y works with energies everyday that encourage awareness of relativity. As we discussed this, a new dimension came to light in me. "Perhaps in your interactions with others you need to be centered in your heart. That is your strength." Y considered the idea, yet I could tell her head was battling with it so I added, "Not the emotions."

We had discussed head and heart often so this was a revisited idea for us both. Y tended to interpret her intuitive experiences as emotional ones. She would identify someone's anger and avoid that person. She would "sense" someone's sadness and sympathize. For Y, each psychic "feeling" just came upon her without discernible cause. To respect her emotional sensitivity, Y would need to still her mind. In order to still her mind, she would need to admit the ego gratification she derived from absorbing others' emotions.

By opening her mind to the possibility that her strength came from the heart rather than emotional connections, Y would have a way to reevaluate Self, a means to admit prejudices. "This way you can expand beyond the emotion, giving it direction and opening your mind to cause." She nodded, seemingly considering the thought.

Meanwhile, my mind opened into Infinite Being.

Like a burst of daylight I saw the image of head-heart more clearly than I had ever before. "That's it! When we as thinking beings try to direct the emotions with the brain the result is emotional reaction. When we attempt to direct emotion from the heart, the result is emotional reaction. When we direct emotion from an entrainment of heart and brain, we activate the glue – the emotion – that unites the soul. We produce emotional response."

Want emotional control? Entrainment is the answer.

I wrote these two accounts three years ago.

Life is what happens on the way to wisdom.

Entrainment

is the refined art and science of Being.

It enables us to be at peace with any situation. It gives us the freedom to be Self while connecting us with others, with the Creator, with all of creation. Entrainment empowers us to respond fully in the present moment with truth and love. It elevates our spirit through wisdom.

Entrainment is one of the essential life skills, in fact it is the omega expertise for developing our potential as a whole, functioning Self. What begins with Self respect, the power to look at your Self again and again in increasingly different and new lights, culminates with a new experience of what Self is. This is the purpose of Psi counseling.

A Psi counselor is familiar with ten essential life skills. These are:

Self Respect

Undivided Attention

Concentration

Memory

Listening

Imagination

Breath

Reasoning

Intuition

Entrainment

Experience in these areas gives your counselor the ability to unite their consciousness with yours. Psi counselors can "feel your pain" without ever allowing it to cloud their vision. They can still their minds thus receive you completely, free from judgement. The same skill that gives them this ability enables them to advise, lead, guide, and teach you to do the same. Some of the ways this is accomplished we have recorded here in this book.

Where entrainment exists, Infinite Being can be experienced. Marriage between a male and female is the physical expression of the desire for this state of being. In a dream, people of the same sex represent aspects of the waking, conscious mind, the part of you that functions directly in conjunction with the brain and physical body. Dream-people of the opposite sex symbolize aspects of the dreamer's subconscious mind. A wedding in a dream symbolizes a commitment between those conscious and subconscious aspects. Commitment means these parts of mind are working together toward a common ideal. This is the natural expression of the mind.

The conscious and subconscious minds have a duty and a purpose to fulfill. These are relative to each another. As they perform their functions, experiences are gathered and greater understanding is the result. Understandings become a permanent part of the individual soul. This is how temporal experience – life experience which comes and goes – takes on eternal relevance and this is the essence of immortality, Infinite Being.

"This above all: to thine own self be true," William Shakespeare writes in *Hamlet*, "and it must follow, as the night the day, thou canst not then be false to any man." Your Psi counselor reveres this thought for Self and offers the perspective that

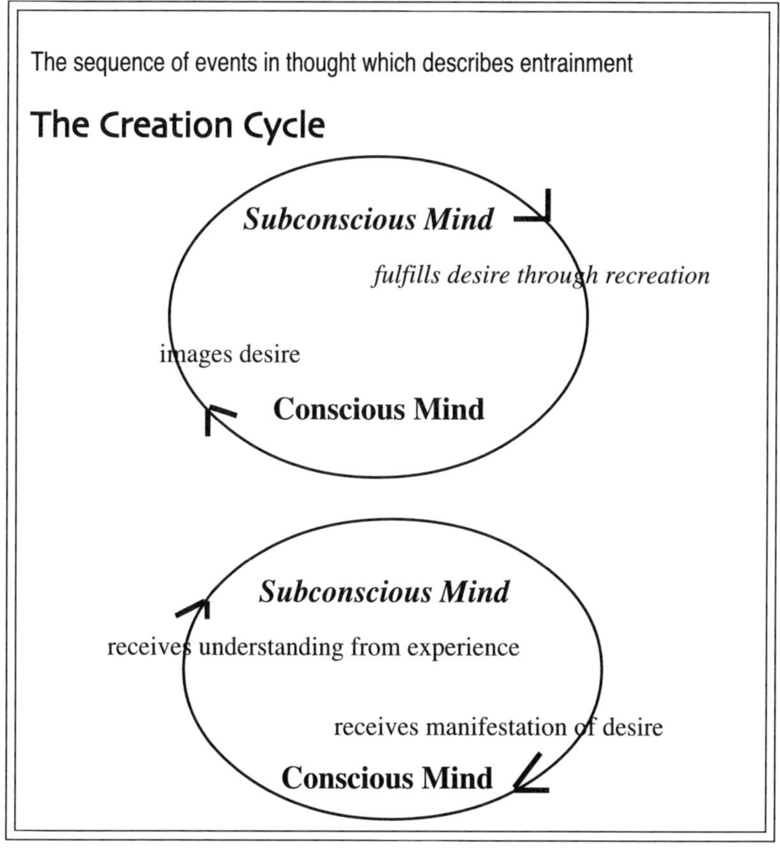

enables you to do the same. She salutes your divinity, giving reverence to you as soul. She addresses this inner essence because she realizes you are a soul experiencing temporary, physical conditions that may have eternal implications. The counselor uses himself as a tool to shed light on your path for transformation.

The secret of psi counseling is the faculty for self counseling. Psi counselors practice what they teach. They remember where they came from. They are attentive to why they are here. They image where they are going. By entraining conscious and subconscious minds they open channels of perception that are at this time supernormal.

Living with infinity affects their being and so they are constantly answering the question, *"Who am I?"*

On Entrainment....

"Entrainment is a scientific term created by Christiann Huygens, a pendulum clock maker. He noticed when he would hang a new clock on the wall that no matter where it started its movement eventually it would move in sync with the other clocks. No matter how long or short the pendulums, they all came to moving at that same vibration. Entrainment is when everything is moving together. This phenomena is prevalent in nature. Breathing in and out is how I look at it, entrainment is breathing in and breathing out – together.

"There is a pulse to the universe that each one of us are either in alignment with or we're not, and you know when you are and when you aren't. When you are, things are going great! When you're not, everything that you touch turns to ashes. Entrainment is being able to cause that kind of rhythm within your being of who you are. One of the ways I am making this conscious is with MultiDimensional Living, a development the School of Metaphysics is bringing into the world. Multidimensional Living describes so well the movement of uniting the conscious mind and the subconscious mind to ultimately reunite what is the soul. Instead of being two pieces, the minds become one entity working together."

–from Q&A session with Drs. Barbara and Daniel Condron during Your Soul's Purpose (Dharma) Session

Infinite BEING …

Making Light in the World

In 1977, I wrote a short book called *Psiology: Evolutionary Step in Psychology* (available now only online at www.som.org). It was the first time I began making connections between what I was learning as a student at the School of Metaphysics and my effectiveness as a teacher. I knew, for instance, that my developed ability to listen with my mind as well as my ears was an amazing asset in counseling others. Part of that ability I had been "born with", the product of past understood experiences, and part of it I was practicing daily in meditation. I was honing this important life skill as well as others.

My mind began to open to the possibilities of the future. A future that was built upon the territory of shamans and prophets, and in more recent times Freud and Jung. This kind of counsel would move beyond psychology. It was more than parapsychology, for this inner, whole Mind experience transcended the physical realms of the psyche. Being seated in the mind – the "psi" – it was quite natural for this kind of counsel to be described as Psiology. Thus Psi counselor is used to describe the one who is adept in using the conscious and subconscious minds, together, to aid/guide others.

I have learned much in the almost 30 years since *Psiology* was written, yet the integrity of the vision it paints of what is to come retains its vibratory impact and the following excerpt paves the way for the real-life story of Infinite Being that follows..

Taking Charge - Your Respond Ability

To the psiologist of the future, the debate of normal versus abnormal behavior will be obsolete. This is primarily because the psiologist or psi counselor will be dealing with the "psi". Psi basically means mind in action. This is a concept which most people can grasp on a physical, conscious level however, few at this point recognize themselves as being more than this physical body or brain. This is most easily evidenced in where society focuses attention.

We are raised and conditioned in the culture where our parents live. We are continually bombarded every day with these social customs which in actuality program, from the moment of birth specifically through age seven, the patterns and responses which will dictate the remainder of our lives until the moment that we choose to change these.

An excellent example of this is the predominant attitude in American society that when we are physically ill all we need to do is consult a physician. At this point, the cold we have can be diagnosed and a symptomatic relief in the form of an antihistamine or a shot of penicillin will be prescribed so the effect can be temporarily relieved. Or perhaps surgery will be recommended to eliminate kidneys stones or cancer. However, there is a high incidence of later reoccurrence of many disorders. With scientific brilliance developed enough to put a man on the moon, modern technology is still unable to cure the common cold.

Obviously we must be looking in the wrong place. This ignorance will persist as long as the attention is focused on the symptom and its relief rather than its cause and understanding. This is true also of any psychological disorder, disease or disharmony. These are directly related to how the individual views himself mentally and emotionally.

The psiologist will recognize that many of the theories previously acknowledged and developed to treat the "abnormal" require an expansion of perspective. He will see that individual as more than the physical mind and body. The psiologist will refer to this part of the individual as the conscious mind. The conscious mind is that part of yourself which functions directly with the brain and physical body. It is the part which functions while you are awake, taking in information from the moment you were born, storing it in the cerebrum of the brain to be used and called upon whenever the information is required. Within this part of mind is also a division referred to as the unconscious mind. This part of mind stores information rarely used. Perhaps it has been used once or twice within your entire lifetime. For instance, multiplying two times two is part of the conscious mind because the answer is readily available. The information required for that correct response has been understood and used frequently. However eight times sixty-four is not an automatic response. Undoubtedly you have multiplied those numbers at some time, but the answer has not been thoroughly understood or used repeatedly. Hence it becomes a part of the unconscious mind. The information stored in this part of mind is not readily available for use because it has not been consistently and constructively used.

This relates much to habits. When you form a habit, there are neuron pathways created to specific brain cells in the cerebrum. These pathways are widened and deepened so specific responses can easily travel that route. Each of you can recognize the difficulty within yourself of breaking an unwanted habit. Perhaps it was kicking the cigarette habit. After many years of formulating that habit, it was difficult to change conscious desire and thought. It also took discipline and will power over your physical body, for the body had become conditioned to that initial desire or impulse to smoke. In the same way, pieces of information filed within the brain and not frequently used, do not have this strong neuron pathway built toward their individual storage cells.

For instance, take a person you met only once, perhaps ten years ago. If you were to meet him on the street you might recognize his face; however, his name might not be as easily accessible to you. Yet at the time you met him, you knew his name and perhaps even repeated to it yourself. This information and the neuron pathway leading to it is not a strong one since it has lacked use. It would take a considerable amount of conscious, concentrated effort to draw this information from the brain. The information has not disappeared. It is still accessible to the brain, but the pathway has not been consistently used. It is not only those things unfamiliar to us that are stored in the unconscious, but also those things we wish to forget.

For instance, if you were four years old and just learning to play the piano--create this scene in your mind. You're practicing, because your coordination is not highly developed, there is much fumbling and many mistakes made in trying to execute movements properly. Your father comes home from work tired and irritable. He walks into the kitchen where your mother if fixing dinner and begins yelling, "Why is he playing the piano now? Why can't he play it when I'm not here? He'll never get it right!" Your reaction at age four would be considerable hurt and disappointment. At this age you lack the sufficient information in your brain to understand the total situation; therefore, you do not understand why your father is reacting in such a manner. At four you are oblivious to the pressures of a job and the irritability it can instigate in your father, so you have an emotional response which is not understood. You might run from the room in tears, not understanding how your father could reject you in such a manner. Your parents would probably not even recognize what you have experienced. Because you do not want to believe that your father would say such a thing about or toward you, you would file this information in the unconscious mind--not wanting to face it, not understanding it at the present time.

When you're nine years old, having attempted for five years to practice and become a good pianist, you still find you have difficulties perfecting the art. You become frustrated, angry and feel you have failed. You do not understand the cause at age nine since the initial incident which is still causing problems occurred at age four. You do not understand the lack of improvement, but buried in the unconscious is your father's voice continually defeating your efforts. This defeatist attitude would eventually cause you to neglect and perhaps even abandon the attempt to develop a talent that at four years you very much wanted to develop.

This is often the way people react throughout their lifetime due to things stored in the unconscious mind. Using the example given, it is quite obvious if you will honestly create it and relate it to perhaps a significant incidence of your own or someone you know, that it is definitely related to the emotions and the reaction to that particular situation. *The psiologist of the future will begin to recognize the full import of emotional response, recognizing that this is not a function of the conscious mind, but the subconscious mind. This subconscious part of mind holds only understood experiences, those you have encountered with the conscious mind coming to a certain amount of understanding. Those situations which you find yourself in and do not understand are placed in the unconscious part of the brain.* Two entirely different and separate parts of the mind; however, both work together to create significant parts of the total individual. The more you understand about each part of yourself, the better you can direct each thought to create your life.

Your emotional responses, no matter what your age, are extremely important to your health and well being as well as your happiness. The key to having a balanced and healthy outlook – mentally, emotionally and physically – is being able to direct intelligently each thought you create. Most people tend to deny their ability to direct and control thoughts. They would rather give the responsibility to the thoughts themselves, seeing the thoughts as having control over them, rather than the other way around. The "I can't help what I think" or "You make me mad" or "These need to be out today because the boss says so" are Self defeating patterns. As long as we divorce our attitudes and emotions from ourselves, we are not accepting them as part of ourselves. This makes direction or control virtually impossible until one accepts and realizes any thought is his creation and since he created it initially he has the same option to recreate it toward a positive and beneficial end. This attitude creates a respect and a recognition of the right to be a reasoning, intelligent being. The reasoning process is one we have developed and earned as a group and as individuals. Each individual has the right to think, to develop this ability; however, most people allow others to think for them. A good example of this in today's society is the news media. There is a great thrust within the journalism of today to report primarily negative occurrences. Many journalism schools and editors impress upon their reporters the importance of being a muckraker. Broad headlines rarely reflect a positive nature. The concept for the modern newspaperman is that this does not sell newspapers. Due to this media opinion whether newspapers, radio or television, the public is continually bombarded with negativity. It is each individual's decision as to whether this negativity will effect him. And, if so, to what degree.

When you objectively view the media, you will find what at one time might have seemed a subtle influence is one of the most obviously powerful influences on society today. This subtlety occurs because we are all too willing to believe what we see or hear without discriminating, reasoning, thinking to see if it makes sense. Allowing others to think for you ("You make me mad") weakens your ability to make decisions. It also gives the control you could have to others. This often occurs in families. A spouse will make his or her decisions contingent on the wife or husband. What at first begins as a noble effort to compromise or create harmony in the relationship often develops into a dominant-passive relationship. The passive partner ultimately sacrifices their own individuality--continually "giving in" to the wishes or demands of the dominant partner.

It can occur with parent-children relationships also. In an attempt to give children what "I never had"--many parents take all responsibility from the child by making all his decisions. This restricts the child building a combination of resentment, dependence, restriction, and lack of confidence, denying him the opportunity to make decisions whether correct or incorrect.

This brings us back to choice. If you truly have a choice, then you recognize that you do have the capability of intelligently directing what you will think and how you will think it. Will those thoughts be positive or negative? Will they foster an "I can" attitude or an "I can't" attitude? Will they reflect quality or quantity? This to the psiologist will be one of the criteria for effectively dealing with any problem that occurs, whether within Self or in individuals seeking their aid. The continual attention will revolve around the individual and that person's capacity to become a whole functioning Self, being the controller of his thoughts, words and actions. The key to this approach will be having the ability to see each situation as neutral, neither positive or negative, detrimental or constructive. Rather the psiologist will view all situations as they are, without emotional attachment or involvement. With this ability in hand, the psiologist will be able to see the value of any and all situations as well as people. He will then reflect this to the person seeking help, offering him this concept through examples and mental tools to aid in practicing this objectivity. This will take a desire on the part of the "patient" to begin to see situations and circumstances as neutral, but it is merely developing the objective perspective thereby strengthening the reasoning ability.

When highly emotional or intense reactions to these situations can be seen, the individual might for instance be asked to put his emotions temporarily aside so that he can view the situation, then the emotions, objectively. At this point he can weigh all factors and reason through the exact process of what is happening and decide what he as an individual intends to do with this situation. With objectivity, the individual can clearly and without any emotional coloring decide if he wants to make this a positive or negative situation. For instance he might be asked to view the situation from the perspective of a total stranger thus causing disturbance.

With this perspective, the individual can begin to see the situation as neutral, choosing a positive response rather than a negative. Once this is determined, the individual can review the emotional response to this situation, beginning to understand what the emotions are and how they can be intelligently directed the next time such a situation occurs. This does not imply emotional repression or suppression, rather it indicates constructively using the emotions and that specific and unique energy within that part of mind.

Each person, within the subconscious mind, has an emotional level of consciousness to work in and through. To deny this part of self its to deny part of yourself as an individual. For instance, say you are an advertising executive. You have been working seven days on a particular layout design. Repeatedly writing copy and drawing illustrations to create an effective ad for perhaps an automobile. At the end of your work your superior comes in and tears it apart, crossing out much of the copy and totally rejecting your illustrations.

At this point in the situation, most people's reactions would reflect disappointment, frustration and anger. However, if the individual can temporarily set his emotional reaction aside and view the situation as neutral, he can see that allowing negative emotions to become involved would indicate either repressing the emotions which in the future would cause mental and emotional disturbance and perhaps even a physical disease, or totally releasing them, exploding and perhaps quitting his job. In the case of a disease, this could incapacitate the individual for months from the working situation, cutting his source of income and sense of self respect for what he is accomplishing. Likewise, if he walked out, he would be immediately without financial support and perhaps go through an emotional period of feeling that he had failed. At this point, if the individual could become objective, seeing the situation as neutral, he could become also objective from the creation he had developed. This is the point where most people tend to allow the emotions to be out of control, especially when their creativity is involved. There is the tendency to become involved or attached to the object which is being created hence when the boss comes in and rejects this manifestation of creativity, it is often taken emotionally as a personal affront.

If the individual can become objective at this point there is no negative reaction involved. The individual can choose while being objective, to act emotionally positive, rather than reacting negatively, recognizing that this rejection is no reflection upon his own value or creativity. Rather, there is something he may learn from this situation if he remains open to the suggestions of his superior. To complete the cycle of value in this situation, the individual would realize what first seemed life self-defeating mistakes, have suddenly become valuable tools to further improve his own ability if the person uses this situation rather than allowing it to use him.

So how would you react in this situation if you could achieve that objectivity? The key is that you would act rather than react, saying "I think I've done a good job. How do you see that it could be better?" or "What do you specifically object to? Why?" In this way, as with any situation you might encounter, whether with family, spouse, employer or friends, the individual can begin seeing himself function as a total self, being the director and controller of his own mind in the mental, emotional, and physical realms. He will recognize that any situation he encounters is a deep and meaningful learning experience from which he can gain much understanding of himself and others. This type of circumstantial reasoning and logic will have a role in the psiologist's therapy.

Unfortunately, most people find themselves on a merry-go-round reacting from the emotions continually. This only reinforces this practice in the future. This technique of placing the emotions to the side could be termed by some psychologists as negative reinforcement; however, this is only true if the emotions are never brought forward to experience and understand. One can move the emotions to the side or even express them, but unless there is conscious attention placed upon either decision the individual will still be reacting.

If the person makes the decision to actively express the emotions or to place them aside temporarily, then an intention is created. If this intention is to bring the situation into perspective in order to choose action, no negative reinforcement occurs simply because the emotions are being consciously understood. At this point, you can begin to see the cause for the emotional reaction, bringing out many unconscious attitudes as well as understanding habit patterns. In this constant watch and observance of our own attitudes and emotional involvements we can begin to understand ourselves and direct our thoughts more productively. It is important to realize that thought comes before the emotional response or reaction.

The major "problem" in anyone's life will stem from the axis of response and reaction. In the example given of the boss--the first examples related were reactions. These were stimulated by someone in the environment outside of Self. The control of the individual's thoughts was given to the employer. He allowed himself to believe that his employer knew his own thoughts, capabilities, and value better than himself. If the individual had responded in this situation, he would have realized his own thoughts and chosen which emotions or feelings he wished to express. A word much abused in our society is "responsibility". It weighs heavy on many minds, conjuring images of doing anything other than what we would rather do. However responsibility is merely your ability to respond. This is not to anyone or anything outside of Self, but rather your ability to respond to your own thoughts concerning what is happening. How often have you found your Self watching a movie and your thoughts say, "I'd like to go there!" Or perhaps you meet someone and you think, "I'd like to have that kind of job." The thoughts are as limitless and varied as individuals, but how well do you respond to your desires and thoughts? You will discover in reviewing your life that the times when you were the happiest were times you responded to your desires.

The psiologist will understand the subtlety of thought and the workings of mind. He will view each individual as mind, recognizing that these two divisions, conscious and subconscious, work together systematically and in harmony if the individual recognizes the function of each and calls upon his creative intelligence to cause the minds to function in that manner. This allows the individual to build self respect and dignity into himself and the life he is choosing.

This is basically how the psiologist will work with the individual seeking aid. It is necessary to understand these two parts of mind to fully perceive the progressiveness and deepened understanding that the psiologist will display....

from **Psiology: Evolutionary Step in Psychology**
©1977, School of Metaphysics

When I wrote these words, I had little idea that almost 30 years later I would live what you are about to read. It is my hope that in some way I can capture the depth of one person's experience of Infinite Being and that through reading this account, you the reader, may be enriched in some way to live your life more fully.

We are each the author of our lives. We are as Shakespeare noted, actors who strut upon the stage of life for but a brief time. To realize multidimensional being is to know yourself as actor, writer, composer, director, and audience. It is to be able to laugh and cry without ever being lost in the emotion. It is being free to accept what life brings with grace even when it may at first appear not at all what you ordered. It is being faced with the manifestations of your fondest desires knowing they are fleeting and unlasting.

To know yourself as a whole being is to understand the transient nature of the physical Self, to set your sights high. "Ah, a man's reach should exceed his grasp, or what's a heaven for?" asked English poet Robert Browning. *I have learned that heaven and hell are here and now, depending upon the direction of our choices.*

The following account of my thoughts, emotions, and choices over five days are some of the choices I have made. It is my hope in some way they bring greater Light to yours.

On MultiDimensional Living....

"It's the ability to be conscious in more than one level of existence at one time. It's being able to function in all seven levels of consciousness simultaneously. This has been an idea that has been openly taught by the School since its beginning in the early 1970s. The ascended masters' experiences were described at that time as functioning in all levels simultaneously, with awareness. So this kind of multidimensional consciousness has been part of the ideal I've held in mind ever since I heard this idea. 'What is that like?' I wanted to know, and I still want to know.

MultiDimensional Living are the steps that you can take to have experiences that are on more than just one level so that you can experience your Self and existence, life, more fully. This may come through a counseling venue. It may come from a healing experience. It may come during a weekend session like this. It may come through receiving an Intuitive Report of some kind. Through the years, the School of Metaphysics has explored, researched and developed avenues that are culminating in the realities of MultiDimensional Living. These are ways that we can help people to experience Self as Infinite Being."

–from Q&A session with Drs. Barbara and Daniel Condron during Your Soul's Purpose (Dharma) Session

Experiences

It's All about Choices

My husband Daniel, our nine-year-old son Hezekiah, and I frequent the Public Library in Lebanon, Missouri, a town close to the College of Metaphysics campus where we live. With Kiah's growing interest in reading, our visits are becoming more regular. Each of us chooses books to take home. Daniel often looks for native American Indian stories, Kiah likes to peruse the brand new picture books with 14-day returns, while I search for easy readers at Kie's level.

Kiah has grown to expect a novel of some sort, something we can read chapter by chapter at bedtime. On this visit as I looked through the volumes I came across a title called The Tale of Despereaux. The description of the story on the book jacket says:

"This is the story of Despereaux Tilling, a mouse in love with music, stories, and a princess named Pea. It is also the story of a rat called Roscuro, who lives in darkness but covets a world filled with light. And it is the story of Miggery Sow, a slow-witted serving girl with a simple, impossible wish. These characters are about to embark on a journey that will lead them down into a horrible dungeon, up into a glittering castle, and ultimately into each other's lives. And what happens then?

"Reader, it is your destiny to find out."

It sounded a bit extreme, perhaps too advanced for Kie's age, so I put the volume back and checked out one on the young Merlin instead. As it turned out, this tale had just begun.

Several weeks later we were at Barnes & Noble in Springfield, the largest nearby city. This was Hezekiah's annual birthday trip and he had a certain amount of money he could spend. While he looked at books, I investigated the audio section looking for a new book on tape for the ride home. Kiah had listened to tapes while traveling since he was about three. They gave him a point of focus which balanced his equilibrium, easing his tendency toward car sickness. Although we owned about two dozen hours of recorded material, we had listened to all of them so many times some of the tapes were beginning to break and we knew the stories by heart.

Today two stories caught my eye: Cheaper by the Dozen, the real-life adventures of a large family, and The Tale of Despereaux. I read the jackets on both. My previous conclusion of Despereaux as a story of good versus evil lingered and with it hesitation about exposing Hezekiah to it. Since I didn't have time to pre-listen, I had to rely on the information at hand and my instinct. I put the tape back and kept searching.

Not finding anything else suitable I pulled Despereaux from the shelf again. Cheaper would let Kiah know about big families with lots of brothers and sisters, a good education for a singular child. Often Kie brought up the subject of "when will I have a baby brother or baby sister" and I knew this book could fuel that desire rather than satisfy it. The story also included life-events taken for granted by most people which are not a part of Hezekiah's life but would be part of his consciousness if we listened to this account.

I looked at the tape in my other hand. The Tale of Despereaux is a story about light and darkness. And since I was writing a book on how duality becomes polarity and how polarity entraps the soul, my mind was filled with images that colored my thinking about whether this was a book I wanted for Hezekiah.

I called Daniel over to consult. He read the jackets and suggested: The Tale of Despereaux. I allowed my doubts to dissipate in agreement. We purchased the tape and a few books, and left.

On the way home we began listening to the story of the little mouse who was not wanted. It didn't take too long to have my fears justified. Within the first hour, the tale turned to the dungeon, the rats, and torture. Material not at all, in my mind, suitable for a young boy's ears.

I'd already made choices like letting Hezekiah watch the *Star Wars* trilogy. That tale had filled his mind with visions of good versus bad without benefit of reasoning maturity or spiritual wisdom. In my efforts to provide Hezekiah with examples and teachings of the latter, I had become much more conscious of my choice in media and its content.

As I write this I remember the movie collector's set was a Christmas gift for Kie from Shawn, a woman you will soon meet. She is the woman who serves as the stimulus for the multidimensional experience I am about to share with you.

Several hours after listening to Despereaux, Hezekiah awoke with a nightmare, the first in several months.

It was of no use to wish we hadn't bought the story. Pandora's jar was open. Now it was only moving forward. Learning. Choosing. Assimilating. For all of us.

Little did I realize at the time how the tale of this little rodent would play such a large role in my grasp of truths I have been courting for decades.

Wednesday, February 18, 2004

Sometimes it seems like others are creating our lives for us. Certainly that is the dilemma Shawn brought into my life. How I would receive her choice to walk out of my life, where it would take me, and the person I became through it, is this account of events.

The need to know who I Am while accepting all people, all things, is strong within me. Life has shown me that it is the ability to watch and observe that lends itself to acceptance. I know I want to accept Shawn's walking out of my life with grace and compassion. Still I am tempted to feel like she has walked into my room, upturned all my furniture, and with cold eyes flashing, stormed out with a defiant, "Deal with it!"

I know the Universe is taking me by the shoulders and looking me in the face. I also know it is holding a mirror before my eyes so I can see myself more clearly, more completely.

I have personal experience with the reality of the statement, "Thought is cause." This is a Truth I live by. Because of this I know that what I see in Shawn is present within myself. She wants to go. She wants to be done. She wants to move on. She wants something new and different and exciting. She wants to finally act upon an idea almost as old as she is. She wants to act on her dream.

In the moment I can accept this and be happy for her. I love Shawn with all my heart.

Then there is the cold truth that right now, little else matters to Shawn. The final step of a thesis for her Doctorate of Divinity matters less. The friendships she has developed in the past few years matter less. The dreams she dreamed with others in her life matter less. Everything matters less than what she wants.

Finally, I get to the voice of the ego, *I* matter less.

I think of Despereaux. The sole survivor of a litter of mice who live in a castle. Despereaux's mother is sure he will die and so she refuses to care for him. It is only because her husband prompts her that she names the little mouse Despereaux "for all the sadness, for the many despairs in this place." She declares that this will be her last child because they are all such disappointments.

Despereaux matters less to his own mother.

I matter less. And I am filled with despair. The thought bruises but it does not break. My heart, my love, goes with her. My heart will deny her nothing. My heart will give her anything she wants. The pain comes from realizing *I* cannot give her what she wants.

Rejection. Disappointment. Despair. So my head aches as it fills with darkness. I am not afraid of the dark. I have learned

This is why I share this story.
It is all in the hope that doing so will
make some light
in your world as well as mine.

---

about the inner light that shines on in darkness. I am willing to look this situation in the eye. It is the still mind that gives me the ability to do so.

"Despereaux is born with his eyes open. Something that does not occur with mice," author Kate di Camillo says. "He is an exceptional mouse. His ears are big like donkey ears. He is ridiculously small.

"And he is in love with light."

I understand Despereaux. I, too, am in love with light.

I will receive this experience. Shawn has given me no other choice. I know my experience is dual. I am proud of her choice to go for what she has always wanted. I am hurt by her choice for she is choosing a way that separates us. With this thought my head is saying "Hooray!" and my heart is wounded. How these two will end up in harmony, head and heart entrained, fuels my writing. I write to empty my head of thoughts in the hope that I will find medicine for the pain. I write to fill my heart with grace that I might experience divine love.

When Despereaux ends up in the dungeon where he is sure dinner for the rats, it is Gregory, the jailor, who protects him. Gregory says he'll make sure Despereaux remains safe because he can tell stories. "Stories are light." he says. "Light is precious in a world so dark." And so the little mouse Despereaux is spared.

This is why I share this story. It is all in the hope that doing so will make some light in your world as well as mine.

"Dr. Barbara," Paul Blosser said, "Shawn's on the phone for you."

I glance at the clock in the office. Three o'clock. Shawn is expected in for dinner at 5:30 so I wonder why she would be calling.

"Hi, how are you?" Shawn asks.

"Good, how about you?" I reply.

"Oh, okay." The tone of her voice paints a clearer picture than her half-hearted words.

The connection is choppy so I know she is on a cell phone. When I ask where she is she says Joplin, a town on Interstate 44 at the border of Oklahoma and Missouri almost three hours away.

"I just wanted to see if I could maybe meet with you and Dr. Dan tonight."

I am puzzled. Shawn is coming to stay for three months and I figure we will have lots of open time to talk. But I don't say that. I say, "We have play rehearsal tonight right after dinner. Dr. Dan will probably be with Hezekiah. Can it be tomorrow?"

"I'd really like to do it as soon as possible." It is strange that she is calling to ask for time.

I can feel the immediacy in her voice.

I feel torn between feeling obligated to respond to her emotional need and the commitment I have to the ten people who are creating the play we call *The Silver Cord*. I want to be both places at the same time. I realize that I will need to choose.

I don't want to in the moment, so I am silent.

Then, it is as if it is before I can even think them, the words come out of my mouth, "Are you going to quit?"

"Yes," is Shawn's response. In rhythm, no hesitation.

I tell her I will see what I can do, and ask if she wants to talk with Dr. Dan. She says yes. After giving the message to Daniel, I go downstairs to prepare supper.

I have heard this kind of response many times before. Students come and go frequently in this study. By the time they embark on this course, people have learned how to take or leave education. Even so – owing to the transformative power of knowing yourself – most learn much more during their time of study than they ever expected. Most students I am happy to have known, to have shared some part of life's journey. Then there are those who seem to *be* my life's journey.

It is now abundantly clear that Shawn is one of those for me.

I feel like Miggery Sow.

When Miggery Sow was six she looked into her mother's dying eyes and pleaded for her mother to stay with her. "I want you to stay with me." Her mother's reply, "Ah, child and what does it matter what you are wanting?"

No matter how many times I experience people departing, a part of me still feels like Miggery Sow. A part of me experiences the leaving as a one-sided choice. *Their* choice. Not mine.

My choice would be to continue to learn together. To love together. To grow together. In many cases, particularly with the expansion of the College, to live together. My heart bursts with hope when I think of others. This is the same hope that brides and grooms feel on their wedding day or parents experience on the day of the birth of their child. I feel this same expectation, this same sense of wonder, with many others, in many situations.

The reality of my learning is often harsh it seems. Painful. It is, in the world of Despereaux, like "a good clout to the ear".

Miggery Sow is sold by her father for a tablecloth, a hen, and a handful of cigarettes. Her new owner is fond of thinking for her and uses her as a place to dump his emotions. When Miggery Sow displeases him, or actually whenever he takes a notion to feel displeased, he gives her a good "clout to the ear".

Over time Miggery Sow's clouts take their toll on her ability to think clearly as well as to receive sounds through her ears. She is handicapped, limited mentally and emotionally as well as physically.

I think back over the people I have learned from and those I've taught over 29 years.

Twenty-nine years! Of all the blind spots I may have had this is certainly one of the biggest. How could I have forgotten that my own Saturn return of studying and teaching with the School of Metaphysics quickly follows the School's Saturn return? I realize this may mean little to you, and if that is the case I apologize and hope it may stimulate an interest in expanding your body of knowledge to include astrological diagnosis.

For now, let it be said that this moment is a great epiphany of the realizations I share with you here. It is perhaps the driving force of why I am compelled to write this account and to share it, although I know I run the risk of piecemeal judgement in the mind of the reader. A counselor told me years ago that this kind of judgement is "unhealthy for you so you are tempted not to let anyone know anything."

Yet I am driven by forces beyond astrology. I want to understand the whole, and to understand I must think more deeply than my astrological makeup. I must see its value in perspective not giving in to its compulsions, its tendencies and limitations, rather like the magi of old who saw the star of Christ consciousness and followed it, I too must interpret the signs for my own enlightenment. I so firmly believe in the light, that every story is worth telling. Every awareness is worth celebrating. Every ray of light is worth embracing.

I trust, dear reader, that you believe that also. I trust you will in some way see yourself in these people, and come to value your own choices in a new light. For that kind of growth is the greatest hope of all. A line from Despereaux comes back to me:

Reader, do you think that it is a terrible thing to hope when there is really no reason to hope at all? Or is it (as the soldier said about happiness) something that you might just as well do, since, in the end, it really makes no difference to anyone but you?

Dare I hope that Shawn is not serious? She has never said the words before. Does she mean them? Will she walk out of our lives?

Shawn has delivered to me a good clout to the ear. This requires from me an open mind. I realize how every student I have ever known, will ever know, has required the same from me. My journey has been in maturing that mind. She has made her choice. Now, I must begin making mine.

A little before five, I go upstairs to check the emails that have come into headquarters. Just sitting here in the library, in front of this computer, reminds me of Shawn. She has taught me the basics of everything I know about cyberworld. "Will I always think of her when I enter the library to work on the internet?" I ask myself. I know the answer is yes.

I have come to realize that much of the work I do in the world is paving the way for others. That's how I saw the work I have been doing with the websites. I thought of it as establishing their presence so Shawn would have something to build upon when she came to live here at the College of Metaphysics.

Now Shawn will not be here to receive her inheritance.

Did I really do all this for her? I have to ask the question. I know the limitations of making others your purpose. "I made your favorite meal just for you and you're not going to take time to eat it?" Or "I work all day and this is the thanks I get!" Or "Look at what I have done for you and you treat me like this." Many of the problems people encounter in life are caused by building their dreams, world, identity around someone else. This is an open door to disappointment, accusation, depression, and the like. Purpose, the image of how I will be when my ideal is achieved, has been a lifelong learning for me. I know my answer to this question is yes, and no. Yes, I wanted to give Shawn something of value. No, I wanted to give the world something of value. It is both. I am happy and proud of what has been produced particularly with the Peace Dome site. I am sad Shawn will not be here to share it. Really sad. I had looked forward to creating with her and now it is not going to be.

As these kinds of thoughts go through my head well over 100

emails fill the inbox on the screen in front of me. Shifting through them I find two that I will share with everyone at dinner. The first is from Lorena our SOM director in Dallas. Mid-20's Lorena is forging a new identity for herself and reevaluating what is "cool" and why. She wants some feedback. I send her request out to all SOM directors to initiate a discourse on the virtues or vices of "cool" which will draw upon people in over a dozen U.S. cities. I know this can be great illuminating fun for all of us.

The second email is this one from Stacy, our Webster Groves director.

> on 2/17/04 12:31 AM
>
> Hi Dr. Barbara.
>
> I want to share a recent series of experiences with you and everybody else in SOM world. I have had the need to learn to be with myself for most of my life. Within the last few months I have had the experience of loneliness even when surrounded by many people. I asked about this on a recent health analysis and the answer I was given is that there is nothing wrong with loneliness and that I need to learn to receive myself.
>
> The whole report was about how I need to mature mentally, emotionally and physically and create an attractive image of a mature woman. So far the image that I am creating for myself is that I want to be a Godly woman. I can explain more about that some other time. So anyway...
>
> I went to visit my parents this last weekend and as I was driving home I felt loneliness come upon me. I came back to the School, talked to Sebastien, made a grocery list and went to the grocery store, feeling lonely the entire time. It's a sinking, empty kind of feeling. I was driving in my car going to the grocery store, thinking about what my health analysis had said about needing to receive myself. I also thought about how I had the radio on to dull myself to the loneliness and I very consciously decided to turn it off. I turned off the radio and continued to drive in the lonely silence.

I got to the grocery store, still thinking about how I need to receive myself and still having no idea how to do that. I finally came up with the affirmations "I receive myself. I receive God into myself." So I shopped for my groceries, I needed more than usual. I finally found everything I needed except two items and I went up to check out. The very friendly checker saw me putting my list away and asked me if I had gotten everything. I said, "Yeah. Pretty much." He said that that didn't sound like I had everything and he asked me if I found everything. I am an honest person so I told him that actually I couldn't find the flour tortillas. He told me to hold on and he picked up a little phone and asked for someone to bring me some tortillas. I was surprised. Then the person came up with two bags of corn chips which is not what I wanted.

I had not meant to receive all this attention and help and I tried hard to tell these guys that I was fine and that I would get it later, and we all ended up getting into this conversation about what I really wanted and the three different locations in the store where they are and finally the guy behind me in line said that he would get them and takes off running to get them for me. I didn't know what to do with myself because I was getting all this attention that I didn't expect or necessarily want. I even remember thinking at one time "this is what I get for being honest".

So then the first guy who brought the corn chips and the guy from behind me in line come up with 10 different kinds of flour tortillas for me to pick from. Laughing I picked the one I wanted and was finally on my way. As I was walking out of the store, I couldn't help but smile and wonder if God sent that experience to me so that I would know that I really wasn't alone.

So, there was one other thing I couldn't find at that store and that was avocados. So I went to another grocery store that always has them. When I went inside, I found out that all of their big avocados were green. They also had bags of four little avocados, but two were ripe and two were green. This was a bummer because I had planned my fruit day meals with avocados in mind so I looked around to see if I could find some substitute snacks.

I was walking out when a produce person asked me if I needed help finding anything. I told him that I had just come in for avocados and that there weren't any ripe ones. He said he knew and that that was unusual. I agreed and told him that usually this is the one store in town where they have them. He then said that he would help me out and he began cutting the little bags of avocados open and put the ripe ones in a plastic bag for me. He must have put eight of them in a bag and then put a price tag of $1.49 on the outside of the bag and told me that if I had a problem to let him know. (Usually avocados cost $1.50 each).

I thanked him and as I walked toward the check out I smiled very big because there was no denying my experience now. God was shining his light upon me to let me know that even though I didn't know exactly how to be or what to do so that I could change and grow, I was on the right track and that I truly never am alone. As I walked out of the store I wondered if I would have had those same experiences if I had not been thinking the thoughts of "I receive this experience. I receive God into my-self." Then I wondered how many of these kinds of experiences I have missed out on.

Magic is all around us. Waiting for us to receive the experience of it.

I love you all!

Stacy Ann

My heart is overflowing,
filling my eyes with tears.

I know the magic Stacy is talking about and gratitude washes over me. Countless times I have been blessed by the powers that be. Stacy is such a bright light in my life. She is in her early twenties and unfolding like a lotus blossom. She loves the School of Metaphysics with a passion equal to mine and I look forward to the times when she lives here at the College.

I realize I am feeling a bit lonely in this moment. I know it will be a while before Stacy's return. I had looked forward to sitting in this room kibitzing with Shawn to create wonderful new ways to reach out to people who want to know. I think of the many early morning hours I spent preparing for that time, a time that will never come. My mind wanders into an endless stretch of future nights of just me at the computer. I enjoy working alone so I don't think of the emotion I sense as loneliness. Not until I read Stacy's words.

"I receive this experience," I choose to say Stacy's words outloud. I realize this thought is how I came to terms with the loneliness of my early years.

Then, "I receive God into myself." I realize this thought is how I know I am never alone.

"I receive this experience." These words open my head and my heart.

"I receive God into myself." These words open my mind to the infinite possibilities. I choose to hold my mind open to what God has in store for me. Today the Creator has brought me a friend who is leaving and my heart threatens to close.

Both of these emails are perfectly timed in my world. They offer great comfort without knowledge of the loss I am experiencing. They help keep my head on straight in a way I will be eternally grateful for. They keep me focused and centered on what the Truth is. They help me with satyagraha – the ability to hold onto truth – at a time when my heart could break into pieces and get put back together all wrong.

Chiaroscuro, a rat in Despereaux's tale, experiences a broken heart when the Princess tells him to return to the dungeon, the darkness, where he belongs. Ms. di Camillo writes, "There are hearts, reader, that never mend again once they are broken. Or if they do mend, they heal themselves in a crooked and lopsided way, as if sewn together by a careless craftsman. This was the fate of Chiaroscuro..."

The author chooses her names well. They have great meaning in her story, in our lives. Chiaroscuro means the arrangement of light and dark. Like a Renoir painting or illuminated buildings against a midnight sky or the yin-yang symbol, chiaroscuro is darkness and light together. Together they represent separation, and that is what I am feeling now.

I am fighting it. Denying it. I don't want it to be.

In the moment, I am like Roscuro, the rat in Despereaux's dungeon who is in love with light.

As darkness threatens to close around me, I am thankful to Lorena and Stacy for shining my way. For also like Roscuro, I think the meaning of life is light.

Shawn arrives near the end of dinner. It is 6:40 before we get up from the meal and play rehearsal is at 7:30 in the Peace Dome. I want to give time to Shawn, yet I don't see how to make it.

Our play *The Silver Cord* has been developing for four weeks. It is like a baby learning to walk and it needs me. I could excuse myself and expect them to carry on in my absence, but it is not right for me to leave these ten people who are committed to their learning and growth for one who is not. The Truth seems cold to me and my heart aches.

I compromise, trying to do both. I rush around gathering the equipment I need for filming tonight's play, a notebook, and a coat. By the time I return to the great room Shawn and Daniel are sitting on the couch talking. I bring a chair near and sit, listening.

Shawn is saying something about not wanting to disappoint us but she knows she needs to do this. There are so many thoughts going through Shawn's mind that they come out in sentence fragments. She talks about some of her failures, her negligence toward others. She begins to talk about someone asking her if she loves Adam, her newlywed husband. She says she told them, "Yes." Then they asked her if she loves the people in her life, and she again says, "Yes."

After listening for about ten minutes I say, "Shawn, however you feel about all of us, I wouldn't call it love. I don't know what it is. It's something else. People who love each other don't treat each other like this." My words are edgy. I know I am hurt and angry. I also know what I am saying is the truth.

Perhaps Shawn does too, but it doesn't change her thinking.

She offers to stay to teach me – or whoever – the responsibilities she has been fulfilling.

When I suggest she stay a week, Shawn bristles. "I won't stay a week."

I tell her if she is going to leave with integrity and dignity then she will stay a week. She knows why I am saying this. The next four days are filled with over 3 dozen people coming in for meetings, classes, counseling training, Intuitive Reports and so forth. These cannot be shelved for a crash course in websites and accounting.

"I won't stay a week," she repeats, slamming a door.

At that point I let go. There is no reason for this to turn into something dark.

I still my mind and hear her clearly.

Shawn is going to leave. She wants to leave as soon as possible.

I think of Despereaux's mother. When she learns that Despereaux is to be condemned to the dungeon where he will certainly be eaten by rats, she swoons, then she says, "Adieu!" "Adieu!" is the only word she has for her child.

"In French it means farewell," the author writes. "It is not the word you want to hear from your mother as you are led to the dungeon. You want to hear, 'Take me instead! I will go to the dungeon in my son's place'."

Shawn is saying adieu. No matter what *I* want to hear. No matter how I see it can all be different.

My thoughts do not matter.

Adieu.

I look at the pendulum clock on the wall, 7:20. I have ten minutes to walk to the Peace Dome and set up filming. I excuse myself saying, "I need to go."

I am letting go with a newfound grace.

As I walk under the stars to the Peace Dome, a part of me lingers with Shawn and Dr. Dan. Hopeful thoughts return. Maybe if she would stay she would reconsider. Maybe talking with her peers will stimulate new ways of thinking, new perspectives. Maybe when the time comes for her class to meet she will realize she hasn't missed class at all, and she doesn't want to, and so reinstate herself by being in class. Maybe she will see what she is throwing away. Maybe.

They are fleeting thoughts from the heart. Hopes.

When Miggery Sow first sees the royal family – the king, the queen, and their daughter Princess Pea, the love of Despereaux's life – she is enchanted. She tries to understand "the perfect family, the brilliance of them." She searches to put a name to this new emotion. And she realizes it is exactly the opposite of a good clout.

"Hope is like love," De Camillo writes, "a ridiculous, wonderful, powerful thing."

As I watch *The Silver Cord* unwind before my eyes, I wish Shawn could be with us tonight in the second floor of the Peace Dome. I wish she could see these ten people bring to life their memories from past lives. What might she see in Chris Sheehan? Chris is a student of her student's student. In the School of Metaphysics we realize that teaching creates lineages of the spirit, similar to those more familiar which reflect the body, the bloodlines. One person initiates another into this study of consciousness and mind. Then as that person learns, sometimes the desire to share with others wells up from within and that person passes on what he has learned. In this way a lineage of teachers is created in a matter of months. Shawn is a part of such a lineage. What might she see in Chris's enactment as Ha Tu, the earliest of scientists searching for a means to create a genetic form then becoming entrapped by his own creation?

Or in Dr. Pam Blosser as Alnitaka, the Mayan shaman who believes in the divine and suffers from humanity. In Aaron Krieshok as Ying Ku the Egyptian mathematician who is Plato's contemporary, or in Dave Rosemann's, Nekatu, Ethiopian charmer of the fire.

What awarenesses might Talina Woods' embodiment of Lolinka – the Persian snake charmer whose dance pleases the master without and within – bring to the surface? Or Greg Brown as Boris Nyevsky, the Russian who gained fame and wealth in China only to lose it all.

Might Paul Madar as Katchewa, the Hopi Indian father who teaches his son the actions of peace, or Tad Messenger as Joshua ben Yochem, a carpenter in Nazareth in the early days of Jesus, strike a chord in her heart? Or perhaps Laurie Biswell as Erin Lofk Ainshey, the Irish girl born in poverty who becomes a benefactor to all children, might speak to Shawn.

I will never know, for I did not ask Shawn. I did not insist. I chose instead to come out on my own.

This week accounts of Mel Gibson's movie *The Passion of the Christ* are everywhere. The reviews talk about it not being a movie, not entertainment, but an experience. I understand movies as experiences. Years ago *One Flew over the Cuckoo's Nest* was like that for me. Like Gregory, the jailor in Despereaux, I understand how stories bring light.

Creating experiences of depth and meaning is what we are exploring here at the College of Metaphysics. We call them emperiences. We know that how people receive what we give – be it time with Mohandas K. Gandhi and Nobel laureates or classical Christmas music – particularly here in the Peace Dome, is the reflection of the consciousness we are willing to invest. When we are present-minded in the experience others are drawn to it.

I am having trouble with this tonight. I struggle with thoughts of being a hypocrite as I urge them to be present-minded when part of me stayed at the main building with Shawn and Dr. Dan. I struggle with being distracted the entire time we are together.

I wish Shawn was with us. I could have asked her to join us. But I didn't. I wish she wanted to be with us. But she said she does not.

Something else is more important to her.

Perhaps, if she were asked, she might say the same about me. She might say that this rehearsal was more important to me than she is.

The reality is she is not here. Now.

I look at the circle of people in front of me. I concentrate on each one. I love them as much as I love Shawn. My head and my heart, working together, get me here.

Tonight, these are the people I am choosing to be with. These are the people who looked forward to Shawn's stay. These are the people who have no idea that Shawn has made a choice that excludes them. These are the people with whom I am striving to create a tale of our own, about the soul and its journey into light. These are the people who will help me to see the infinite possibilities in this most finite of experiences.

Rehearsal is over early. As I walk back to the main building I am watching my thoughts. This is a seasoned skill developed through concentration. After three decades of practice, being able to separate Self, the thinker, from the thoughts Self creates is natural for me. Second nature, it's called, when you know something by heart.

As I exit the Peace Dome, the orchard is reflected in the starlight. I remember standing here four months ago when we dedicated this structure as a "universal site for peace". Following the Peace Dome Dedication in October, I remember starting to experience the energies of 2004, what we would later describe as "The Open Heart".

My journey into open heart began in November with a berating phone call from Shawn, the first and only of its kind. Now I saw what I could not see at the time – how this was a perfect gift for me to begin the process of consciously moving from lower heart to higher heart. Lower heart being the manifestation of the need to care in the human being and the battle of indifference and sympathy that eventually evolves into compassion. Higher heart being the expression of mental concern and embodiment of divine love.

At the time, the hurt I experienced from Shawn's sharp words were like arrows. The pain was devastating. I felt misled. I felt misunderstood. Mostly, I felt falsely accused.

These were all thoughts and emotions from *throughout my life* – they didn't begin or end with this woman, she was merely a tool through which the experience was coming into my world. Memory is experience resonance, the scientist in me says. The stimulus for this recall was a phone conversation. What my mind then did with it, how my mind became polarized was the manifestation of the lower heart energies.

I watched my mind go to extremes in the hours following that conversation. I was able to separate ideas of good and evil which I had been working with quite consciously for some time. I had to become aware of my own thoughts. I had to gain mastery of undivided attention and concentration so I could elucidate what my thoughts are. I had to become aware of my imagination and when I was becoming distracted by creative ideas. I had to know when I was falling into memory which had nothing to do with the present moment. All of these were skills I learned in the School of Metaphysics and had honed for years. I had applied them with myself and others.

I became very clear, bringing to myself the ability to be awake and aware of the content of my thinking. I knew what my thoughts were beyond any doubt. This told me that Shawn was projecting her ideas and thoughts onto me. In psychology its called projection, which is an appropriately descriptive term. In effect, Shawn was giving her thoughts away in full belief that I was the source and not her.

I knew my thoughts of her were open and creative. My thoughts were directed in terms of how we were with one another, how we interacted together and what we were able to create together. My thoughts would often go to future possibilities, future projects that we might share.

This line of thinking was similar to what I watched Christine create. She too saw a bright future with Shawn, her husband and her yet-to-be-born children, a part of it.

Now in this phone conversation, Shawn was telling me, in a way she would never suspect, to *still my mind*. She was instructing me to *open my mind to the possibility* of anyone filling the place she had occupied.

One of the Universal Truths that I understand and live by is: *the nature of the physical is change*. I can understand that openness is a part of that process. I can then see that the open mind, the willingness to be open in your thoughts, to entertain the enormity of the resources available, leads to an open heart. In November, I was being given a wonderful opportunity to prepare for what was happening in my experience now.

Just a couple hours ago when Shawn was telling Dr. Dan and I about her reasons for wanting to leave, she said "I could have left last fall after that phone conversation." She looked at me for confirmation that we both knew which phone conversation she was referring to. "But I didn't want to leave angry." Although I will never know the construction of her conscious mind thoughts, of what the anger was about, I can sense the energies and identify them.

Beyond all that, I am grateful that her learning was compatible to mine. Before I have experienced guilt from someone else being angry. "What could I have said or done that would make this outcome different? What do I need to change? How could I have done better?" This time, quite miraculously, there is no guilt. There is no regret of any kind because I know the cleanness of my thoughts and my intentions. I have always respected Shawn and her choices. Because of that respect, I can give her the space that she wants.

Because I trust the universe to supply my needs, I am confident in my ability to remain open through this experience. The degree to which I can do this has proven to be a blessing to others. Remaining open brings a deeper understanding of abundance as infinity – the essence of "more". This is Infinite Being. Being an example of what I believe, of what I know, of who I AM.

The truth is

I am the only one who can deny me

forgiveness, or freedom, or friendship,

whatever is my most heart-felt desire.

After Hezekiah, our nine year old, is asleep, Dr. Dan and I sit together for a while. There isn't much to say yet. It is all too new.

I have begun to think of who-can-learn-what-quickly so Shawn can leave as she desires. The thought enters my mind, *"I am always helping other's fulfill their desires."* It appears to be part of my function in the world. I am learning to fulfill it without attachment. With grace and ease, compassion and equanimity.

The heat generated from my earlier hurt has faded. I think of Botticelli Remorso. What a name!? Botticelli is the rat's rat. The one who rules the dungeon of darkness. The one who teaches the new rats how to be rats.

It is Botticelli who tells Roscuro that light has nothing to do with the meaning of life. For Botticelli the meaning of life is suffering, particularly the suffering of others.

" 'Do as I say and your life will be full of meaning,' Botticelli tells Roscuro. He proceeds to teach Roscuro how to torture a prisoner. 'First, convince him he is your friend. Listen to him, confess his sins. When the time is right, tell him what he wants to hear. Gain his trust, then deny (refuse) him. You withhold what he wants the most. Forgiveness, freedom, friendship. Whatever it is that his heart most desires, you withhold.

'You are not a friend, you are a rat.' "

I am beginning to understand light and dark on a whole new level of awareness. Botticelli's description of how one becomes a rat is succinct. The wolf in sheep's clothing enteres my mind. I think of what this really means. How many times did a friend tell a secret, or a teacher withhold a praise, or a parent an allowance or the car keys? Simplistic, do you think? Perhaps. Yet this is the reality of most lives. To realize friends, teachers, and parents who follow the teachings of Botticelli are "rats" is to begin to awaken from what tortures us through life.

The truth is I am the only one who can deny me forgiveness, or freedom, or friendship, whatever is my most heart-felt desire. Does this sound far-fetched to you? One of the ways I came to realize the truth of Self possession is through other's experiences. The reality of torture became clear to me when I learned how Mohandas K. Gandhi purposefully went to prison. And Martin Luther King, Nelson Mandela, and a host of other people who believe in their cause. With all of these people only their bodies were in prison, never their minds.

For suffering to rule you, you must believe in it. You must give it existence. In the past two years I have had a very personal, revelatory relationship with Gandhi's ideas. I believe him when he writes there is only good, that evil has no objective existence of its own, only that which *we* are willing to give it. I choose to see the good in this situation.

I am not a rat in this, nor is Shawn. Neither of us are bad guys. Even though part of me feels betrayed, I know better. She is merely doing what she wants to do. How I choose to respond will be my choice.

Much later in Despereaux, the Threadmaster tells him, "You, friend, are on a quest." Despereaux doesn't understand and the Threadmaster says it doesn't matter, the little mouse need only "feel compelled to do the thing, the impossible, important task at hand."

I am compelled to understand and so I begin to write.

Pisces are symbols.

This is what I am thinking at 1 a.m. I have always felt ill at ease when something has upset my equilibrium. Even as a child I would be restless, unable to sleep, when something was on my mind.

One of the first benefits of the mental disciplines taught at SOM is the ability to recall the day's events clearly and in detail. The memory exercise opens the door to realizing causal points in your life. Strengthening my memory has given me access to the cause of what I experience. Knowing cause has brought me forgiveness, gratitude, and resolve.

Through the years I have used a growing variety of methods for self-counsel. Of these, writing tends to be favored. So it is I find myself writing these words, long after most everyone is asleep. I am seeking resolve of my thoughts about Shawn. I am coming to terms with what I have learned from having her in my life, and what life without her may be.

I am receiving this experience in the most personal way, and I am receiving it in the most universal sense for I know that Shawn is both a reality in my life and a symbol of many other people, places, events, and circumstances in my life.

Pisces are symbols. The classic description of the final energy of the zodiac is expressed in two words, "I believe." I have studied energies for three decades now. The energies of our universe as they manifest through astrology are therefore of interest to me.

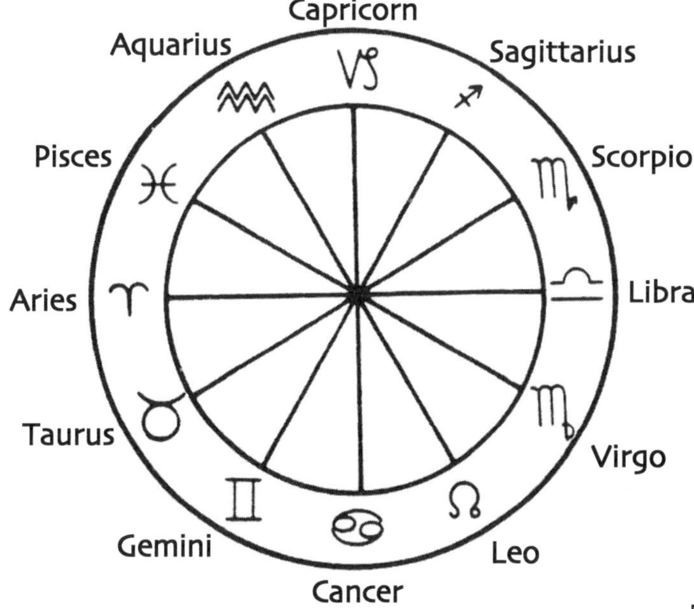

The classical words for Aquarius, which precedes Pisces on the astrological wheel, are "I know". I have often given consideration to how believing can follow knowing particularly since in the School of Metaphysics teachings we describe the Universal Law of Creation as the "Law of Believing and Knowing". Until tonight, I have settled with Piscean believing as indicative of the reaching for a new cycle. Coming up out of the wisdom of knowing through experience, we now imagine how to share that wisdom. We believe anew.

Through this experience with a beloved Pisces, my mind focuses on believing as the mutability that follows the fixed Aquarian quality. "To be in the world" is Aquarian. "Not of it" is Piscean. For understanding there must be both. To be brought to their doorstep means using the life you create.

I feel my head clearing, my mind opening to new awarenesses.

An insight into the Virgo (the zodiacal sign opposite Pisces in the astrological circle) quality comes into my mind. The words classically employed to describe that quality are "I analyze" or "I discriminate". Some years ago I worked to synthesize my understanding of astrological influences in a way that would reflect the movement of consciousness in Human Man to become Spiritual Man. This resulted in new descriptive words for each zodiacal sign. I was at peace with each one I had chosen except Virgo. The clarity of perception for Virgo eluded me.

Today, with the reality of a good friend walking out of my life where I *believed* she was walking into it, I see the Virgo energy quite clearly. The more evolved energy, the energy of the reasoner who courts intuition, can be described as "I assess."

Let me explain for a moment. Virgo is an earth sign operating in the sector of the astrological wheel which deals with self and another. The signs of Leo, Virgo, Libra, and Scorpio all are relationship signs meaning the learning is associated with intrapersonal relationships. What is begun in the first earth sign Taurus (the influence of my sun and rising signs) as value is carried on by the Virgo in the act of determining *relative* value. This is best described as the act of assessing. While Tauruses learn to give and receive value, Virgos assess the value of anyone or anything based upon its relativity to them. This is why they are inclined toward service positions as this affords them constant opportunities to assess. This process then continues into the final Earth sign, Capricorn, where the assessed value is experienced between Self and humanity, the much greater whole. This expression I picture as Albert Schweitzer's "reverence for life", the key words of Capricorn "I respect" reflect this.

In this moment I can see how the Earth signs all fit together. How each leads to the next. Putting this into the context of what I know about the inner levels of consciousness, it tells me a great deal about the emotional pulls I am experiencing in the present moment. The temptation to become polarized into good-bad thinking – to judge Shawn, to judge her choice, to judge myself – surfaces like a knee-jerk reflex.

An image of my dad, a Virgo with a Sagittarian moon, comes to mind. He can assess in a BIG way. He has always had everything and nothing, at the same time. His ego has quarreled with this every day of his life. From money to marriage, he assesses credit and blame on everything and everyone, including himself. I see this so clearly right now. He has a tremendous grasp of emotional truth. He can also be like Ahab railing at Moby Dick. Obsessed with his version of the truth.

This reminds me of something Shawn said. In a self counseling tape Shawn made just a week before today she said, "I guess I don't want to face the truth. I want to keep my version of the truth, and I don't want anyone to mess with it." Such a lucid assessment of how the Piscean loses sight of what is real is striking to me. Yet, as evidenced in my life today, there is often a large gap between grasping the truth intellectually, in ideas, and living that truth.

I hear the words "beauty is in the eye of the beholder" inside my head. Beauty is a word I associate with Shawn. When I first met her she had Rapunzel hair that cascaded down past her waist. I knew the investment it takes to grow your hair that long, and to have it in radiant condition. "Here is a young woman who can commit to something," I thought. The observation became one of the cornerstones for my perception of Shawn.

Upon meeting her, most people receive Shawn's goodness. Her dharma centers on serenity. *Dharma* comes from the Sanskrit *dhr* meaning "to sustain", "to nourish". In my experience, Shawn's dharma is the epitome of the meaning of the word. I think of dharma as dual. It is both one's duty and the divine order of the universe therefore dharma transcends the pairs of opposites.

"Pairs of opposites" is a term used in ancient Indian writings to describe the physical nature of existence. "Free thyself from the pairs of opposites – the changeful things of finite life;" says the Bhaghavad Gita. "And careless about the same dwelleth thou in the consciousness of the Real Self. Be free from worldly anxiety, and the fierce cravings for material possessions. Be self-centered and uncontrolled by the illusions of the finite world."

As Jesus said it, "Be in the world, but not of it."

Buddhi yoga, arising from the teachings of the Buddha, describe dharma as "action that pleases the lord." These are the actions that lead a soul to union with God.

Who am I to say that Shawn walking away from years of investment toward a Doctorate of Divinity and Metaphysics will lead her astray from her dharma? I know it is not for me to decide. It is not even for Shawn to decide. She will live the truth of her thinking wherever she is. She will reap what she sows. As am I.

Dharma implies where you stand. It is your point in evolution. I know that Shawn's choice to no longer be a part of my life is being accepted by me as a yardstick, a measurement of where I am in evolution. How this will all end, I cannot see fully. I have faith that it will reveal itself in the hours to come. What I know is how to learn, and I will learn as much as I can from this situation.

I have learned how to make

the most of every experience.

I know the sequence of events in thought that produce understanding which unites the soul. I know I will miss Shawn in my life. All the things that "could have been." Most of all I will miss her presence. It is a profound experience of peace to be with her.

From what I have learned of Shawn in the past six months, I now realize what a confusing experience this must often be for her. To have others drawn to you like a magnet when your mind is filled with dark thoughts of rebellion, lust, self-condemnation and the like must be troubling. I think back to my own trials with worthiness. The night of the dark soul I prefer to call it, pun not intended. The reasoning mind is challenged to separate the light and dark. Being blinded by Shawn's inner presence, her dharma, I had only recently realized the ugliness.

From the soul's perspective it would make sense that one whose dharma is described as serenity would find the self in the midst of many experiences of the pairs of opposites. War, battle, conflict of mental, emotional, physical, or spiritual calibers would arise for such a soul because their presence can neutralize the energies in those situations.

On one level I realize there is little of this kind of conflict in a place where the world's Peace Dome lives.

On another level, I know how individual dharmas help build community and sustain it. I feel it more potently each time someone physically leaves the College and I am learning to appreciate it more when it is present.

On another level, I am just beginning to admit how Shawn's presence had given me an ease that I relished. One way this manifested was in just talking. I talk with people every day. Usually the conversations are centered upon what they want to learn, explore, do, create, and so forth. Shawn was a place I found where I could often talk about ideas of personal interest.

I remember a conversation we had on Leonard Orr's book *Breaking the Death Habit: The Science of Everlasting Life*. Leonard describes the Eternal Father as Goraknath. Nath means "Lord" and gorak means "garbage". The name is descriptive of the Holy One's coming to earth in the form of a discarded babe who died of starvation, the result of infanticide.

"God incarnated as Goraknath 9000 years ago," Leonard writes, "He is the great Kali Yogi – the destroyer of time, limitation, evil, and death. He is the bringer of truth, simplicity, love, and immortality. .... Goraknath lives in the world for a few decades, absorbing the karma of his disciples into his own body. Then he disappears into the Himalayas for a few decades to do spiritual purification – setting an example for us. He heals and rejuvenates his body and comes back again to participate in the world."

The idea of being a psychic vacuum cleaner for humanity is one I can wrap my mind around. This awareness is largely due to Shawn. She would sometimes describe experiences where she would indiscriminantly absorb other's emotions. I noticed that these in turn would manifest as rashes on her hands and face.

Through counseling with Shawn I began to study how my dharma in the world performs a kind of cleansing function for individuals. I am often a discharge point for people to release polarity and see themselves or their situations in a new light. I can see how the Piscean influence calls upon one for this kind of work. That is why the 12th house is the house of karma, of the mysterious and unexplained, of institutions and the like. My sun is in the 12th house of my chart. This is why I am reminded of the story of Goraknath.

Something my favorite astrologer Bill Herbst said to me in 1975 comes back to me, "Whatever hasn't gotten done by the soul gets dumped into the twelfth house." He explained it to me as "You've come back to tie up loose ends." Seeing few connections between the Taurus sun and all other planets in my chart he added, "That's not easy to do when there are no ties."

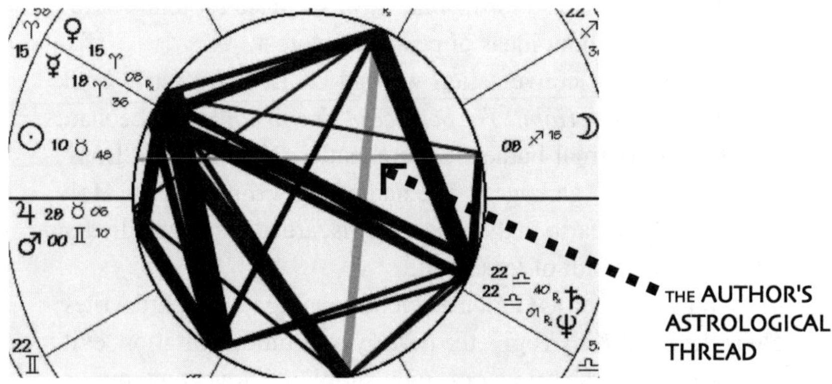

THE AUTHOR'S ASTROLOGICAL THREAD

Part of my life's work has been grasping what he meant. I have grown to see the single connection, like Despereaux's red thread, as an amazing blessing in the cause of enlightenment. Changes can rock my world and there is a part of me that receives it in stride. That's probably why I consciously desire equanimity. In light of yesterday's events, I can sense that I'm about to go to a whole new level of understanding of what this means for my soul growth.

Late in the Tale of Despereaux, the little mouse is on his way to save the Princess who has been kidnapped and taken to the dungeon. The Threadmaster, the one who tells Despereaux that he is on a quest, gives the mouse a spool of thread and a needle he can use for protection. He then does something miraculous. The Threadmaster frees Despereaux of the thread around his neck. The thread that would lead him into the dungeon ***against his will****.*

"You're free," the Threadmaster says. "You see, you're not going into the dungeon because you have to. You're going because you choose to."

It is Desperaux's destiny.

I understand destiny. That urge that arises from within one's soul, calling, and in its beckoning commands to be heard. In the hearing, the spirit is freed into life itself. Into duty. Dharma.

Destiny is neither-either, yet both. This moment in my life, stimulated through a thread with one person, holds the heavy lightness of destiny. Once again it is emotion that opens the door. Surprise. Denial. Hurt. Anticipation. Anger. Blame. Thankfulness. Regret. Gratitude. I move along the astrological thread to bring light to my netherworld. I am grateful for the hurt, the anger, the disappointment I have experienced today.

In gratitude I am free to choose. I know I embrace the darkness so I may become light.

I've written enough for tonight. I feel good about the resolve I have. Scarlet O'Hara's classic line from Gone with the Wind sweeps through my consciousness, "Tomorrow is another day!" I smile because since I read the book at 16, I have seen the character as incredibly strong, secure and amazingly heartless, childish. She is like a baby creator, self-indulgent, wishing away what she does not like and pretending that what is too hard to bear never happened.

I know this is making demands on my ego. It is testing my understanding and the maturity of my heart. I welcome the test.

I am committed to stilling my mind and completely embracing whatever comes. I understand quest. I know it is the result of choices well made. My quest is for truth. This night truth comes in my thoughts and in my dreams.

Dharma Profiles are an intuitive report on the individual soul's mission in life. Often they bring clarity to why we are drawn to others and they to us. In today's climate of uncertainty and insecurity, Shawn's dharma of serenity is magnetic for many.

Dharma Portrait

...serenity. We see that there is a great power within this one for centeredness and for the capacity to allow energy to flow through this one.

We see that this has been built over many periods of time. There have been many investments that this one has placed in a kind of environment where this one needed to be disciplined and needed to be Self aware and Self controlled. We see that this was done in training fashion in many cases whether in religious monasteries or in schools such as in Greece and in Japan. This one has brought to the Self the education that was needed to refine the vibration of the Self and we see that this one has absorbed this and has brought it into the Self in great abundance. Therefore there is a great capacity within this one for peace and for tranquility that is quite magnetic and very soothing to the Self and to others. It is this capacity for stillness and therefore peace that does give this one the greatest sense of fulfillment and the capacity to influence other ones to a great extent. It is a power that this one needs to realize and to cultivate. For it is the essence of magnetism and therefore of charisma.

What would be the relevance of this one's dharma to the present lifetime?

This one has a sense of what has been spoken and even a sense of a kind of urge toward responding to it. However, there are several ways in which this one doubts it or does not believe in the Self, not so much in the capacity as in the presence or reality of what has been spoken. There is a very real need for this one to cultivate Self acceptance and to do so with a vision in mind. There is a need for this one to begin to embrace that which has come before and to realize that that which this one is today is the accumulation of all of the good that has happened. That which is not understood or a source of pain or turmoil for her is temporary in nature and has not been longstanding, nor has it been accepted as a permanent part of the Self. This understanding brought into the awareness will aid in this one being able to separate that which is real and eternal from that which is illusionary and temporary. *It is when this one is still that the serenity fills the Self, this one need not do anything, it merely occurs and there is a need for this one to be accepting of this, attentive to it and to allow it to grow and to permeate this one through every movement, through every thought.* There is some idea that immersing the Self in the serenity will mean losing other things that this one holds valuable, this is erroneous. Serenity does not require the forfeiting of liveliness. In fact it is the threshold for truly being alive. This is all. *(7-21-2000-BGC-4)*

Thursday Morning

Daniel and I are in a glen floating through a tunnel made of ivy and foliage. It is like a tube. Hezekiah comes and goes. He moves in and out of the pathway, weaving in front of us, beside us, behind us, then moving out into the woods, then back. There is a rhythm here, like a dance. Light comes through the ivy streaming on our faces and clothes.

I hear Hezekiah giggle and say "Probably Right there!" Then I don't hear him anymore. I stop going forward and look around, seeking him. I know I've lost track of him. I look to Daniel, but I know he doesn't know where Kiah is. I start panicking. I'm afraid.

I become lucid and it takes a moment or two to calm the emotion. To realize this is a dream. I hold my attention on Daniel's face and reach for his hand in the dream. We embrace and I hear Hezekiah's giggle again. Kiah emerges from the shadows and he seems a few years older now. He continues his weaving out and weaving in as we continue in the same direction along the path again.

I have been interpreting dreams since I was 22. I have had conscious, lucid dreams since I was 24. This dream is about being in the present. Hezekiah represents the idea that I can be fully illumined in the moment. Yesterday my attention strayed from this ideal because I allowed my emotions to get the better of me. I know this is the anger and hurt and disappointment and loneliness I felt. The dream tells me it was through consciously aligning the inner and outer selves that I could pass through this emotional sea. I had to reestablish my purpose, to align my conscious purpose with my inner urge. Doing so caused a maturity in that ideal. A maturity in me.

I am grateful, for I sense that I will draw from this newfound maturity often in the experiences ahead of me and that doing so will teach me what I need to know.

I look at the clock. 4:20. Still an hour and a half before I need to get up. I lay there in the darkness for some time, thinking.

Thursday 7 a.m.

We congregate in the Great Room for the Teacher's Guide class. Shawn does not come.

The topic today is the "Student Guide", a four page introduction to the School of Metaphysics that students read the first night of class. Interacting with this wonderful group of people keeps me focused on how I am needed. Teaching, the sharing of love and truth, is a transcendent experience for me. I am especially grateful for the opportunity this morning.

My heart keeps hoping through the entire class that Shawn will walk in. It is not until after class that I give myself time and space to take stock of this. In the reality that she did not come, my heart sinks and my head comes forward.

"Of course she wouldn't come!" I hear the chiding words in my head. "Why should she? She doesn't want to teach, to learn with us anymore." I hear the truth in my words, and acknowledge that they are not clean. My heart isn't in it. My heart is wounded. My heart is cloaked in rejection and hurt, and this taints my thoughts. My words are both truthful and self-wounding. The feeling is Shawn doesn't want us anymore.

In earlier times, with other students, the sinking feeling at the pit of my stomach would have affected me throughout class. It would have constantly pulled on my attention like a beggar. Like a thief, it would have robbed me of my greatest joy. I take stock of the difference. I have learned how to live in more than one level of consciousness. I have learned how to be in the moment. I know how to forgive. I can more completely love. I am a better teacher for it.

When Despereaux is brought before the Mouse Council to be tried, they insist that he renounce his actions so he might go to the dungeon with a pure heart. Despereaux refuses. He loves the Princess.

He wonders what difference love makes. He wonders what went wrong. "Wasn't it a good thing to love? Happily ever after? Did the knight and fair maiden not live happily ever after, after all?" He wonders about the distance between what he has read and what he is living.

"Reader," de Camillo writes, "do you believe there is such a thing as happily ever after? Or like Despereaux, have you too begun to question the possibility of happy endings?"

The famous words of English novelist Samuel Butler – "It's better to have loved and lost, than never to have loved at all" – come into my mind. So does a man named John Clark.

John's death at 42 swept through our extended community. He was a close friend and beloved student/teacher. His passing, the result of medical management of diabetes, was not a shock to most of us. This intellectual knowledge, however, did not resolve how his passing touched each of our lives. I knew awareness of what John's death stimulated each of us to think, feel, release, resolve, and do, could be found through psi counseling.

I created a Raja Yoga exercise centered upon this common experience of losing a loved one. We explored our ideas about death, in a personal sense and a universal sense, making sense of our individual experiences and revealing connected patterns. In every case what we had been told as a child about death was significant in our inclination to accept mortality or reject it. My learning about this continued in a Taraka Yoga exercise following the stillbirth of Christine and Paul's eight month old, which she writes about in the *Infinite Manifestation* volume in this series.

These exercises were profound in developing the consciousness of self counsel for those pursuing Psi counseling. Since the first of the year when the current group of nine had begun training, I wondered how I was going to give them the benefits of this Raja Yoga experience. Since it cannot be heady for it is not an exercise in intellect, its potency depends upon a shared experience, in this case a common loss. I had no idea what that experience would be. I certainly did not image one of our members withdrawing from physical life.

I knew this needed to be a whole mind experience to reflect

what Raja Yoga is. I knew the answer would not be found in my brain, in physical knowledge only. I didn't know where it would come from, but I believed and knew that something of the same calibre as John Clark's death would occur. A common experience would come and it would be a stimulus for deeper understanding.

As I write this the full realization swells within me. This is the full mind experience I wanted. The stimulus is Shawn. The desire and all its fruition brings is of my own making. Does this mean I in some way influenced Shawn to quit? I know the answer is no. I was no more a part of Shawn's decision as I was a cause for John Clark dying. It does mean I will choose what Shawn's leaving means to me, how useful it is for my soul growth and the progression of others.

In Despereaux, Princess Pea's mother dies because a rat falls into her soup. The king loved the queen and without her he was lost. "This is the danger of loving," di Camillo writes. "No matter how powerful you are, no matter how many kingdoms you rule, you cannot stop those you love from dying."

Or going. My husband often says, "Everyone you know will eventually die or move away." His point is the nature of the physical is change, and our ability to accept change is the beginning of causing change in Self.

Until yesterday, Shawn was one of nine people training to become Psi Counselors. She and seven of these people have been studying metaphysics in the Third Cycle of SOM lessons with Dr. Daniel Condron for over two years. They have lost a classmate, a friend. How they receive this change will become part of their training in Taraka Yoga. Here is the Self counseling Raja Yoga I prayed for.

Shawn's passing is like a death. Certainly no less profound than John Clark's passing. I recall a line from *Anne of the Thousand Days*, a play about the life and death of Anne Boleyn. After Henry VIII has had her beheaded for alleged adultery he says, "It would be easier to forget you living than to forget you dead." For Henry, it is a thought of responsibility, of guilt, of realization, of the need to understand. Because he had her killed, she will remain with him, haunting him. There is no forgiveness there and so there is a holding on.

I will forgive and I will remember. How I will remember Shawn will become clear in the days ahead as I put my thoughts in order. For now, I am beginning to see the layers and the connections, in and between, and among us all. I am continually in awe as my reverence for life deepens. Thank you God for sending Shawn to me. And thank you for the wisdom to make her light my own.

Shawn comes upstairs about 10 to let me know she will be able to stay as long as we need her. She explains she has been concerned about her possessions. She had packed up her things to move here, to the College, for three months. Now she will be taking them to another town where she plans to enter a school for midwifery.

She says she has made arrangements with Ernie Padilla, the owner of a nearby store, to keep her things there for the next few days.

Given the reaction from the night before, I know this is not what Shawn wants or had planned. I don't know why she has changed but I respect her right to do so. Shawn's fears of being at war or controlled or at odds with me is a fiction within her own mind. As long as she will let me know what she wants, I can respect and honor it. She had let me know what she wanted very clearly the night before when she said, "I won't stay a week."

Last night I spoke to my husband, chancellor of the College and also Shawn's teacher, about the need for others to quickly learn what Shawn knows so she can be free to leave as soon as possible. We talked about how that might be implemented. This was set into motion so it didn't matter that Shawn was changing her mind.

I explain this briefly and she agrees to whatever might be needed.

When she mentions Ernie, a thought that had gone through my mind in the past 12 hours returns. I ask Shawn, "Does Ernie know?"

"Yes," she says.

"I wonder how he's taking this." It is an open-ended remark rather than a question I expect her to answer.

Shawn replies, "He's not particularly happy, but he's okay."

I find this so strange to hear her say. Ernie has spent almost two years training Shawn to be an intuitive reporter and they have recently given their first Past Life Profiles. There are only a handful of people on the planet who give this service. Giving intuitive reports is incredibly insightful and so very helpful in the development of consciousness – to be a part of giving that service as well as receiving it.

This is something I felt certain Shawn is aware of. Yet in the moment I am open to those beliefs of mine disappearing.

The next statement is very telling. Shawn says, "Ernie knows how I am."

I have known Shawn and I have known Ernie to be quite headstrong and self-centered in what they want. This is the thought I was receiving from her. I note it, let it register, and still my mind to any further judgement.

"Come on, Mommy," Hezekiah says, trying to pull me to the stairs. I know he is hungry and I encourage him to go ahead of me.

I turn back to Shawn saying, "Dan and I would appreciate it if you would tell Kie when we are around." She nods seeming to understand immediately. "We don't have to be there, but it would be good for us to be close by in the room in case he wants to talk or go somewhere." She agrees and I go downstairs to find Kie.

Following lunch Jay, another student talks to me about the Society for Intuitive Research. Out of the corner of my eye I see Shawn go past. Kie is sorting his toy sea creatures into types. Lines of sharks, tropical fish, whales, jellyfish and the like stretch out on the living room floor.

I can hear Shawn talking, and I think it is good that she is giving Kie attention. I believe she'll wait until an appropriate time to tell him the news. Dan notes the interaction and brings my attention fully to it. "Shawn's telling him now."

I ask Jay if we can talk later, but it is really too late. By the time I turn around, Shawn is standing up and walking away from Kie.

Because of how she described her choice to him, which I hear about from him, he seems to take it in stride. Shawn doesn't linger with him, she leaves.

I ask Kie about what Shawn told him.

"Shawn's not going to be a student anymore," he quickly replies.

I say, "Yes, I know."

"It's okay, we'll still see her," he says. "She'll still come. It just won't be as often."

At the time I just nod. I know he will need time to assimilate what he has heard. He has experienced people leaving the College and not seeing them again yet that is not in his mind concerning Shawn. Kiah believed Shawn would be living with us for the next three months. He looked forward to it. In a few minutes seeing her every day has turned into seeing her less than he does now.

I keep a line of attention on Hezekiah from that moment forward. He seems to fair well throughout the afternoon.

I talk with Shawn after lunch, pairing her with people so she can pass on to others what she knows throughout the afternoon. Laurie will attend her until she leaves, being present whenever Shawn is teaching someone else and learning web design at other times. With a dharma of magnaminity, Laurie will absorb the entire picture. Paul Blosser will learn the mechanical side, Paul Madar the financial, Christine how to submit our sites to search engines. I say a prayer that each will give and receive completely in the time they have together.

Later in the afternoon Laurie seeks me out. We began working on the final scene of *The Silver Cord* day before yesterday, on Tuesday. Laurie's past lifetime is the most recent of the ten lifetimes we are illustrating and, being the final lifetime to be told, it will need to connect with all the other lives. Laurie wanted help in imaging this. I suggested she create a sketch, a kind of mini-mind/

treasure map, of the significant events in each person's lifetime. She now wants to go over what she has created so she can further develop her part.

Laurie tells me about each mind map sketch she has created. I am surprised. I expected her to do one map with herself at the center and the other nine souls around her. Instead, she has created individual maps of each person's life, nine separate sketches. I smile at her willingness to do things in a BIG way. It is her dharma of being magnaminous working through her.

Quickly I realize what Laurie needs are ties, the connections between the people.

I ask her to tell me the main events of Erin Lofk Ainshey's life. "My mother could not feed my brother and I," Laurie begins. "So she looks for homes for us." Laurie speaks in first person because she has memory of these experiences from another time and place. "It is the best she can see to do. She leaves me with a well-to-do woman. I am expected to be a servant. The woman is kind but I am at a loss. I don't know these people. The house is huge and rich to me. I am out of place. I miss my mother. I fall into a deep depression."

The images move before my mental eye of perception as Laurie talks. She is there more than she gives herself credit for. The distance between belief and knowing is what I must help her bridge.

"It is the kindness of the lady of the house that eventually brings me forward. Out of my gloom. She nurtures me, coaches me. She treats me more like a daughter than maid. She teaches me how to walk and talk and dress and conduct myself as a lady. She even finds me a husband, of abundant means. He has more money than he knows what to do with. He gives me anything I desire, which is actually little. I am still in awe and gratitude of what is before me.

"We have children and one of them is killed. It breaks my heart and threatens to destroy all the beauty I have been shown. I pull out of my grief with greater resolve than I have ever had. I commit to helping others, feeding the children who are hungry as I once was. I become quite respected in the community for my efforts and die at an advanced age."

"It's a beautiful lifetime, Laurie," I say. "So gentle compared

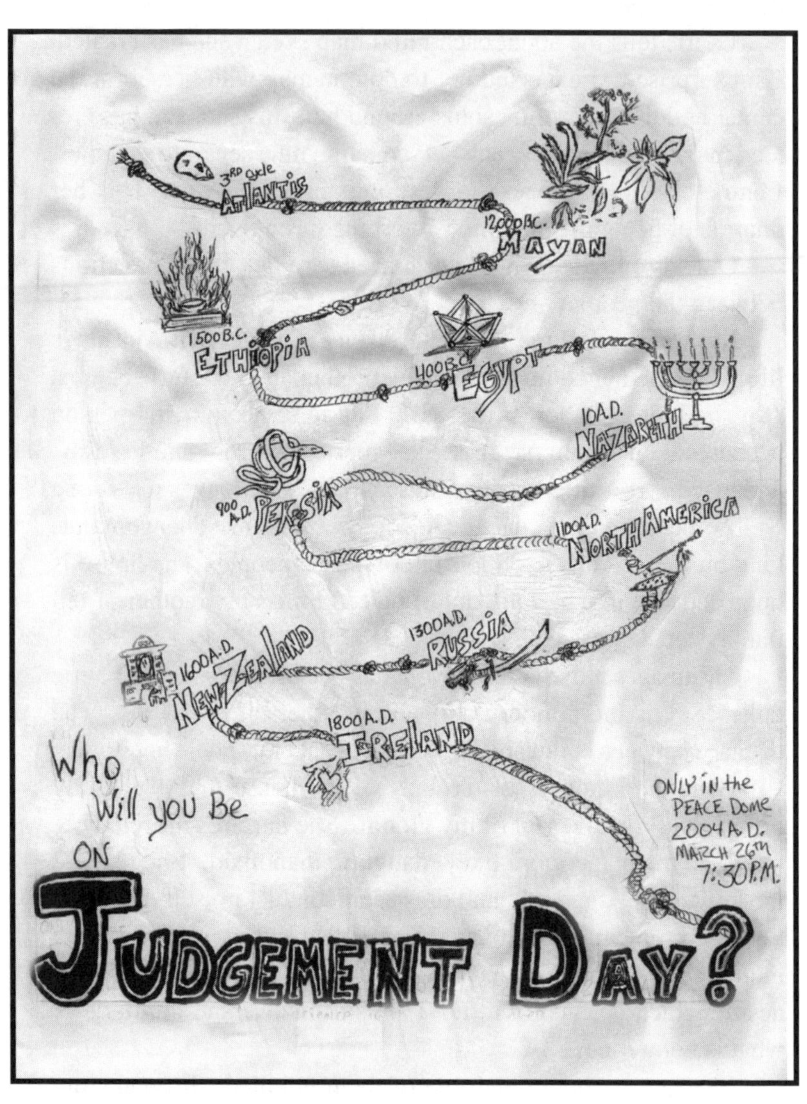
3RD cycle
ATLANTIS
12,000 B.C.
MAYAN
1500 B.C.
ETHIOPIA
400 B.C.
EGYPT
10 A.D.
NAZARETH
900 A.D.
PERSIA
1100 A.D.
NORTH AMERICA
1300 A.D.
RUSSIA
1600 A.D.
NEW ZEALAND
1800 A.D.
IRELAND
Who Will you Be ON
JUDGEMENT DAY?
ONLY in the
PEACE Dome
2004 A.D.
MARCH 26TH
7:30 P.M.

to most of the rest we portray." I suggest we list the names of the others. I ask her what she sees as each one's major learning. As we talk about the keys in each of the others' lives the connections begin to form. Ying Ku was taken from his parents at a very young age to be trained as a scientist in Egypt. He becomes disoriented from his experimentation with forms. Here is a connection of losing a parent. Lolinka blames her mother for her own loss of power, just as Erin blames hers for abandoning her. This is another point of relativity. Josiah ben Yochem returns home to find his wife and son dead, the victims of war. Josiah must return from the abyss of grief to serve the living, just as Erin must following the shocking death of her son.

One by one the connections unfold before our eyes.

The lady of the house in Erin's life parallels Nekatu's Ethiopian teacher. Erin's attachment to her son is echoed in the Hopi's life as much as in the life of the Hebrew carpenter from Nazareth. Her drive to make a difference is reflected in Briar Kain's search for perfection, and her need for connection is a fitting partner to HaTu's loss of it.

The details of what I foresaw are before me. Every day I think of how we are all connected. I live with this reality. A few weeks ago I believed we could illustrate this connection, today I know. The evidence is laid out before me in the very real connections between the past lives of ten people. When put together, these illustrate well the journey of one soul toward Enlightenment.

Laurie and I feel very good about what we have seen. Life is about learning, about how the choices we make either feed or starve our souls, and we are going to be able to illustrate it.

Feeding or starving our souls. Shawn comes into my mind and I allow her to be there. I wonder how many times we have known one another. I wonder if we will meet again. Finding no answer in the past or future, my mind moves to something tangible, something practical and immediately useful – choice. I choose to learn from this moment. I choose to learn the lesson Shawn has helped me create. I choose life. I choose love. I choose to feed my soul.

When Despereaux is being led to the dungeon he thinks "I cannot die....because I'm in love. I love somebody and it is my duty to serve her."

I understand such love, and duty, and service. I know what the inner choice is even when outwardly I feel like I am being led to a place I do not want to go.

Thursday Evening
The Still Mind is an Open Mind

"Dr. Barbara," Ivy says, "I'm having a hard time with Shawn leaving."

Ivy, a college student completing the requirements for her Doctorate of Divinity, and I are in the library for the purpose of teaching her how to respond to the School's daily emails.

I acknowledge by simply saying, "Yes." There is a moment of silence between us, each giving each other space to mourn. And to appreciate.

Then Ivy in true heartfelt and Piscean fashion asks, "How are you doing with it?"

This is the first time anyone has asked and it is quite a relief. I realize in that moment that much of my experience with Shawn had been that same kind of relief. The energy between us was such that it was easy for me to be honest and to completely give. I experienced acceptance with Shawn, a willingness to receive whatever I had to give without condition, without judgement. I felt she understood.

Through this moment with Ivy, I see that my greatest pain is the realization that this receptacle for my love, my thoughts, will no longer be present in my life.

In this moment I realize I had actually lost this four months earlier. An associated memory thought surfaces:

As the dedication of the Peace Dome grew near, I realized the information on our website would seem out of date after October 11, 2003. Much of the information was timeless yet the entire site was a historical account of building the dome. It would need to change otherwise it would appear irrelevant to the present and future.

Shawn was living in a Chicago suburb and came in once a month for class. I knew these weekend visits were not enough time for her to regenerate a site and since she planned on coming to the College after the first of the year, I was not inclined to ask her to come for a week. Rather, I decided I would devote every spare minute to this endeavor.

By the weekend following dedication, I was far enough that Shawn could create an index page directory to help visitors get around the site. Shawn and I discussed the categories of information and the ways they would be presented. She worked on it intermittently and when she said goodbye on Sunday she said the template was ready to be used for the pages I would create on the site.

I was so appreciative. Shawn has a wonderful sense of balance and rhythm that expresses itself well on the internet. After creating the elaborate sunburst on the School of Metaphysics site over a year earlier, she had begun designing websites for others as a source of income. Plus Shawn had skill. She could quickly grasp what computer programs are capable of producing. She thought in "computer language". Some of our best conversations were about this ability to perceive on different levels of reality beyond the physical world. Just as computers work like the human brain, so I have learned the web has counterparts to the conscious and subconscious minds.

Because we were invested in developing mind potential the level of creativity between us was high and could easily travel at warp speed. I relished this kind of rapidity for it causes me to reach, to excel, to respond fully in the moment. These were all part of the experiences I shared with Shawn – what she had come to represent to me in my life – that now I had to be responsible for in a way far from what I would ever choose.

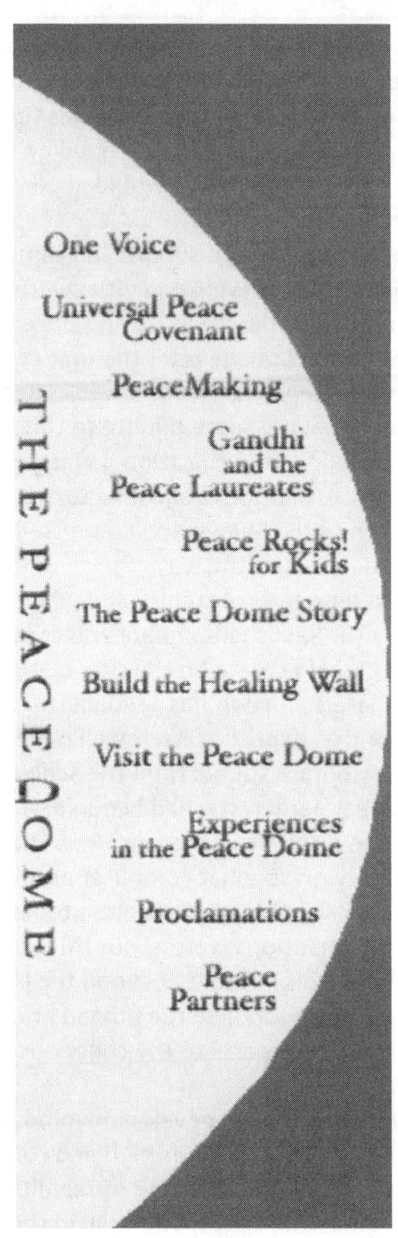

THE PEACE DOME
One Voice
Universal Peace Covenant
PeaceMaking
Gandhi and the Peace Laureates
Peace Rocks! for Kids
The Peace Dome Story
Build the Healing Wall
Visit the Peace Dome
Experiences in the Peace Dome
Proclamations
Peace Partners

PEACE DOME NAVIGATIONAL BAR CREATED BY SHAWN AND USED AT www.peacedome.org

When Shawn left that Sunday, it didn't occur to me to ask her to wait a bit longer so we could review what she had done. I hugged her, said "Great!" and told her to drive carefully.

A few days later when I was ready to use the page, I opened it so it would appear on the computer screen. The image was of a Dome flush to the left side of the screen/page. Ten horizontal segments divided the Dome to reflect the sections of information available on site. "One Voice", "Gandhi and the Nobel Peace Laureates", "The Peace Dome Story", and "Peace Rocks Kids" are examples of the sections.

As the image came up on the screen the top half of the Dome appeared, the bottom half did not.

I was dismayed. It would be four weeks before Shawn returned. I tried to figure out what might be going wrong. I wondered if it was something I was doing. I decided to contact the source. Shawn's email replies gave me several ideas to try, which I did with some success. The pieces still weren't in order though so Shawn suggested we could get on the phone and she could talk me through it.

One day early in November she did just that. By then I had resolved enough of the problem that I felt it could wait until her return in the middle of the month. I always enjoyed talking with Shawn although our distance communication was more likely to be through emails since both of us spent considerable time at computers. Today, was different.

What began as a simple tech-support call from Shawn turned into a bitter analysis of what Shawn did not like, understand, or accept about me.

I am having trouble recalling the specific words Shawn used in the conversation, but its emotional legacy continues to live with me.

I know it was in part this experience with Shawn, and my understanding from it, that led to the desire to explore judgement day in my Tuesday morning <u>Bible</u> study class. The idea of judging, the idea of discriminating, and the idea of separating and identifying and what these are as mental actions which produce learning and growth, are an integral part of my understanding how to be whole, and the temptation to become caught up in the pairs of opposites. This thought tells me the greater truth of the memory that has risen in my mind. I return to that memory:

After learning some of the thoughts Shawn has toward me, I have a difficult time reconciling the fact that Shawn and her fiance chose me as a minister for their wedding. Why would she choose someone who sparks such polarizing ideas to officiate at her wedding? The thoughts are incongruous. Throughout 2003, we counseled together in preparation for the marriage. Never was a word of dissension, of mistrust spoken. The talk was about marriage and children, and wanting to raise souls in a spiritual environment.

Christine and Paul Madar had moved to the College and were expecting a baby at this time. Christine was Shawn's matron of honor. It was quite shocking to me that what appeared to be a close friendship would be disrupted in this way.

Eventually what I learned from my reactions to Shawn's words came to me in a simple statement: **"I must still my mind."** I knew that having her best interest in mind first required me to have no thought. No creative thought concerning her.

This put me in a very interesting place because as far as I knew Shawn was coming to the College for three months after the first of the year. Since learning this, my mind had often drifted to what we could create together during that time. Sometimes I thought how Shawn might love it here and want to make a home here with her new husband. Internet development was a subject Shawn often talked about. She said she wanted to redesign the SOM web bookstore. We had dreamed of creating a membership site for the Society for Intuitive Research. When I thought of Shawn I thought of these kinds of activities that she might enjoy, learn from, give through, and that we might be able to do together.

There was a great deal of peace, of joy and excitement I experienced with these thoughts. This combined with my knowing that our son Hezekiah has a great love for Shawn.

On his list of best friends, she ranks #6 even though their time together is sparse. This was a demonstration of the profound influence Shawn had upon our son, and as I was discovering now – me.

In the face of being accused of trying to control her, what she does, and who she is – which I knew was not true – I knew that I needed to stop dreaming. I needed to stop actively thinking of Shawn in any way.

And so I did.

I didn't know until this moment how important that choice was, for me and for other people. What a step "stilling my mind" was in me being able to receive the experiences of today with equanimity. What I am realizing in this moment with Ivy is that stilling my mind produced something in me that only now do I recognize.

All of these thoughts come to me the moment Ivy asks her question. Rays of light flood my mind when she opens the door for me to talk. In that moment, the realization comes to me that God has sent me an elevated form of the energy that Shawn has been in my life *through the person of Ivy.*

Outwardly I tell Ivy, "I can accept Shawn's choice to leave the School of Metaphysics. My pain is experienced through Hezekiah, and through Christine. I have seen it coming," and you, reader, know some of the reasons why.

I explain briefly to Ivy that last fall Shawn let me know what she thought of me in clear terms, and that what I received from that experience was the need to still my mind concerning her. In this moment all of the puzzle pieces begin coming together on one level of this experience of parting.

As I talk, I begin to realize that what stilling my mind with Shawn meant was that I had stopped imaging with her. In essence, *what I had done was remove her from my images.* I still imaged the world moving. I still imaged website development. But it was no longer linked to her. It no longer depended upon her and it no longer included her. It was not that I was excluding her, pushing her out. I was seeing in my mind's eye what needed to be done without seeing any particular person doing the activity. My visualizations were open, the forms faceless.

I remember Jerry Rothermel, one of my teachers of metaphysics, explained the refined use of something we teach in the School of Metaphysics classes. "This tool for setting into motion the Universal Law of Prosperity works according to the images you produce," he said. "Image the condition or situation you desire, do not put faces on your pictures. People choose." Jerry said this over and over, partly because we needed to hear it, partly because he wanted to hear it as well. By creating in this open manner, the Laws of Creation reach into the infinite universe to fulfill your desire. Put a particular face in your desires, and that result is finite.

Over time, through teaching others and through my own experience, I began to see that imaging clearly what you desire in this way allows people to choose to be in the situations in your life and this is respect. There had been many occasions throughout my life to understand this. In concept, in theory, I could grasp it immediately for I realized that by imagining particular people you want in your life immediately you cause a finite condition of the mind. It makes you poor for you can no longer be open to the abundance of the universe and this was a concept I could readily grasp. I could understand it even at 22, with little experience in the physical world.

As a teacher, time and again when students learned of this prosperity tool they would image a relationship with a particular person. What would happen to many of these is that so-and-so did not want to cooperate. They were not interested! They did not share a compatible desire with the student. When the student woke up to this reality, he would often be put in a tailspin, going to extremes of anger, jealousy, lust, envy, disappointment, or even revenge. All of the human shortcomings would make themselves known.

I taught students how to use their imagination productively and in the process how to be prosperous.

This was all familiar to me but back in November, I did not want to remove Shawn from my pictures. I love her and enjoy her company greatly. She gives and receives with me in ways that few people have. So it was quite difficult at first to still my mind. My need was clear. In order to respect her and give her space I had to do this. So I moved myself to accomplishing the mental and emotional task. In succeeding, I had become free to accept her as she is.

My desire to give Shawn complete freedom so she could learn, and move and grow, had a negative description originally. Immediately I knew I *did not want* to warrant another emotional outburst. I knew I *did not want* to produce any images that she would interpret as controlling. Since Shawn is highly psychic, it was important that I direct my thoughts and calm my emotions, as well as control my words and actions. The transition in me would need to be complete.

In this moment, sitting with Ivy, I realize I had ceased to dream dreams with Shawn some time ago.

This is followed by an incredible moment of despair, for dreaming dreams with people is in large part what I live for.

I am reminded of pure exhilaration that moved through me of thrill and joy as we moved through the growing communication and connection worldwide that became the dedication of the Peace Dome. We began building the Peace Dome in the spring of 2001, months before the New York City events of 9-11. What we were building was much more than a physical structure. It was even more than a sacred site. With the Peace Dome, we were constructing a conduit for consciousness that will become a magnet on the planet for people of all backgrounds.

In one way, the Peace Dome is a symbol. In another, it is a channeler of energies – of light, of love, of peace.

Throughout 2003 we prepared ourselves for the time when we would give this structure to the world. I had a strong sense of wanting to unite us, here on the campus and throughout the School of Metaphysics. I began reading speeches from Nobel Peace Prize laureates. The words of people like Albert Schweitzer and Martin Luther King, the Dalai Lama and Mother Teresa, touched my heart and illuminated my mind. Here were people like you and I. People with lives very similar to anyone's. People with challenges and hardships and dreams.

I explored these people, and shared what I was learning in a form well catalogued in the book PeaceMaking – Nine Lessons for Changing Yourself, Your Relationships, and Your World. I had learned a great deal in those months of preparation. That learning is reflected in *The Invitation* and *Satyagraha* – both multidimensional experiences in the form of plays. The first intertwines the words of eight Nobel winners with the *Universal Peace Covenant*, a document penned in 1996 by two dozen spiritual teachers. The second is the life story of Mohandas K. Gandhi and his influence on those eight people.

I will think often of influence in the next hours. I will grow in appreciation of how I have practiced keeping my mind open to possibilities.

We presented these "plays" in the Peace Dome even before it was completed. In film footage, the bare wooden floors in the upper chamber are quite visible in *The Invitation*. This was all in an effort to elevate our thoughts, to reach for the highest each of us are capable of. I saw people transformed through portraying Linus Pauling and Jimmy Carter and Alva Myrdal. I watched people absorb their truths each time we would give these people life.

I experienced waves of powerful emotion each time I would describe Gandhi's death. I knew I had been in his presence each time I watched him walk out the Dome into history. Like my feelings about Shawn, I wanted to say, "No! Stop, don't go!" Each time my heart would expand to hold him wherever he is, whoever he might be now. Just as Gandhi's time had come and gone, so there was a part of me that understood Shawn's time had passed as well.

In a general sense many of my life lessons are about love, as I believe is true with all human beings. In a specific sense my life lessons as a reasoner revolve around the perception of value, particularly self and other appreciation. Studying the laureates, being in their company several times a week, living with those who were bringing these people to life, was an advanced course in love. I learned from each of these people the qualities which together we call love.

By summer 2003, I was experiencing adulthood. I had applied my mind single-pointedly, devotedly to the idea of peace, to understanding the idea of peace and living it, and to encouraging others around me to do the same. Now it was time to receive.

The world began to respond. This came to be, in large part, through the efforts of working with Dr. Laurel Clark. We began contacting members of the World Peace Prayer Society in Japan, Australia, Rumania, Brazil, and Israel. This expanded the number of people willing to join us in reading the *Universal Peace Covenant* beyond our own network of friends. In fact, two days before dedication, people on six continents had made commitments to be included.

It was Shawn and Ernie Padilla who would make email and phone connections with people in Argentina and New Zealand to finally make the Antarctica connection. Lynn Arnold and a friend, both living at Amundsen-Scott South Pole Station in Antarctica read the *Universal Peace Covenant* at 1pm CT making "One Voice" a truly global event.

The moments of reading those timeless words – describing peace, what it is and how it is made – with the world are imprinted in my consciousness. My vibration changed that day, as did that of many of us. It was like living in the future. This moment of giving and receiving with Emeka Onyekwere in Ghana and Hagit Radanan in Israel and Yashio Mochizuki in Japan made my heart soar with the doves that flew up and back and circled in the Peace Dome energy before flying home.

Shawn is a person who understands this kind of energy. She doesn't have to be convinced. She knows. She allows herself to be a tool for this work as much as I do.

It is dreaming these kinds of dreams of uniting the world, of being a force for good in the world, that I link with Shawn. So it is natural in my way of thinking that because of who she is and her willingness to help and serve that she had the same kind of commitment to our work that I do. What she was giving to me in the fall was a reality that this was not the case.

One of the final lines in *Satyagraha* comes into my mind as I write this. The narrator, who appears at the beginning and at the end says, "*Gandhi hoped that the satyagraha movement that caused*

India to win her independence would also serve to unite his people. But this was not to be."

I hoped Shawn would move through the anger and misunderstanding she displayed in November. "But it was not to be."

The present moment is like the end of a marriage for me. The surprise ending, where the spouse who has been brooding in silence for some time comes home one evening to announce he or she wants a divorce. The door is closed. There is no changing his/her mind. The finality is deafening. All hope sinks and only emptiness remains.

The dreams are gone.

Although the attitudes of despair are present, they do not overwhelm me for I have had many lessons in what the Buddha teaches as attachment. Ever since I began teaching at the age of 22, I have experienced people coming and people going.

In the beginning, depending upon my level of investment in them, whether it be mental, emotional, physical, or combinations of the three, the separation would leave me clueless and shocked. In the beginning I saw it as though I was torn from their picture without my permission, without any consideration for what I might have wanted or needed.

A parade of people - young and old, rich and poor, Christian and Muslim, of short duration or of many years - moves through my consciousness when I think of this kind of divorce. This divorce is not of a male-female relationship. It is not of a human marriage. This is divorce, or separation, between people. For years it had been very difficult for me to receive completion with grace and dignity although from the very beginning I tried.

Each successive experience of receiving people
and needing to let them go
added a richness and fullness to my love.
It afforded me learning opportunities
for unconditional love.

To learn about forgiveness, acceptance, and how to allow others to be who they are and where they are. Ultimately, I have learned to allow myself that same respect. To the degree that I have succeeded, I know infinity.

What helps me in this moment, sitting in the library with Ivy, is the memory of a lesson from five years ago. When I think of dreaming dreams, I think of a profound moment of revelation I had during a one of a kind weekend where we invited to our campus SOM students studying in the first cycle of the course.

Seventy or more came from Chicago and Dallas and Indianapolis and places inbetween. Five sessions of Intuitive Reports were given. It was the first time these people had experienced the research the School of Metaphysics has conducted for decades.

This was a weekend of openness and discovery. Everywhere you turned there were new faces, new people, eager to learn, curious. It was like having the campus filled with children of all ages. Their willingness to trust was beautiful.

On Sunday, Dr. Daniel Condron, College chancellor and my husband, and I walked with the group to what we call the Octagon field. This is the intended site of a very large, octagonal building that will serve as the world headquarters for the School of Metaphysics. Dr. Dan asked if I would talk about this building, this dream that had begun in 1993. I was thrilled by the opportunity.

In 1993, students came together and created plans for the 75,000 square foot structure. A model was constructed by students in Oklahoma City and transported to Chicago for the Parliament of the World's Religions. This was where the dream began.

On this Sunday morning, the dream had existed for five years and was no closer to being built. Previously I would have felt embarrassed by this, ashamed that our efforts had not made more progress. But this morning, standing in the sunshine with the crisp autumn foliage around us, it was different.

I was different.

The large field is huge. Up on a plateau, you can see in every direction. To the south is the existing building we use for headquarters and the road that goes into town and to the river. On the west are the hills where the pyramid will eventually be built with clusters of domes around it. The north is wooded, leading to the healing pond, and another road. To the east are the bluffs along the Niangua River.

As I began to describe the vision of the College – a place where people from all over the world can come to learn how to apply metaphysics, how to use consciousness, how to be a whole, functioning Self anytime, anywhere in the world – new thoughts moved through me. As I spoke about the potential of the people standing before me, I also described the potential for all of humanity to evolve and grow. I had said the words before, but on this day the images came together in a new way.

I looked at the faces of each of the people present. The energetic exchange between us could be seen. I was reminded of so many talks I had enjoyed on my travels in the 1970's and 80's. Through lectures, classes, and intuitive reports, I experienced many groups of people in many cities. The experience was always similar. I had the ability to stimulate idealism in people.

It was in that moment that I realized just how important this is to me.

I was always awake to the importance of sharing ideas. What was new on this day was how important the process is to me. The dreaming dreams together.

All of a sudden all of the attachment to accomplishment, to acquisition, to having, to manifesting, fell away. When the attachment was released, what was revealed was the truth that it is the process not the goal, the journey not the destination as the Tao teaches, as the focal point of illumination. I had taught this idea many times. Today I lived it, and it would forever be in my heart. I understood that dreaming dreams is what life is about. This is what happens in the present moment.

I had our son to thank for lessons in present moment that prompted this realization. These lessons were the stepping stones to this greater look at the world. The best way to direct your attention to the present moment is to have a child that you love with all your heart.

I know truth is in the doing and the being, the magic of believing together. This is what I have always loved about the School of Metaphysics. By its very nature, SOM is a magnet for those who love to dream. It produces an attractiveness to and from like minds. This magic is present in the Peace Dome.

I loved the weekends in 2003 when an increasing number of people would come to prepare the College for dedication. It was like they were being called. New people were coming into classes and finding their way to this little hamlet called Windyville. All because of a common dream. I received emails from a St. Louis mother who combed search engines at 2 am for organizations who needed to know about the Peace Dome. Experiences like these are not rare in my life. They come often. They are the manifestation of the power of dreaming together that I experience over and over.

It has become easy for me to dream with people.

I know thought is cause and the manifestation of it through the Peace Dome involves light workers around the globe. The light the Peace Dome adds means darkness has faded that much more. There are many on the journey to know how to be that light and teach others the same.

So when people I have dreamed with walk away, in the past I have tended to be wounded by that. I've tended to feel rejected, to mentally look at the empty place they are leaving. Through the years I've experienced a variety of reactions, of darknesses and each was an opportunity to illuminate, to bring light to those areas. Sometimes the light would come immediately. Sometimes it would take days or weeks or months for the forgiveness to be complete. The lessons have been rich.

Sometimes I would be angry when people would leave, because I felt helpless.

Sometimes I would be depressed because I felt hopeless.

Sometimes I would be hurt because I felt careless.

Sometimes I would be resentful because I was thoughtless.

It didn't take me a great deal of effort to put the responsibility on my own shoulders when people would leave. I've had lessons in giving credit and blame elsewhere. However, the understandings in me do not allow me to abide it for too long. I would always look to see how I could make something right. Resolve is very strong in me.

I've known for quite some time, what makes me restless, indeed what makes me sick, is when I cease to seek to resolve before I go to sleep. This is the essence of what staying awake means to me. My inner drive to assimilate experiences while awake is strong. Most people will go to sleep to assimilate, they will not be present consciously but will rely upon subconscious mind to provide that for them and give feedback in a dream. Many people don't even remember their dreams so the feedback is like a conversation that is never heard.

I understand the steps to becoming attentive. The steps to becoming awake and the ability to remain awake. I have learned this by devoted practice to spiritual/mental disciplines learned in the school.

Each opportunity when people would leave offered a lesson for learning. To learn how to give more, dream more, love more, create more. Shawn had given me a lesson. That lesson was the application over a long term and amidst attachment – both mental and emotional – of the STILL MIND.

The more in this case, was less. It was the ability to create infinity. Openness. So anyone could walk into the very vivid pictures that at one time she had occupied.

It was a lesson in space. Giving it. And receiving it. To open in my mind the space that at one time Shawn had occupied. Now my mind's pictures were open to an infinite number of people.

Thursday evening
More

Just as Ivy and I finish our work, Chris arrives at the door, college report in hand. Chris serves as this month's editor of the article that will be published in the School's monthly newsletter, *Vibra-*

tions. I offered to help him put the lengthy article into a layout program and this seems the best time to do so.

As we begin to work, he says, "Dr. Barbara, I just heard that Shawn is leaving." I turn away from the computer screen so we can see each other. "I don't know what I think about it."

I understand Chris's experience. In a symbolic lineage, Chris is Shawn's great, great spiritual grandson. Shawn moved from Oklahoma City to Dallas to teach and direct a School of Metaphysics. Because she taught a class, John became a student. Because John started a class Erika became a student. Because Erika taught a class Chris became a student. Because Chris started his study, he now found himself a student at the College of Metaphysics, here with me at this place and time.

I gaze at him with great love. He is like a child who learns that their great grandmother has died, who is just realizing she won't be around anymore. I know that how Chris views and embraces this moment will forever be important to him, particularly in the way he will receive in the future others' coming and going.

"I understand," I say. "I remember very well how I felt when I heard that my teacher quit. I admired her greatly. She set me on a disciplined path when it would have been very easy for me to be lax with application, strong in intellect. For Thelma this was unacceptable and I knew it. So I did my mental exercises, as assigned, no excuses and no apologies. It was Thelma who started me on my path of application."

Similar to Chris, I was into the advanced part of the course when I heard that Thelma was quitting. Unlike Chris I never got to say goodbye. My interaction with Thelma was about as distant as Chris' was with Shawn, we saw each other on occasion. It was the memories that were profound, such a high level of gratitude.

Thelma was a lesson for me in respect. Self respect, as much as respect for her and her choices. I know this will be true for Chris.

I can see in his eyes how we impact one another's lives. All the layers and depths that are infinity. It is accepting the more, reaching for the more, understanding the more, being at peace with the more. In that moment I can see the essence of more that I have always wanted. It's core as it evolves through the development of the thinker, of man.

Beginning with the animal tendencies for survival, we reach to fulfill our needs oblivious to others' needs. At first, we are like a child who takes a toy from another child with no thought of how it will effect that child. Without caring, the thought is merely survival.

For the human, survival turns into desire. The overtaking of the mind by desire is the reason why all marketing works in the world in its present state. Easily this more conscious ability to want becomes greed, the concept of "more" is born. Thus the Buddhist concept of desire-less-ness makes sense. It neutralizes the "more".

In this moment I can see clearly how the "more" evolves into prosperity for the reasoner. The person who begins to see that we are all connected. Who begins to care, who builds upon the humanity with love. A philanthropist. An Altruist. Albert Schweitzer. Mother Teresa. His Holiness, the Dalai Lama.

"More" evolves into the stage of wisdom as abundance. Infinity. Where the world, indeed the universe, is available to meet your needs. The practice of giving unconditionally so that you can receive in like form – the ability to expect to receive an abundance through this kind of giving – is an experience of infinite possibility.

In the School of Metaphysics we teach this principle as a willingness to give of your physical wealth. We teach a way to save a sum of money every day over a period of time for the purpose of giving it away. This is a practice in understanding how to harmonize with the Universal Laws. We do not expect repayment from the person we give the money to, we may not even know who you are. We expect our return from the abundance of the universe, and it comes according to Law.

Sometimes that return comes in the most unexpected ways, in unexpected times and unexpected places. According to your faith, your knowing that Universal Law exists and works in your life, you come to understand more. That understanding removes all fear that your needs will be met. It neutralizes the survival. It neutralizes greed. It neutralizes prosperity, so that one can experience infinity.

Infinity is what inheritance is all about. Fame. Reputation. Being remembered. They are finite experiences masking infinite possibilities. For Shawn teaching has become a finite experience. As long as Chris, and others like him, continue to teach, there will be infinite possibilities.

I may not have "more" with Shawn. I will have "more" with Chris and John and all the people they teach. Through this very real connection I will fulfill every desire. I will lose nothing.

"I am so grateful for having had Thelma in my life." I tell Chris. "I am grateful for having known Shawn as well. She is one of the reasons you and I are together now."

We smile, the smile that only gratitude brings. Then we set about creating – together.

Thursday evening
Board of Governors meeting

After dinner, the Board of Governors of the School of Metaphysics gathers for our regular monthly meeting. Until tonight Shawn has occupied one of nine seats in this group. Her work with the Internet earned her the privilege.

Shawn had not contributed much verbally to the meeting for she had not been as involved as she was capable of being. The times when she did speak were usually argumentative or accusatory in some way. These times were few and far between but when they occurred it was like a dose of reality. I slowly began realizing who Shawn is and what her thoughts are. These were not as I believed.

This was part of my opening mind, a waking up that had occurred within me the previous year.

I miss Shawn's presence tonight while at the same time acknowledging that the reality of her absence opens the door for all of us to be closer, to be more aware, and to be more invested in what we have in common. Terry and Christine, who both tend to be quiet at these meetings, are much more verbal and giving tonight. A certain tension has left the air and we talk of the present and future.

The meeting brings forward a memory from January, 2001. I know I wrote about this experience at the time it happened. I search for it and am glad for the effort. Reading it today, I can see more clearly the journey I have taken to get where I am.

"The tension had been building, flowing like a river under the land. I had sensed it in springs that would at times bubble to the top, watering the surface. Particularly through Paul, one of the male board members who shares the experience of a moon in Sagittarius, the most volatile of all places for those day-to-day moods to be. Directed by positive thought a Sag moon can expand into the vision of prophet, when left to least lines of resistance it can be a smouldering volcano erupting at the most inopportune moments.

When I was talking about what needed to be done to teach directors, Paul said, "Sometimes I think, Dr. Barbara, that no matter what we say it'll never be what you want."

This was an idea whose time had come. I had thought it myself, at different times, with different people. My response to hearing Paul voice it in this way was to shut down, to refrain from speaking.

There would be more to that story the next day. And I would reverberate with the impact of his emotion to mine, even to the point of crying about it the next moment because I wasn't sure what to do until I realized it wasn't up to me to do anything. I couldn't change someone else so all I could do was love and wait.

Christine chose this meeting, while I was reverberating intensely, to announce the 10 most wanted list for the publishing portion of the School of Metaphysics. A move I would have commended, since it was after all what I was asking for - setting goals, moving forward, visionary thinking, had the timing been different and the manner been a bit more evolved. She proceeds to read the list and at number three or four stops, saying, "It occurs to me that something is not right. That we haven't talked to you Dr. Barbara about this." I can't say anything. Whatever buttons might have still been in order have been pushed now and I'm about to fragment right there. I say nothing. Bearing down and keeping it together a few more minutes. I train my mind upon what she is saying fully aware nothing is really going in and the emotion coming up from within me is overpowering.

Some time later I find escape in my room. I let it flow. Hurt. Rejection. Despair. Anger. What have I done to deserve being treated like this? I'm hopelessly at a loss. I keep working it. I breathe, then let the images rise from memory. I am standing at Gayle Matthes' presidential inauguration ceremony. I am announcing the new list of officers, naming myself as president emeritus. Jerry Rothermel immediately insists with great authority that that has yet to be determined. Inside I know it doesn't matter what he thinks, the truth is I have served the School of Metaphysics as its president, which is what the term means. But outside, I am mortified. My place has been taken away, I have been publicly embarrassed. Someone was against me and I didn't deserve it. I deserved better. It's the same feeling just the flip side. Jerry-Christine, teacher-student.

Then I realize all of this is in my own mind. The others didn't even know what was going on. Even my husband Daniel didn't know how upset I was when he got home. Yet in my mind I believe others lack compassion for me, lack consideration. And I am hurt.

These thoughts are a major revelation for me. Very long in coming. I begin to release the burden. The idea that I have to teach, to be right, to know. I begin opening to redefining my image of a teacher. Upgrading it as we say. Who you are is the imprint – **who**, not what!

Dr. Pam has taught me about elevating things, in a comment she made to me months ago concerning my influence upon anyone and anything. Since then conscious awareness of that quality in me has been stimulated. I have noted in the past two years that "elevating" is how I do what I do.

I receive something, internalize, integrate, and give it back in an elevated form. It is the way I invent. That's why the media love affair with "re-invent" increasingly chafed at my consciousness because I understood it as copying, as imitation, as somehow cheap, not authentic. To elevate is to create anew and it is, I now see, how evolution evolves. Nothing is ever completely made new or destroyed.

The next morning Daniel informs me that one of our field directors has spoken to him about discontinuing study with the School. Dan and I "expect too much", and he's tired of being in an "abusive situation". By the afternoon, just fifteen minutes before I am teaching the counseling class Paul is a student in, Paul asks to talk to me. He tells me of his decision. I am silent, giving him space to talk. He speaks of rejection, "can't do anything, never satisfied, never do enough." I see the polarity working between us in this moment, the openness-rejection. And I love him more. He has struggled with love recently.

I tell him I love him, and if that's what he really wants, what he thinks is right, I'll continue to love him and I will miss him because he adds a great deal to our common efforts. If he feels I have abused him I am sorry. I know that's never been my intention and what I have said and done has been from love, not to take anything from him in any way.

He acknowledges that it is my place to be a visionary, to see more, to expect more than what is. That opens a door later for me to learn I can love midst the high standards I hold. It is indeed love that unites. This is the means by which I can accept "as is" people. This attitude releases my disappointment (the Sagittarian influence) and any residue of fear of rejection (the Taurean tendency to "take the ball and go home"). This in turn will help me with teaching Kiah in the next few weeks, about emotion and disappointment.

I tell Paul I hope he will reconsider, that I know Dr. Dan loves him and has never done anything for the purpose of hurting him.

Accepting is the key to happiness, to feeling good in life. Fear of things being too good to last has run my consciousness too long. It's the "bushwhack" idea that when things are going good it's just temporary because someone or something will come along to end it. This is a dependency that the ability to respond at will – self-trust – will cure.

I see the whole situation with Paul as a test. Where am I? Part of Self can let go, love regardless of choice. This understanding has been built over twenty-five years and is real. The heart and head are entrained because I know we are always connected. It is the lesson of Dermot and Denise, both former students of mine. I am comfortable with this. My head still reacts, stirring up emotion, trying to imagine the past thus moving me out of acceptance into loss and anger and sadness.

Three years later I sit here thinking about Paul's relationship with Shawn. He has been her field director for over a year. I think of how much he can offer her concerning her current misgivings, grievances, perspectives. He has been where she is. He worked through it. Perhaps she will too.

Thanks to Paul I have a way to clearly determine my growth. The lower emotions which tore at me three years ago are at peace in the present situation with Shawn. My heart will love Shawn no matter what. This understanding in part I owe to my experience with Paul.

My head, although preferring something else, is willing to accept a choice differing from my own. This was not so with Paul. With Paul some of my motives were murky. Incomplete thoughts had been behind some of my words. My conscious awareness needed to change, to become more present, precise, steady. This was what I learned from Paul, and I have applied it with Shawn. Three years later I knew what my intentions were. When Shawn expressed her grievances on the phone, I could say, "I don't deserve this. What you are saying is all in your imagination."

When you know your own thoughts,
those of others become clear.

Hezekiah has trouble going to sleep tonight. Part of it I attribute to having played a feisty game of marbles up and down the hallway. Part of it I know is because I did not arrive until shortly after 10. Typically, it takes Kie about an hour or so to wind down after this kind of boisterous activity. Eventually, sometime after 11, he falls asleep.

One of my last thoughts before going to sleep is: Shawn is on Hezekiah's 10 Best Friends List.

The next morning I slowly awaken to the impact that Shawn's leaving is having on a nine-year-old boy.

Friday Morning
Hezekiah's Sixth Best Friend

Before Christmas Hezekiah made it a point of asking me one morning, "Do you know who my 10 best friends are?"

Realizing I hadn't been updated for a while I started with the list I remembered, "Let's see, Briana is number one." I looked at him for confirmation.

"Yes."

"John Crainshaw is number two." He nodded. I was at a loss as to who came next.

"Laurie!" Kie was playful.

"Oh yeah," I said with a smile. Laurie and Kie spend at least two hours every day together. She is like a nanny, friend, playmate, sister all rolled into one. "I would think she'd be number one, the way you look forward to seeing her every day." Kie wasn't budging. He had his priorities and I am forever curious how long Bri and John will remain at one and two, since they see Kie infrequently these days.

This is the nature of life at the College of Metaphysics for all of us. People come and people go, frequently, and for all kinds of reasons. Some are students committed to 12 months of study, fulfilling their degree requirements. Some are grad students who have returned for a period of assimilation and higher learning with those who are experienced in areas they want to explore. Some are long-term residents raising young souls.

Some are teachers throughout the United States who come to the College for Doctoral level classes once a month or biannual teacher conferences. Some come from other countries to attend Spiritual Focus Sessions for a weekend. Some are visitors who are curious, checking out the College of Metaphysics and its Peace Dome.

This is the world Hezekiah has known since his birth. He has lived with people from 11 to 60, from Chile to Czechoslovakia to California. He has lived with a wide variety of people: an anthropologist, a nurse, a mechanic, a geologist, a bail bondsman, a factory manager, assorted musicians, artists and scientists, and many teachers and college students.

I have been most sensitive to Kie and the people who come and go in his life, the relationships he forms. I consider those he spends time with relatives, spiritual brothers and sisters. I consider them teachers for until recently they have been predominantly older than he is. I trust they have his best interest in mind and repeatedly I have taught, encouraged, insisted that others be honest with their thoughts and actions when interacting with him. This is in part to give an example to him, but as he has aged I realize this advice is more for the well-being of the adult since Kie does not tolerate any form of deceit.

He has been quite close with several people who have moved away. In most cases he still sees them, more often than some of his blood relatives. We talk often about his thoughts and feelings. This affords both of us a means to identify where we are in learning the love lessons coming and going bring.

It was hard when Shawn left after studying at the College for 14 months. I know that I must be attentive, available to Kie as he digests Shawn's change of mind, and change of heart.

Waking early, I go to check the emails that came in overnight. This can often take as long as an hour. I knew with all the activities planned this weekend, it would be best to respond to this now so my attention could be free.

I wasn't completed until shortly after 8:30. Most mornings if I spend this long, Hezekiah will awake and come find me so we can read, study, or just talk. When I came back to his room, he was still solidly asleep.

I came over and sat on the floor by his bed and, as I often do, I started talking to him. He was difficult to rouse, but eventually I got a response. He seemed to come back and talk a bit, but within minutes he was asleep again. Soundly.

I thought, well, he was up late. I also knew he had a lot to assimilate. I have learned that sleep for anyone at any age means assimilation of the day's waking experiences. It was not unusual when Kie would visit a new place or embark on new activities that he would sleep more than usual.

Shortly after nine, I tried to wake him again. He roused, then went back to sleep. Shawn's leaving was affecting everyone at the college. It was affecting the people who had been in class with her. It was affecting her teacher. It was affecting people who had had interactions with her, who depended upon her. It was affecting anyone who had ever been in her presence and had experienced her touch.

I wanted to be with Kie when he woke so I brought in a notebook so I could be with him. I started writing these notes about my experiences.

As one Shawn is leaving my life another is entering. That in itself is an amazing sign from the universe. Two people, opposite sexes, both with the same name, even spelled the same. Amazing!

Shawn S. is male. Recently he had told me he planned to move to the College in a year. S, I will identify him by for your clarity, is another one of those people who has a particular cluster of understandings that I have learned to identify over the years. These clusters make them powerful people, as I see them, with great influence without opening their mouths. They have a presence. Shawn has this, and so does S.

S called the College on Wednesday and I happened to pick up the phone. He had attended the Atlantean Awakening session the weekend before, here at the College, and at that time had mentioned he had pain in his ribs from a kick he had sustained in martial arts class. Now, on the phone he said in spite of time, care, and healing, the pain was getting worse not better. He wanted to get an Intuitive Health Analysis because he was concerned about his liver. I asked if he'd seen a chiropractor, he said no. I suggested he do so today and get the Health Analysis.

On Thursday morning, he called again. This time he asked for me. I mistakenly thought it was about his ribs.

"No they're better today," he said.

"Did you see a chiropractor?"

"No."

After chiding him for not keeping his word, we got into the reason for his call. S said he had been experiencing severe depression this week, the worst he had ever had, and he needed counsel. I sensed his urgency and the connection. When I asked why me since Fayetteville is a good four hours away, he said he trusted me and he just needed to be in my presence.

Presence. The word has come to mean a great deal to me, particularly since the Madars first experience with pregnancy. I could receive the sincerity, the honesty with which he meant it. I noted the difference in me. Before I would have demurred, or denied, or even fought against receiving it. Today, now, my mind was still and I received with little judgement.

In fact, I could see this affirmation of someone needing me was the balance for the thought that Shawn did not need me. Within twelve hours I had experienced the complete cycle, the attraction and repulsion, the push and the pull, the pair of opposites revolving around influence.

Recently, I am realizing greater truths concerning the existence of healing presence. Counseling depends upon it, which is why training begins with self counseling, becoming familiar with the self, at ease with the still mind. This is the essence of counseling itself. No words, no brain thoughts, mind-centered questions on occasion are usually all that is needed for someone in need. These realizations are making me better with everyone and at everything I do.

S was willing to drive up whenever I might be free. There was no question that I would make myself available. We talked about several options and ended up with 9 pm tomorrow night.

One Shawn no longer wants me, another Shawn does. The Universe is working perfectly, showing me the Truth.

As time passes, it dawns on me that what Hezekiah is dealing with is not so much *his* thoughts and emotions because in his world nothing is changing that much. What he is trying to assimilate are all the emotions and thoughts of everyone else. The energy is trying to move through him.

Sitting there I realize this is the reality of being nine years old. The cycle between seven and fourteen is the time of adolescence. This is when a person's humanity needs to be brought forward and matured. When it is, 14-21 is a very productive period. When the youngster is shut down, thus learning to suppress thoughts and emotions instead of understanding them, 14-21 becomes a time of rebellion and trouble.

At 10, I try again. Finally, about 10:20, something grabs his attention enough that he wakes up, gets out of bed, and immediately goes to the bathroom to get dressed. He comes back to the room, lays on the bed, and starts talking about how his stomach is upset. Not one to let his body rule him, he says he wants to go downstairs and see everybody. I agree thinking a bit of food in his stomach might be what he needs.

I prepare a boiled egg, pineapple (which has helpful enzymes), and a bit of bacon in case he feels up to eating it. I sit at the table as an encouragement for him to eat, but Kie shows little interest in the food. He grabs a pineapple chunk, then goes to lay on the couch or look through his books.

On one return trip I comment on his indifference toward the food and he replies, "I don't like the same old foods."

I know this is opinion rather than factual. "What would you rather have?" I ask.

"I don't know."

I list several of his favorite foods.

"Nothing sounds good to me," he replies.

I remind him that his stomach hurt and eating a bit of something might help. I ask if he will eat a fried egg if I make it. Kie has some time ago decided Daddy's fried eggs are the best and *only* fried eggs in the world! So this is a major request I am making. We both know it. Since daddy is teaching class and Kie really is hungry, he graciously said he'll try.

He agrees to give me a try on the fried egg. He eats a few bites of it and some pumpkin bread.

After a while he comes over to me, leaning against me as he often does when he doesn't feel well, and says, "Why does my stomach hurt?"

I put my hand on his solar plexus. The moment I touch him I know what he is experiencing. I center my attention and ask him to breathe with me. We establish a rhythm that brings balance to this area which connects mind and body.

"Hezekiah you are absorbing the thoughts and feelings around us," I say softly.

"So?" he asks. "I often do that."

Kie is self aware in this for we had spoken of the reality of thought transference many times. He practices it purposefully through drawing pictures with people, creating stories, and games like Mastermind. Kie knows those experiences do not make him feel sick. I know he is ready to know more.

"Hezekiah, this part of the body is called the solar plexus, do you know why?"

"How come?"

"Because there are many nerves that come together in this area. They are like telephones allowing the different organs to talk to one another." Kie listens intently. "When the emotions are disturbed it interferes with that communication. It distorts it like when you can't hear someone very well on the phone."

"Like when people are on cell phones?" Kie asks, remembering a couple of crackling and hissing phone conversations.

"Exactly!"

"So how come my stomach hurts?" It is a good question now.

"Because emotions are interrupting the communication between the stomach and your brain. There are an increasing number of emotions not being expressed openly as people find out about Shawn. There are many people who are in pain about her leaving."

"How come? She said she would visit."

"She may, but not as often."

"I'm okay with her leaving," Kie says.

I hold him close. He has no idea what the future holds.

Neither do I. Two days ago I thought Shawn was going to be living at the College of Metaphysics. I ask myself, "Who am I to say anything about what another will or will not do?" In the moment, Kie is helping me to remain still minded and clear. There is no benefit in making up stories, "Shawn will probably come as often as she can", or "yes, we'll probably see her quite a bit", or the protective negative side, "well she's quit the classes so she won't be invited to weekends for students or teachers, and she won't be having class with your daddy anymore." What purpose do any of these serve, for me or for him?

What is important is the love I have for Hezekiah. Even with that I cannot promise I will always be with him. Truth. Grasping Truth that is universal is a passion for me. Is there a difference between honesty and Truth? Can I tell Hezekiah I will always be here for him when the Universe may make a different choice? These are more than lofty philosophical matters to me. These are the real life of a nine-year-old boy and a 51-year-old woman. Here is where enlightenment happens, in the questions of a child and the answers they provoke.

For now I still my mind and focus upon how much I love this soul. I merely say, "It's good to have a mommy and daddy that love you a whole lot and not just a little, isn't it?"

Hezekiah nods, color back in his cheeks, a grin on his face. He is better, and ready to play.

With Hezekiah happily playing with Laurie I feel free to give my attention to others. Four of us meet to discuss ways to better organize access to our worldwide members. Jay has recently purchased a computer program that will better suit our needs and we are brainstorming how we can create a useable database.

I am having trouble keeping my attention on the project so I ask myself, "why?" Two reasons immediately surface. The first is Hezekiah and the second is the lack of necessity for me to be here. Between them, the others involved can answer any question, and they can create a sound plan of action. I am not really needed, although at a different time and day I would love to create with these people. After this bit of self-evaluation I say, "I think I need to check on Kie, so keep working and let me know later what you come up with."

Being sensitive to the pace of the weekend and it's unexpected features, Paul B., Teresa, and Jay graciously agree.

I find Kie with John Harrison. John is preparing to play a game of dominoes while Kie seems restless getting up and down from the table. I asks if he has eaten anything, and he says no. I figure toast is the best choice now. So much time has passed since his last real meal and with the upset, acids will be released that will cause more hurt.

I bring the toast over and leave it at his place then I return to the kitchen. He nibbles, then eats it quickly. It is easy to see he is hungry. I bring him blueberries, and he eats a few. The food seems to perk him up and when I see he is willing to play, I go upstairs.

That's when I run into Dr. Sheila in the hallway. She is another level of this experience.

After talking about our books with Teresa Padilla and Paul Blosser at brunch, I go upstairs to organize materials for tomorrow evening's Taraka Yoga class. Laughter floats from the library and I glance in as I pass by. Paul Madar, Laurie and Shawn are eagerly engaged in the transference of internet information and know-how. My heart cringes at the gaiety that masks thoughts unsaid, feelings suppressed. The room is thick with the pairs of opposites. The eagerness to learn juxtapositioned with the denial of the lessons that bring soul understanding bring a Salvador Dali painting to mind. I feel the pain.

Always the compulsion to do something to ease pain is present within me. I have learned to accept it as an incessant urge for resolve. In the end, it has served me well. It has motivated me over and over. It has made me keep asking questions of a teacher long after others have abandoned the quest for fear that they will be judged as foolhardy, pesky, or stupid. Through the years I have seen this compulsion as the desire to shed light – "You could try this....", as balancing energies – "Have you looked at it this way?" I have learned from others that when my intention is the least bit self-centered, taking action in this way can easily be resented and labeled interference.

From my gut the instinct rises to rush into the room and say something to clear the air. I know this is lower heart energies, emotional energies, less than my best. Whatever I might say would probably make Shawn uncomfortable. I live with Paul and Laurie. They will be here tomorrow and the next day. There will be plenty of time for us to talk together. So I conclude that the motivation to "interrupt" is ego-centered. I know this. Eliminating this distraction, I return my mind to the commitment I have made of maintaining a still mind with all things concerning Shawn and I continue down the hall, never breaking my stride.

I think of Laurie, examining my motives. I have paired her with Shawn, seeing her as a Siamese twin who will go wherever Shawn goes, experience whatever Shawn experiences. Laurie will listen, learn, ask questions. She has the aptitude to think in progressively multidimensional ways, creative ways. She lacks information, knowledge, and experience that Shawn will be able to give her. Laurie also has a desire to learn. The word used to describe her dharma is "magnanimous." This constant urge expands her spirit to receive anything.

Paul B., already a computer expert and familiar with many of the backgrounds, can absorb the more technical information Shawn has to offer. The accounting end of Shawn's work falls to Paul M. Monthly updating of SOM web pages will be in Jay's hands. There is a beauty in this movement. Through Shawn moving on there is an open door for others to walk through.

Yes, there could have been one replacement. I could have learned it all. Or Laurie. What elevates this from just finding someone else to do the work, is the nature of the work we do. The ideal of the School of Metaphysics is very real to me. It lives and breathes, and so I allow it to influence every thought, every decision. I did not make these choices based upon convenience. Nor on a job to fill. These choices were based upon individual's aptitude, area of interest, and background. In other words, their understandings combined with their desire to learn. In this way several people are using this situation for their soul progression.

With this thought I realize what it is that disturbs me about the laughter in the library. The learning, the transmission of necessary information in as short a time as possible, leaves out the soul. The people in the library are there to do their job. To get what they need to done. This is the same thing that happens in offices around the world every day.

The lack of multidimensional learning here at the College of Metaphysics troubles me. Identifying the cause of the separation in my mind eases the reaction. I do not expect a person who has elected to quit studies before completing to provide this kind of learning. This would be unreasonable. I have learned how to respect people's choices in this regard. I know how to disagree with someone's choice while defending their right to make it. In my understanding this is a beautiful expression of "being in the world but not of it," of being conscious of the pairs of opposites working in your life.

With my mind now centered and emotions calm, reasoning comes forward. I ask myself, "Did we wait for Shawn to leave before giving others an opportunity to create, learn, and give?" Earlier in my life I had experienced just this. Directors of schools or teachers would leave their positions and only then would others be offered a chance to try their wings, prove themselves, to learn. Looking with physical eyes only, it certainly appears that this is happening again.

I know better. This is a perfect example of appearances being deceiving. The truth is all the people now interacting in this way with Shawn have already been moving in this direction. There is no need for Shawn to leave in order for this expansion to occur.

Jay is already working on the branch school's web pages. He has recently designed an animated clip on the Peace Mandala, housed in the Peace Dome, for that site. This clip is beyond Shawn's current learning. Paul Blosser is becoming more instrumental in our video productions. He has worked for weeks on *"The Invitation"* video. Laurie is learning the photography end of web design. Christine has learned what she needs to know to take the reigns of the Dream of the Month Club, an internet membership for learning the art and science of dream interpretation. Paul Madar is making SOM a presence on ebay and is moving into forms of marketing SOM goods. All of us are involved, and we easily adapt to the added responsibilities.

No, I resolve, Shawn's leaving is by no means a cause for this expansion. From what it necessitates in me, however, it opens my mind to another part of infinity that has been maturing for years. How many times have I felt abandoned by people? Left to cope? Dumped on? Most often it has reared its head through the thought of "cleaning up someone else's mess."

This has been a demon at my door repeatedly. Each time he appeared I learned something new. Forgiveness. Acceptance. Allowing. Respect. Generosity. Honesty. Each lesson had been rich.

Today, I can appreciate this moment rather than fear it. That is an amazing culmination point for me. Each time the situation arose in the past, I might be able to see the good in it but I never was able to move myself to appreciating it. In this moment, I am there. At the same time I do not like, desire, need, expect, hope, dream that Shawn will walk out of my life, I can appreciate wholeheartedly the experience of her doing so is giving me. And others.

Having accepted this as truth, I have to make the step to appreciate Self. This is all happening because of me. It is my choice to involve all these people, not Shawn's. This is a major step. Self as cause. It is clean. No blame. No credit. Just the truth. Before I have always wrestled with the credit-blame serpent. From the inexperienced thoughts of a 22 year old girl: "How can so-and-so do this to me?" to the 30 year old's thoughts of "What did I do to deserve this?" to the forty year old thoughts of "I should have seen it coming", I ask and answer each of these questions each time a student leaves without completing what they have begun.

In the past, my limitations in feeling responsible caused me to compulsively want to take on whatever people were leaving behind. I felt it was an obligation. It took me a long time to see that this feeling on my part was a limitation for *other* people. I have had progressive learning experiences in this regard which now enable me to discipline my own ego to allow other people to move forward, rather than me rushing to fill that space and in that action - however unconsciously - stealing from someone else an opportunity.

This time, unlike times before, I have no guilt associated with asking others to learn what Shawn knows.

This time is different. This time I have a still mind, and I can clearly see.

Friday
Lessons in Friendship

I am in the kitchen when Paul Madar walks in looking like he might have been up all night with three-month-old Alexandra. I project love to him, smile and ask, "Are you doing okay?"

He shakes his head, and I can see the tears close to the surface although being a proud man I know he will contain them. He says, "It's getting hard."

"Alexandra?" I ask, remembering well the challenges of the first year of hands-on parenting.

"Between Christine and I."

We have spoken of their marriage off and on since the baby was born. About the adjusting between two becoming three, the movement from being a couple to a family. I know the change has struck him in a similar way it entered my life. Although there was intellectual awareness of what a child might bring, the reality of the first newborn is often entirely different than what is imagined. Shocking is the word that comes to mind.

"I feel like I can't do anything to please her," he says. "I can't seem to do anything right."

This is not the first time I have heard this sentiment from Paul. Years ago when he worked as a foundation planner and directed a School of Metaphysics in St. Louis, he said the same words. This was long before he and Christine were married.

In the moment, I suggest that it might be time for the three of us – meaning he, Christine and I – to get together and draw some pictures.

He knows this is a reference to a Taraka Yoga session, free of the little one so we can have some space. He doesn't jump at the offer, but I hope he will think about it.

As I hug him I whisper, "Try not to take what Christine is going through personally."

A few hours later it dawns on me that much of Christine's current brooding has nothing to do with Paul. Paul is serving as a point of discharge for her pent up mental and emotional energies. Energies she naturally tries to spare her newborn daughter. Energies that, as a result, build up. Energies that seek a safe place of release and find him.

I understand this movement of energy between the Madars, having a similar astrological makeup in my marriage. Christine's pain in part has nothing to do with Paul. It's origin is all of the thoughts and emotions attached to losing her best friend – Shawn. Just four months before Chris served as Shawn's matron of honor. Friendship had been growing between them, or so Christine believed.

Chris dreamed that Shawn and Adam would move to the College after they married, have children and raise them as she and Paul are doing. She dreamed that their children would grow up together, a new breed of soul-aware thinkers, and that they would be able to help each other in the process. We all knew about Shawn's interest in children through her desire to be a midwife.

She was a nanny for two children.

What Christine is slowly allowing to sink into her consciousness is that now, none of that will come to pass. In this, I realized that Christine had put Shawn in many of her desire-pictures.

I remember Christine recently talking about her Friendship Profile saying something about how she experiences friendship through her imagination. I want to better understand so I research the report. It opens with:

"This one's experience of friendship occurs largely within the imagination. We see that this is the avenue by which this one experiences the greatest expanse, the greatest willingness to give and the greatest abundance. We see that it is through the incorporating of others into the image that the most is gained and this is intermittently accomplished."

Comments Christine has made in the past few months about things Shawn said or did which surprised her come back to me. I remember Chris saying, "I didn't realize Shawn thought that way." It wasn't so much a statement of judgement. Rather it was an awakening, a realization that what Christine believed of Shawn was different from the reality. This I understood, having been through a similar awakening process myself.

So I know today, Christine's pain and anger belong to Shawn and not Paul.

When I leave my room, I pass by the library again. Paul, Shawn, and Laurie are still sitting there. These thoughts flood my mind, I stop and walk back. I stand at the doorway. The room becomes still, and they turn toward the door. I look directly at Paul and say, "What Chris is going through doesn't have anything to do with you, Paul. It has to do with Shawn."

Two hours later, Chris arrives for dinner. She is standing alone in the library, her back to the door. The computer glows and I can see she is checking the dreams that have come in for interpretation. I stop to give her real attention and love. "How are you doing?" I ask.

She looks up, the traces of tears still on her face. "Not so great," she replies. I come into the room and we embrace for a long time. Immediately she allows the tears to flow. Then, as is her tendency, she says, "I didn't think I was going to do this."

I remind her it is good.

In the moment, thoughts of my influence with others comes back to me. Much of this comes from my capacity to be honest. I am fearless in the face of emotion. To allow emotion, to admit them, to accept and appreciate them so the lesson at hand can be learned, is an amazing power. Many times this manifests as merely being present. I offer Christine that while giving her the space for her own experience.

Christine and I had both looked forward to sharing our lives with Shawn. I sense, as happens so many times in relationships, this shared "loss" will, as it changes the shape of our future, bring us closer together.

During Christine's Friendship Profile she asked, "What is meant by this one's experience of friendship within the imagination?"

The answer was:

"It is through the workings of the imagination that the greatest sense of friendship is experienced, when there is something that this one images that can be both given and received. There is much that can be accomplished in regards to causing there to be a continual cycle in this for it tends to be experienced in the manner described - where this one is either receiving from another or giving to another rather than there being a complete experience. However, nonetheless this is the means by which this one experiences the most profound truth of friendship and it is the means by which this one can expand and grow in the awareness. The imagination when pooled with the will and with the capacity for recall is a very strong factor in being able to utilize the unification of consciousness toward the growth of Self and others. This one understands (this) in many ways, particularly in regards to the power of imaging. It is at times when this one is attempting to move in the moment or is attempting to interact with those whom this one considers peers in any endeavor, on any level, that the imaging falls short and this one becomes mired in that which does separate the mind rather than unify it. When this occurs there is a similar action that occurs in this one's relations to others. There is a separation rather than unifying." (11700BGC1)

I do not know what Christine may see in this for herself, but it is – as is true with every Intuitive Report I have ever heard – of great value to me. I understand a greater application for the still mind. I realize the resolution I made back in November to maintain a still mind with Shawn is the reason why my consciousness is remaining unified in face of separation from someone I love.

In fact, the response to another question asked during this profile speaks to the still mind:

"This entity would like knowledge or wisdom on how to function as a whole individual or as a whole being.

To still the mind to the point of being able to hear the whisper of the inner guidance and having done so to seek this consciousness in every moment regardless of activity in the outer sense. To realize that activity in the outer sense is the furthest extension of motion and therefore to reach with the consciousness toward the innermost source of motion. In this way this one will come to understand the innerconnectedness that this one seeks." (11700BGC1)

Friday
Dr. Sheila

A Bit of Background

Four days ago, Shawn went to Tulsa where Dr. Sheila Benjamin lives with her husband. Sheila is a spiritual teacher and member of the School's Board of Governors. She is a field director for several of our branches, and was in fact Shawn's field director when she first became a director of a school in Dallas. Their relationship spans several years. I have known Sheila since 1978.

Dr. Sheila asked Shawn if she would tutor her on web design and Shawn obliged. This was the purpose of Shawn's Tulsa visit. Sheila has a tendency at times to be secretive, to hide, in a similar way that Shawn does. I didn't know about Shawn's trip and so I didn't know, once I learned that Shawn was leaving, if Sheila already knew. Since I'd practiced stilling my mind with Shawn, the thought moved through me but it did not linger. And I did not create with it.

Sheila arrived just before Board of Governor's meeting Thursday evening. She learned sometime that evening of Shawn's decision. She was shocked. She told me, she had no clue. This, combined with several other factors in Sheila's life led to a major breakthrough in self awareness for her that I became witness to.

Friday after brunch Dr. Sheila and I cross paths in the hallway. "How are you doing?" I ask her.

"I think I want to talk," she says, tears in her voice. "I think I want to come back on Saturday and talk if you can make time for me."

My first reaction is to affirm her, to support her. "Of course I can talk with you."

As I say the words another time of Sheila wanting to talk with me enters my mental line of vision. Like a negative to a photograph, here is Sheila saying she needs to talk when she returned from attending Christine and Paul during the delivery of their stillborn child. In that situation my mind too was so filled with Christine that I didn't see clearly to make space for Sheila.

I remember clearly there were Intuitive Health Analyses scheduled that night which Sheila intended to provide. Given the events of the previous 24 hours, I knew she needed rest and there was no reason for her to be burdened by this. I offered to give the Intuitive Reports as a way of giving to her and she was grateful.

The sense of relief poured from her in sobs. I held her for a while, and then, in Sheila fashion, she apologized telling me I needed to go. She thanked me again and said perhaps later we could talk after the reports.

I knew Sheila's need, and I recognized it, *but I didn't stop everything at the moment to be there for her.* I said we'll talk later, and by the time later came, the moment was gone for Sheila and I knew it. At that time I vowed I would never do that again. I visualized myself responding to Sheila's need *in the moment*. That was a year and a half ago.

The moment I had visualized two years before is here.

This is that moment.

"What are you doing now?" I ask. She is somewhat shocked. "You want to talk? We'll do it now."

"Okay," she says with surprise in her voice and gratefulness in her heart. Within three minutes I finish what I was doing, grab paper and markers and come into her room.

"Thank you, Dr. Barbara," Sheila's gratitude is both melting and healing her broken heart. She begins talking through tears and I hold her, just listening. I haven't always known the power in listening. It has been presented to me through countless experiences with an array of amazing people. Because my choices have always introduced me to new people – lay and professional, young and old, rich and poor, book learned and street smart, native and foreign – I have learned we, all of humanity, have much more in common than that which seems to divide us. I have learned this Truth through listening.

In this moment Sheila doesn't need the comfort of someone telling her the opposite of what she is feeling. She doesn't need me to say, "Oh, Sheila I think you contribute a lot." She doesn't need rebuttals, "You are, too, smart!" Nor denials, "No one else compares you with others!" Nor encouragement, "Oh, but everyone loves you! You're the only who thinks this." Nor suggestions, "You need to realize how much people appreciate you!"

Sheila needs someone to listen.

I can tell when she reaches a point of completion with the onrush of thoughts. She becomes calmer, quieter. "I thought I had all this taken care of." I nod, we both understand that expectation. Sheila has already identified the root of the problem as not appreciating herself. I know from hearing her talk that this experience, for both of us, will be focused on Taurean energies.

"Okay," I say reaching for the paper and pens. "Draw me a picture of appreciating yourself. Put it in the center of the page."

Sheila draws a big pink heart.

"Now write the thoughts that are in the way of you appreciating yourself." I watch as she begins to write words in a circle surrounding the heart. In the end, there are eight distinct thoughts that, as she places them, completely enclose the heart.

During the time she takes to create her image, Self-reflective thoughts enter my mind. Each is stimulated by the words I have just heard Sheila say. When she began talking she used a word that is magic for me, for it symbolizes the work I am here on earth to do. The word is *appreciation*. When Sheila used the word I felt an immediate shift in my attention. I knew what was going to come during this time with Sheila would be meaningful for both of us in deep and profound ways.

Sheila and I both work with the qualities of fixed earth, both having been born in the spring under the sun sign of Taurus. The more I have understood about the mind, the more I have grown to know that astrology does not dictate, it merely influences. It pays to know what is influencing you, be it people, places, or things. I have a healthy respect for the universal moment people come into this world, and astrology gives us a means for interpreting that moment.

I have learned that the development of consciousness is what frees one from any compulsions of the flesh, be they personal habits, congenital conditions, or astrological makeup. The compulsion for the Taurean to "have", evolves in the mind of a reasoner. Acquisition and possession can be replaced by exploring the nature of creation. When a Taurus learns to value the journey at least as much as the destination, the soul lessons come forward. How much something costs evolves to the value, the usefulness of the item, the person, the situation.

Since turning 49, I have experienced the coming together of different thoughts and experiences over the course of my entire life. When this began occurring, I knew it was in part owing to the nature of seven year cycles. What responding to these cyclical markers is giving me is the ability to be increasingly awake and aware of experiences beyond the physical plane. My ability to receive and interpret energies is refining. I am getting better at separating and identifying others thoughts as well as my own. I have come to realize that my indebtedness to self, my karma if you will, is Self appreciation. Even typing it now I still have an attitude attached to it. The physical part of me – the old ideas in my brain, the conscious ego – still reacts, threatening to carry me away into a whirlwind like the one Sheila is drawing on her paper this morning.

What I am receiving this morning is Sheila's appreciation. Her appreciation for herself which is at the center, the heart, of who she is. Her appreciation for me taking time for her. Her appreciation for having someone to walk with her through a dark valley. Her appreciation for accepting what I have to give.

Acceptance is such an amazing power.

Students practice it in a Circle of Love each time they turn to the person on their right and say the words "I love you just because you are." Unconditional love is a part of appreciation. Both Sheila and I can be conditional with ourselves, and when we are, Self appreciation leaves us.

As I sit here watching Sheila write her ring of words, I remember how I have been tempted this month to feel unappreciated by Shawn. What has kept me from falling down that rabbit hole is my love for her. In January, Shawn failed to complete a simple assignment for the counseling class. I knew in my heart this meant she was not prepared to be with the class which meant she would no longer be a part of it. This she probably still doesn't know because I kept working with her all month, giving her ways to see herself, understand herself, go deeper. All of this was in the hope that she might come to a new level of understanding. Which she did.

I realize how much I have allowed other's assessment of my value to affect me emotionally. I have a strong command of reasoning. I can direct my attention at will. I can recall past experiences, see relevance to the present, and with imagining skills create a different future outcome. Because I love Shawn, the vestiges of lower heart, of the emotional attachment, are few. I compare this to previous experiences of similar magnitude – in other words

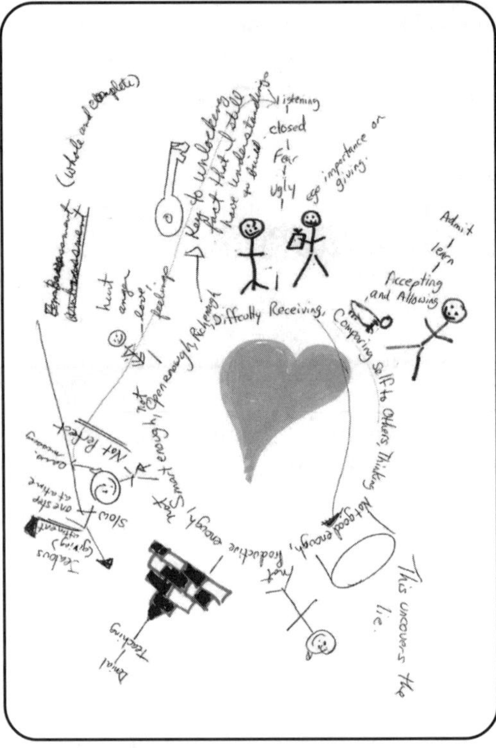

other deep friendships that have been ended not by my choice.

My love for Shawn is centered in how *I* think of *her*, what I think of her. It occurs to me that this is Self appreciation. I can now see the value in my own thoughts in a new light. This is what I am here to assist Dr. Sheila with.

Being a counselor herself, Dr. Sheila knows how to identify many of her thoughts but she hasn't been able to separate these out and that's what she needs me for. I understand that. Our time together is a process of separating, identifying, and admitting so Sheila can make the connections that she wants to perceive. The attitudes in the ring around her heart are laden with emotion and judgement. Each has at least one story to tell that relates to all these thoughts in the present.

"Which of these thoughts trouble you the most, Sheila? The one that in this moment, at this time, on this day, is provoking the most thought and emotion?"

We move in this fashion to each thought she has written around the circle. As we go to each one I ask her questions to help her separate and identify so she can admit the depth of that thought. She draws associated images and writes more words emanating from the original ones. By the time we finish, the entire diagram of her thinking processes is in front of her. Sheila's need to appreciate Self and the ways to change that will bring appreciation forward, that will free her heart, is captured on this piece of paper.

I realize how centering helping Sheila is for me. How as I listen to her thoughts, I am able to hold my mind steady – mind open, heart open – and give her feedback that is whole. The beauty of this whole mind experience sweeps through me. This is the experience I have cultivated for years, that I am making into a science so I can teach others how to produce it. This is what it means to be a Psi Counselor.

By assisting Sheila, I have come up out of the pairs of opposites, the tendency to take sides in the name of helping. I have elevated my heart to a higher heart. I know the experience within me is one of appreciation. It is a growing in value, and to the degree that Self appreciation is my karma I am realizing in this moment, in all of these experiences and how they will ultimately fit together, I am reaching a point of zenith.

I am so grateful.

I am living Self appreciation. By responding to Sheila in the moment when she needed me, in having Shawn S. call and be willing to drive four hours just to talk with me, to as he said "be in your presence." Those words are still with me. "Presence." I am understanding that.

The Healing Portraits that Daniel and I have been giving for several years now focus on presence. They describe the too often elusive quality of a soul, the power of being who you are, and the unique influence that that has upon others. In this moment following counseling Dr. Sheila I think about presence. I think about being present for Sheila and for Shawn and for Kie. I think of being present for the meetings and classes of these few days. I realize that I have been preparing with my still mind for something I never wanted to happen – I never dreamed would happen – and now that the shock of it happening has occurred I can be still, I can be open. I know how.

Although a part of me will forever be surprised by Shawn's choice, all of me can accept.

This is what enables me to be an anchor for others, a stabilizing force.

I realize this is the essence of keeping your heart open. There have been many moments the past 30 hours or so when I could have closed my heart. Times when the brain and head could have gone crazy with denial ("You can't be serious! You're going to walk out right before you earn this degree to begin on another?")

or anger ("How can you treat people so carelessly?") or bargaining ("If you'll stay you can.....") or depression ("It doesn't matter to me, I don't care anymore"), all causal ways to postpone change. I have been to these places in mind before. Instead, I am experiencing the truth that accepting leads to allowing, and allowing frees me to perceive many Truths in a situation only one of us wanted.

Dr. Sheila's story through emails

2-20-04
Today was a breaking point. I've been HOLDING on, at least in my illusionary thoughts, for the past 2-3 months. I observe different stimuli taking me to some deep dark holes within myself that I thought were gone. I labeled myself emotionally disturbed. Today I heard things, felt things, etc. which I interpreted as me being bad, invaluable, stupid. I could no longer contain the emotion inside. Dr. Barbara went upstairs and I purposely followed her because I knew I needed help. I knew that she knew how to unlock me to my self, where I did not know how. I asked her If I could come by next Saturday on my way to Columbia to counsel with her. I could not hold back the tears of the thoughts that were moving out.

She knew me very well and said we needed to do it now. (Thank God) I knew she was right. I would have gotten busy in my life activities and buried my feelings only to think that I was okay again. (Years ago I described my emotional burial dance as being a ball inside of a pinball machine. When it is bouncing all around I felt the imbalance, pressure, pain, etc.... These are the only times I have ever thought of asking for help. Usually I wait until the ball comes to rest and pretend that everything is okay. Then along comes a stimuli that causes the emotion to rise again. And we are off! Repeating the same process.)

Today I was experiencing a great amount of energy. I gauge this by my tears. I was doing more than crying, I was sobbing. What is this all about?

Dr. Barbara entered my room with a box of markers. I don't remember the exact question she asked me and I am learning that is not so important. She had me put in the center (of a page) the image of my blockage, the cause of my pain. Strange though it may sound, I placed a heart. What a thread to pull.

My mind returns to Despereaux.

After the Princess is kidnapped and taken to the dungeon, Despereaux feels it is his duty to rescue her. Thread plays a most important part in DiCamillo's tale. Despereaux knows the dungeon is "full of twists and turns and hidden chambers." The only way to find his way to her and back out again is with thread.

Sheila is on a quest. She has found the thread she needs. Just like Desperaux.

This brought to mind a counseling session I had with A.C. about 21-23 years ago. I met with this woman because it was she – through a series of questions – who cracked me open to myself. I realized that I had a host of feelings I refused to let out. I practiced this for 22 years or so, to the point of not knowing honestly what I thought or felt. I had been living a lie or at least disconnecting (maybe that is my computer's problem ha! ha!).

In the counseling session with A.C. she took me on a guided imagery and asked me to examine the boulder that was in my way. It was Love. Me being able to give all of my love and receive love from others. Here it was today all over again, with a little more light. This is trippy and fascinating all at the same time. There was a part of me that felt dense, retarded for going back to this train of thought. Dr. Barbara was so loving and held my heart and mind as I went on this reminiscent journey.

She instructed me to write around the heart the thoughts that come up when this blockage appears. One of the 1st areas I identified was "being nonproductive." I often think of myself as always short of the mark, therefore everybody else has to compensate for my inadequacies. However on the other side I've remembered the times that I've done something that has paid off that I don't claim. In not claiming, it is as if it didn't happen. Memories of being (a director of a school) in Tulsa in 1980 and me not telling Jerry (Sheila's supervisor/teacher) what I had built there – 3 new teachers, 2 directors, money to send to the college as well as support Wichita, continual reports that the school served, student count of over 25 consistently. Because I didn't talk for myself I failed to receive a teaching certificate. I discovered through this journey how I have used and misused my ego (I did receive the ego award for being introverted; I did break the curse of its recipient quitting before earning their doctorate!)

Where the non-productive thoughts take me is comparing myself with others, those that in my mind I'll never measure up to. The image I put here was interesting as I write this because it was a baby comparing itself to an adult. One of the words Dr. Barbara heard as I was talking was "learning". I discovered how sometimes my thinking is distorted. Honestly, what's wrong with a baby reaching up to be like the adult? Something for me to look at.

2-23-04

Over the past few days, the sun's light has been brighter. I have been able to see my influence in a clearer way. I was looking at my pictures on the counseling wheel and what stuck out to me was the people with no ears, myself with no ears. A memory came to me (it is so fascinating how the threads of our life can be unraveled when still and pointed) and that was when I was young, I don't know when, I started to suck my thumb. Anyway when I sucked my thumb I played with my ears. I would stick my ear inside of my ear. To this day I have very bendable ears.

As Despereaux moves down the dungeon steps he is consumed by the darkness. "I will tell myself a story," he says. "I will make some light."

So it is with Sheila. She, like I, tells a story to make some light.

When I was about 6 or so – shortly after the time when I got herpes and created phobias (dogs, birds, horses) – I was watching the news with my mother. The weather man was talking about tornadoes. I asked my mother what a tornado was. She told me it was a storm with high winds and people sometimes died. After that time and until I was in Little Rock and witnessed a tornado I was deathly afraid of high winds. I would fold my ears (both of them) inside of themselves and lay one side of my head on the pillow while I held the other ear really tight . It was a way of ignoring and blocking out the sounds that were frightening to me.

When I look at this in the Universal language of mind: tornadoes are emotional confusion and there was refusal to hear my own thoughts and express them (no tears). That is really wild!

I think about the richness that Hezekiah, Alexandra,and even Briana are around having parents that understand the universal language of mind and can shed light. I think back on that time in my life and even though there was emotional confusion there was always a trust. I would say that it was in my relationship with God that kept the door open. It was at the age of 6 that I made my communion. This was a strong commitment that I made to my soul awareness.

Thank you Dr. Barbara for taking the time and giving the love to help prime a much needed pump. I feel that my thirst is beginning to be quenched. (I have been having nightly dreams which is refreshing.)

Friday Afternoon
Hezekiah's Sixth Best Friend

After Sheila and I part, I go to my room for the purpose of reviewing my notes for tomorrow evening's counseling class. As I gather my papers, Kiah comes in.

Falling into my arms he says, "Mommy, my stomach hurts again."

"Oh, Kie," I reply, holding him. Hezekiah has been sick a handful of times in his life. All of them viral in nature - flu and colds which are troublesome but easily healed and usually shortlived. When he is not feeling well his energy changes becoming more magnetic. He becomes "easy to love" as some might describe it.

I would trade anything to have him well. It's taken me years to stop absorbing Kie's illnesses, taking them upon myself in order to free him. I know better than this as a healer, I reprimand myself. These lessons for me are not in how to heal. At least not head lessons in healing. I understand the mechanics of healing. I realize as I write this my healing lessons with Hezekiah are about the heart, about using understandings of healing to build new ones.

As I hold him the urge to cry sweeps through me. I let it move and pass. I envelope him in kundalini energy and his breathing calms.

After a few minutes he pulls away to ask, "How come others aren't happy about Shawn leaving?" He has told me the thought behind the stomach ache.

"I think, Hezekiah, it's because of the plans we had all made together." Christine comes into my mind. "People have looked forward to Shawn moving here and living here for awhile." Several of the younger, newer College students come to mind for they have expressed delight this past week in her coming. They looked forward to her living with them.

I understand the centering Hezekiah helps me do and I come back home in my thinking. "I looked forward to teaching her how to be a counselor."

"You did?" He is so open. The power of his willingness to learn always touches me deeply.

"Yes, I did," I say with tears in my voice.

"It's okay, Mommy," Kie says gently, and I know he is right. I think back to my experience in counseling Dr. Sheila just moments earlier. Self appreciation is a strong lesson for me.

A budding reasoner desiring intuition, Kie wants to know. He has a strong inner urge to understand, so he returns to the focus of his concentration. "How come that makes my stomach hurt?" He is trying to learn enough so he can understand the connections.

I ask him if he remembers about the solar plexus being a place of communication. He nods. "The solar plexus is the place where the inner and outer minds come together. This is the place where the waking mind and the dreaming mind meet," I reply touching his mid-abdomen.

"What can I do?" It is a plea.

"It might help to put something in your stomach," I reply, realizing the physical pain needs a physical rememdy. We decide upon yogurt. Then it doesn't sound so good. So we sit and rest. I know he isn't doing too well so we stay in his dad's room listening to a bit more of The Tale of Despereaux. This seems to make Kie feel better.

Our Mennonite neighbors had brought fresh venison as a gift for us two nights before. As an act of appreciation we made a miracle pie in the pan used to deliver the meat and made a handcrafted card which all the residents here had signed. Right before dinnertime, Dan decides to take the gift and entices Kie to go with him. They invite me along, but I need to finish reports for *Vibrations* which are due before dinner. I hope to finish them before the evening meal.

As I sit at the computer completing my work, Hezekiah runs in the door and down the hall not stopping to say hello. I call, "Welcome back! How did it go?" to him.

"Okay," he says, moving down the hall.

Several minutes later I turn off the computer and head down the hallway to my room. I notice the bathroom door is closed. I knock. Daniel is sitting on the floor, Kie's head in his lap. Dan asks if I knew Kie had thrown up and I say no.

Dan stays with Hezekiah for almost two hours. I check on them several times. Kie dozes then wakes to be sick again. His stomach empties very quickly. While he is awake I ask if we can change his clothes. The jeans are somewhat binding and I know looser pajamas will feel better. At first he resists then he agrees. I ask if he wants to go lie in bed. I know he'll be more comfortable and so will Dan and I.

I put a clean washcloth under the cold water and wipe his face with it. He likes that. It is soothing. He drinks a little water, and I make him some ginger tea with honey that he can sip. I am hesitant to give him anything that may interfere with the body's natural movement toward wholeness.

Kie asks more questions. He is now beyond why and into "How can we make it stop?" He is ready for it to be over and since it is not he is scared.

We talk about Higher Power, a wisdom beyond ours, and the reality of infinite possibilities. I synchronize my breath to his. Then lead him in a prayer for God to help us heal. He wants to know about the healing. He wants my hand on his stomach. When I move, he reaches for my hand, replacing it. I am reminded of the importance of being a healing presence.

Dan and I take turns comforting Hezekiah. For a while we talk. Kie wants to know more about why he was sick, why his stomach hurts. I know it is his way of asking to hear the story again. He often asks to hear stories over and over when trying to understand something new. Stories are afterall, remember, light!

We listen to more of Despereaux until he is ready to sleep again.

The final book of Despereaux finds the Princess kidnapped and brought to the dungeon by Miggery Sow and Roscuro. For how this comes about, you will need to read the book yourself. Suffice it to say here that a discourse on the condition of the heart of the princess is most brilliant in this our time of need.

DiCamillo writes, "Reader I am pleased to tell you that the Pea was a kind person, and perhaps more important, she was empathetic. Do you know what it means to be empathetic?

"I will tell you: It means that when you are being forcibly taken to a dungeon, when you have a large knife pointed at your back, when you are trying to be brave, you are able, still, to think for a moment of the person who is holding that knife.

"You are able to think: Oh, poor Mig, she wants to be a princess so badly and she thinks that this is the way. Poor, poor Mig. What must it be like to want something that desperately?"

"That, reader, is empathy."

I readily empathize with Hezekiah. He has few defenses for the very adult thoughts and emotions around him. The present situation gives me cause to evaluate where I am in understanding the difference between empathy and sympathy. I think in the past I have been more of a sympathetic healer with Hezekiah. This is why I have gotten sick a few days later than him each time he has a cold.

This makes me more curious about empathetic healing. I know it fits into what I was realizing the night before, the psychic vacuum cleaner idea. I will think about this many times in the days to come. For now it is enough to know Hezekiah has fallen into a sleep.

Friday 10:30 p.m.
Shawn S.

Earlier in the day I told Daniel about S's (the male Shawn) call. I needed him to be prepared to put Kie to bed, then as you have learned Kie became ill. About 9:00 pm Friday, I sent word to S, through Daniel, that I might be able to meet with him later if Kie settles down and sleeps. About 10, it seems like that is going to happen.

I ask Talina, a College student and S's girlfriend, if she will bring him up to the library, just a few doors down from where Kie is sleeping. In the library, I will be near my husband and son in case I am needed. Before we begin talking I tell S I may be called upon to leave. He understands which frees me into giving my full attention to him.

Our time together is insightful. It is helpful to him in the present and it ends up giving me information about Shawn.

He asks about Kie, and my heart is warmed from his concern. "It's all the emotion," I say.

He looks surprised and I realize he doesn't recognize the connection between the other Shawn's leaving and Kie's stomach problem. There really isn't any reason for him to physically know, I tell myself. He has no knowledge of the nature of their relationship and he is just beginning to learn about the levels of consciousness – what they are and how they function to create thought.

Shortly I will learn that much of the reason S wants to meet with me has to do with solar plexus energies. The same energies that have been giving Hezekiah fits all day.

S says he has lost motivation during the past week and been plagued by strange, wild thoughts about packing up and moving, quitting his studies. That morning he says he woke up angry for no reason. He wants to make a change but he doesn't know what kind.

As we explore the way he sees his world, we begin to realize that the loss of motivation is tied to his heart. He speaks of being betrayed by his wife. An action that led to a divorce. Since that time he has not been able to trust in relationships.

I listen while he describes his thoughts and I can clearly see the origin of his difficulty. "I don't believe you lack trust, Shawn," I tell him.

"What do you think it is?" he sincerely wants to know.

"A fear of being gullible," I respond. His problem concerning being close to others is not a heart problem, it is a *head* problem.

At first he looks at me, absorbing the idea. I am allowing it to sink into my consciousness as well. Images of the road I have taken to reach this conclusion flash before my third eye. Perception is everything, a Sagittarian once told me. It took me a while to free my ego from *that* statement. As I separated how things look from how things are, I slowly began to see the manifestations of thought into the matter of our lives. To perceive the truth, to live that truth, is one of the highest ambitions we can know.

I could say that life taught me this, but that would not be true. The truth is I taught myself through what life has brought me. How to be your own teacher forms the intent of the counsel I offer others.

S cocks his head slightly to one side and asks, "What does it mean to be gullible?"

His question causes my mind to choose specific images as a point of focus, like selecting and examining photographs. I search for words to describe the picture of gullible. "Someone afraid of being tricked, afraid of being taken for a ride." His expression tells me he is with me. He understands.

I move on to describe the reaction S has to feeling gullible,

"So you shut down – your emotions and your heart."

We talk of his dreams of snakes earlier in the week. Interpreted in the Universal Language of Mind the messages about creative energy are clearly associated with the injury he sustained in Tae-Kwon-Do class over a week before. The injury is to his solar plexus.

We talk about attention, of concentration as the means for connection, and about the solar plexus chakra's link to the seat of the conscious and subconscious minds. As we exchange questions and answers, the room grows brighter. Both of us are learning, our consciousnesses are becoming enlightened. In S, I can see my own need to believe. Through him I am given a picture of the temptation to be hurt, to shut down "feelings", to justify, to establish distance, to become cold, stiff, and hard. I know the temptation, and I have seen what it can cost.

S is here tonight because he wants to change all that.

S is here tonight to help me claim the ways I am able to assist him.

At one time I, too, feared being gullible. Finding it impossible to shut down my "feelings", I tried to hide them. I did not yet understand lower heart energies, emotional energies, and judged them as a weakness that my head sought to hide. "Weakness," my head told me, "means you can be hurt."

Not knowing what else to do, and intent upon doing more than surviving, I would hide the fear, in essence hide my innocence. To others nothing seemed to be wrong. I became adept in giving the "perception" that everything was fine, controlled. Yet, I could not hide from myself. I could not lie to myself about this fantasy, this illusion. My heart knew of the head's deception of others and found it objectionable. When alone, the truth my heart knew would surface again refusing to allow me rest until I could find some point of resolve.

Resolve. There's that word again. Having the means to create that resolve is one way I used what I learned in the advanced part of the SOM course. The knowledge of the structure of consciousness gave my head direction. The other way I used the course was developing consciousness so I could draw upon understandings no one had taught me this lifetime. Learning the fine art and science of intuition has brought me into the multidimensional world of consciousness. Practicing mental and spiritual disciplines for years has strengthened my command of attention, memory, listening, imagination, energy, reasoning and intuition. All of these are at one time or another employed in my quest to be open-minded.

This is what enables me to remain open in my thoughts about the Shawn who is leaving. From this discussion about desertion, faithlessness, and healing, thoughts of her enter my mind. I do not see her choice to leave the School of Metaphysics as a betrayal. My first experience of it was as a relief as much as a wound in the outer rim of my consciousness. My love is so deep for Shawn, my belief in her so strong and unconditional, that I want her to have what she wants.

The hurt in me is from feeling that I cannot be of help to her in accomplishing it. In this moment, I know the help I am giving to this new Shawn in my life is empowering me to let her go. Without grief. There is relief for us both in that.

The power of the still mind returns to me again.

One Shawn no longer wants what I have to offer. One door closes. Another Shawn is just beginning to ask. One door opens.

I think of the Tao Te Ching,

> *"The Tao is the breath that never dies.*
> *It is a Mother to All Creation.*
> *It is the root and ground of every soul*
> *– the fountain of Heaven and Earth, laid open.*
> *Endless source, endless river*
> *River of no shape, river of no water*
> *Drifting invisibly from place to place.*
> *...it never ends*
> *and it never fails."*

S's presence tonight, with the contents of his thinking, is a healing balm for me. I realize I no longer need to pull away, to separate, for my soul to be fed. Everything I ever need is here in the moment. The universe, God does provide.

Female Shawn's closing of her heart has to happen for her to follow through on the choice she has made. The closing of heart is the disconnection that allows the head to prevail.

But it is not the only answer as S is beginning to understand.

It's alarming when your child is sick. I can see how so many people get trapped into medicating their children, as if the medicine will make the pain or the fear go away. Between us, Daniel and I have an extensive amount of knowledge and wisdom concerning the connection between mind and body. We also know the power of the mind to heal.

By 11:30, the time of Hezekiah's last attempt to purge his body, I realize that his problem is not (as I have believed) everyone's emotional state. Hezekiah is tied to Shawn. After my time with Shawn S., I can see her stubbornness and the closing of her heart. My attention has been wrapped up in Hezekiah throughout the day so I have not been aware of all the people Shawn was telling her story to. I have, however, received enough feedback to realize she is letting everyone know, pretty much one person at a time. The question on everyone's lips, "Why?"

I know she's had occasion to revisit the answer, to look at it again and again, over twenty times in the same day. My mind boggles with the enormity of the task. It would be like telling the same story over and over and over. Would the story change with the telling? How would the teller change? I could image the ideas and thoughts that this diverse group of people must have offered Shawn. Mental fare for consideration. The only way anyone would be able to maintain his own line of thinking would be to close his mind and – in light of many of these people and their affection for Shawn, their love for her – to close his heart.

Hezekiah and Shawn have a tie, a connection. Even though in the past year since moving so far away she has spent few hours with him, she remains number 6 on his *"Best Friend List"*.

Hezekiah, the little boy who has repeatedly purged his body, is in part reflecting Shawn's mental and emotional state.

I look at the digital clock. 1:02. As I sit in the darkness next to his bed I think back over the few hours before. It was like a Fellini movie. Down the hall in the bathroom, Hezekiah laid on the floor, head in his dad's lap, trying to escape through sleep while less than twenty feet away Shawn, Laurie and Paul were in the library acting as if it was just another weekend at the College. In the room beyond them, Dr. Pam and Christine and a rotating group of people played with newly-born Alexandra who seemed to be faring well. Their laughter spilled down the hallway. "Perception is everything." The repression of all the things that could be said was increasing and I could see it through the cyclical violent reaction of a nine-year-old boy's body trying to rid itself when there is no longer anything there.

I now know either I need to remove this child from this environment or the environment needs to change. In this case, it means it is time for Shawn to leave the college. I admit I am the reason she is still here, and because of this I can also be the reason she leaves. Weighing Hezekiah's health with whatever we have yet to learn that Shawn knows makes the choice quite clear. My head and heart are in agreement. I will share this with Daniel first thing in the morning and ask if he will let her know.

Kie wakes up on and off through the night. I lie on the floor by his bed so I can more easily hear him. He dozes for increasing lengths of time. I make more ginger tea in the hopes it will help balance his system. Each time he wakes he drinks a little bit of water, a little bit of tea, then after half an hour or so he goes back to sleep.

My mind reaches out to each of the students who live here. Having missed dinner, our common communication time here on campus, I feel slightly out of touch. I wonder how each is receiving this turn of events. I wonder if Shawn has been a meals, if she has talked with others, heard anything that might bring light. I think of her classmates who have started to arrive from cities like Lexington, Des Moines, and Fayetteville, and wonder if and how they have learned of Shawn's choice. My mind goes to counseling class which will meet tomorrow evening. This shared experience will bring a reality to that gathering. I send all of these people love as I drift in and out of sleep, as dream thoughts blend with waking thoughts.

Sometime in the middle of the night I feel it safe to give Hezekiah a homeopathic herb for his stomach. I also remember an effective healing tool Daniel and I have used in the past. I apply color therapy to the weakened areas of his body. This is something he responds to very well, and I'm certain this helps him recover.

Eventually in the early morning hours, somewhere around four, Kie is able to sleep for two hours straight. It is a blessing and the sign that the healing is well underway.

Saturday Morning
Hezekiah's First Best Friend

Notwithstanding what he has been through the night before, Hezekiah wakes early, before eight. He bounds out of bed, very quickly discovering his energy is depleted. He says his stomach still hurts, and he is weak. He is able to drink some water and a cool washcloth on his face makes him feel better.

"Let's take it easy, okay, Kie?" I say softly. This morning, Daniel is teaching the class Shawn has been a student in for over two years, so I am prepared to do whatever it might take to continue nursing Kie back to health. "Maybe we should lay on Daddy's bed and watch a video." This is a special treat and I feel certain he will respond favorably.

He goes into his room and comes back with a Beatrix Potter video, *"The Tale of Samuel Whiskers"*. Potter's story is about how a curious kitten gets separated from its family and is finally spared from certain death. I note for the first time that Hezekiah uses this video when he is recovering from feeling out of sorts or ill. Its story is comforting to him.

We are in the middle of "*Samuel Whiskers*" when I realize the <u>Despereaux</u> tie. The kitten wanders into two rats' abode. The female begins to make a rare kitten pie for their dinner. I comment on the meanness of ignoring the kitten's pleas for mercy and wonder out loud how the rat got so mean.

Hezekiah says, "It's because their hearts break and are not put together right."

I look at him with amazement.

"Like Roscuro," he adds. I know the rat he is talking about. In that moment I realize how much Kie has learned from listening to this book about a mouse, a princess, and the light and the dark of the dungeon. He has heard and remembered things I have not. I start going back over the story for what else I might have missed. That's when my mind begins to open to the lessons of a mouse named Despereaux and that's how Despereaux became entwined with my experience of Infinite Being that I record for you to read here.

By 9:30, Kie is ready to go downstairs. When he is determined, little can sway him. The extremes of health/illness are still going on within him. Buoyed by the presence of Dr. Laurel, Dr. Pam, and a young 20-year-old visitor, Kie decides he is very hungry. "Grits and peppermint tea would be just fine," he says. I persuade him to try plain grits with salt and butter instead of the heavier and richer sausage-and-cheese kind he asks for.

While waiting he introduces himself to the young visitor from Springfield. He takes to her right away, talking to her as if she has been to the college dozens of times. I listen from the kitchen as he describes how the Peace Dome was built, how the doves flew overhead at the moment of dedication, and how people come from many states and other countries to classes here. In these moments I receive a glimpse into Hezekiah's being. I find out who he is and who he is becoming.

When I serve his grits, he eats the entire bowl full. His appetite returning is a good sign.

I am continually amazed by Hezekiah. We sit on the couch. He says he wants to watch a movie he's been making with Paul Madar – a great dinosaur epic. In the process of cueing this, a program on air sharks appears on the Discovery channel. These sharks are huge. They leap into the air to catch seals.

Hezekiah says, "I'm rooting for both of them!"

"What do you mean?" I ask, wanting to know his complete thought.

"The shark and the seal. It makes no difference which wins. I want each to have what they want."

I smile, basking in the wisdom this child has. The ability to hold all things in your mind, seeing the good in all is present in our son. This is a level of awareness I have worked to understand all my life. Something I highly prize and strive for each day. To have it reflected back to me through our son is the richest form of thanks.

Reenergized by the food, Kie goes to visit the young girl again. This time he invites her to tomorrow's PeaceMakers, saying that people come from Springfield every Sunday. When Dr. Laurel wants to show her the Peace Dome, Kie asks if he can go too. I weigh my response. He seems to be doing better. He has eaten and it looks like the food he has eaten will stay with him. With Laurel's consent, he accompanies her to the Dome.

A half hour later I am delighted to see S at brunch. I thought he might have left early in the day. Here is the opportunity to share the insights of the last few hours. What I want to tell him is a heart-centered thought concerning Shawn's eminent departure. It arose as I tended to Kie throughout the night. What S doesn't know – and therefore cannot take into account – are all the relationships that female Shawn is altering with this one choice. Her choice to quit the School of Metaphysics is not like quitting Harvard or the University of Illinois. It is not a distant head choice. It is also a heart choice.

I am understanding this as well about myself and about Shawn. The head and heart choices are all through this experience: all through the connections in seeing the different people, thoughts, and lives that are coming together in this one moment of time.

"This is not just a choice to stop studying," I explain to S "This is a choice to severe relationships. This is a choice of the heart."

I'm not sure how he is hearing what I am saying so I add the following, centered on purpose, "I felt the need to tell you this because you are endeavoring to open your heart again. And opening the heart is a choice."

All of a sudden, Kie resolutely enters the room, still in his heavy coat. He grabs me by the arm and says, "Come on! Upstairs." I excuse myself from S and I follow Kie. I am both grateful the powers that be gave me these few minutes with S and I am regretful of missing yet another lunch with the others, particularly with those attending classes this weekend. I allow the remorse to pass in the hope I will be seeing these people tonight in counseling class. I wonder if Shawn will be at brunch.

For the next two hours Hezekiah and I rest. Through the physical noise and mental bustle of brunchtime, we stay in the safe quiet of daddy's room listening to Despereaux. Both of us, I think, are deepening our understanding of the nature of light and the need for darkness.

On occasion, Kie says, "How come my stomach still hurts?" I explain it all again, each time he reaches a better resolve, more light. Each time he understands it a bit more, as do I. I wonder if his inner self, his soul shares my incessant need for resolve.

About the time everyone finishes brunch and has gone off to their activities for the remainder of the day, Kie decides he is ready to go find Briana who is number one on his list – his first friend. Seven years older than Kie, Bri has a magic and power with him that no one else will ever have. Although often unconscious of this, she repeatedly is willing to give to him.

Bri is in town with her mom Teresa and dad Ernie but she will be leaving at 3 o'clock. Hezekiah heard this before brunch. He might have missed brunch – the thought occurs to me to wonder how intentional that was – but he is not about to miss an opportunity to be with Briana. This is a Godsend. It is perfect timing because Bri's presence gives Kie somewhere productive to place his attention. Bri's presence aids him in using those solar plexus energies toward his own desire. He goes downstairs in search of her.

Finding Bri, Kie is happy. They take off for the Peace Dome and to play in the woods.

As Kie goes on his way, Daniel comes up to ask if I want to see Shawn before she leaves. Of course I want to see her, my heart thinks.

Being so attentive to Kie I have had no awareness of where she has physically been at any given time unless I happened to see her or hear her voice. I didn't even realize she was off campus all morning until Daniel tells me.

I am intent upon being still and nonintrusive. "Not unless she wants to see me," my common sense gives the reply. This is meant as a point of respect, a courtesy to her, not as a rejection.

"She does," he replies.

I take in a deep breath, "All right."

This is the first moment I have considered the real possibility of sitting down with Shawn. I have no idea what I should or need to say so I am willing to listen to whatever she has on her mind. This no-thought, no-perception land is a new experience for me. I have known about the potential for this meeting for days. I have not given in to the temptation of reviewing the possibilities in my mind, playing through different scenarios, replaying, revising, improving what I might say. I have kept my mind still about Shawn the entire time.

I am learning without judgement.

Saturday Afternoon
Ernie

As I walk toward the stairs Ernie and Bri are coming up to give hugs and say goodbye. They are on their way back to Kansas City. The impact Shawn walking out of our lives has on Ernie (Bri's dad) – the conductor who has invested so much into Shawn becoming an intuitive reporter – will probably make itself known over many weeks and months to come. Being capable of insightful and deep thought, I'm sure he will evaluate it.

In our brief conversation, Ernie says he has intended to send an email to me that he *will mail* when he gets back to Kansas City. I tell him I look forward to it.

What he sends is an insightful piece that is almost precognitive in its message. Its essence: the still mind and the conscious ego. As you read it, keep in mind that although Ernie sent it to me after Shawn had decided to leave us, he had written it a week before.

on 2/24/04 2:10 AM

Dear Dr. Barbara,

These last few months have been very incredible for learning how to go beyond extremes. One thing I am realizing is that when dealing with extremes I must be patient, loving, kind and gentle to myself and others.

I am very grateful for what I have learned in the School of Metaphysics because I have learned to still my mind even when I experience extremes.

I was teaching Simone this week concerning layout for *Vibes* this weekend. We were joking around talking about how to deal with anything in life -
stuck in traffic...still your mind
upset about something...still your mind
want to understand cause...still your mind
scattered thinking...still your mind
having fun...still your mind
teaching...still your mind
feel sick...still your mind.

Stilling my mind since becoming a student in the School of Metaphysics has enabled me to begin understanding my ego and how events in the physical are opportunities to learn from past karma. These events many times appear as things that happen to me and seem unrelated to my learning. These debts to myself provide stimulus for volatile reaction or a reaction of I don't care in myself. This ultimately leads to interactions with others where I don't get why someone else has a reaction of extreme emotion or indifference to me.

When I stay stuck in my reaction it leads to the desire of attempting to change my self by changing my physical environment in an extreme manner, thinking I have to choose between this or that. Avoiding, ignoring those in my environment or putting physical distance between myself and others is a way to unconsciously deal with what I don't understand. This ultimately leads to pain.

A still mind allows me to experience my reaction without pushing it away. I can then create the desire to learn from the experience and change myself through the use of imagination, using ideal, goal, purpose and activity. This is the secret of the aggressive and receptive principles of creation.

When I try to make a change in myself by changing my environment in an extreme way I experience a temporary means of avoiding change in me. It is similar to what is experienced in *Revelation* (in the Bible) with the 1st beast. (This is why someone drops out of the school, moves away, changes all their friends or goes back to the same old environment, it is an extreme way to avoid the self by blaming the environment or being indifferent). This is identifying with the 7th level of consciousness only. This is being stuck in a catch 22.

With a still mind I have the opportunity to cause change in myself. I can identify cause, I can see what has led to the event, I can respect the situation for what it is, I can respect those involved and I can respect myself. This gives me a way to be honest with myself and others and begin to implement what is necessary for the successes that will aid my soul as well as others involved. I am free to use my imagination to change myself and be of greater influence, a Master Teacher. (This also leads to forgiveness in self and for others). This is the mark of the 2nd beast.

My ego can motivate me in the physical or I can motivate my self through desire to be compatible with my Creator and direct my ego to be a Whole Functioning Self in alignment. How cool is that!

When I let my ego motivate me I can be sure I will stay stuck in the reaction of denial, blame, anger or indifference. Directing my ego leads to freedom with responsibility and allows the reaction to be what it is...a wake up call to evolve, instead of a falling back to unconscious sleep waiting for a bigger wake up call.

Imagine all this from a still mind!

May peace be with you all ways

Ernie

As I sit reading Ernie's words, images of the decade or more that I have known Ernie, his wife Teresa, and his daughter Briana, move in my mind. Each of them holds a special place in my heart. I have a respect for the way Ernie thinks; we share a certain hunger for truth and for mastery of the pairs of opposites. Teresa has revolutionized how I understand the Virgo influence in my life and given me such freedom to be comfortable with interpreting energies. And Bri – she is a daughter to me. I love her in the same way I love Hezekiah. Memories of times with each of them fill me with gratitude.

A new dawn is rising in Ernie's mind. His mind is opening after a dark night and I am thrilled. Another reason to rejoice. It makes the sadness easier to accept. Through the bitter with the sweet, we come to appreciate both.

Ernie was such a great partner for Shawn. Shawn had said, "Ernie knows how I am," as if that excused what she was doing to his life. Shawn was walking out of a dream they had created together.

The thought goes through my mind of something Maya Angelou said once, "When people tell you who they are, believe them." Shawn kept trying to tell everyone that she wasn't as good as we thought she was.

I'm glad I never believed her.

Saturday Afternoon
A Few Final Moments with Shawn

When Shawn and I meet in the library we hug, then sit just looking at each other for a moment. My first words are, "I love you."

She smiles that Mona Lisa smile of ambiguity, "I love you, too."

"I am so appreciative of having known you, of having you in my life," I add. The tears well up. They will be present intermittently throughout this encounter, and they are in many ways a measure for the completeness of my attention. I am thoroughly in the present. I have not put any forethought into anything I will say. I have been faithful to still mind, and here with Shawn in what I fear may be our last time together I remain so. Like breathing in and out, thoughts occur for either of us to say.

Having understandings of space, Shawn is as willing as I to give us the time we need.

After a few minutes I say, "I will always carry you here." I lay my right hand on my heart and allow the tears to spring from there. With this one simple thought and action, I am connected with all the people I've ever loved. Images of all the people my head would convince me that I've lost, my heart today is telling me that I have never lost anything. I have only gained. I know this with every fiber of my being.

Shawn says with complete candor, "You are amazing."

I don't question it as it might in the past. I just receive her words. I'll never know why she said them, and it really doesn't matter. This personal truth in itself is a revelation. Before, the why's mattered a lot. They were everything.

I am seeing "why" on a whole new scale these days. I am seeing connections that are far beyond the conscious mind and its reasons for fabricating the things we do in our lives.

When I respond to Shawn I tell her, "I am a symbol." I explain to her the last time Adam, her husband, and I had talked – here in the library – he spoke of me being a symbol. He said, "You're not really a person to many people." This was not a new thought to me, but hearing someone else say it opened a door in my mind. I knew people often thought of me as their mom, or former teacher or an employer they had known in their past. With that kind of projection – and to the degree that it is warranted – relationship in the now changes from what is possible. *Infinity leaves and the finite situation takes over.*

Today, in this moment, Joseph Campbell's work and Jungian archetypes come to mind. The door opens to realizing how the archetypes – the hero, the maiden, the martyr, the villain, the magician, and so forth – are the key to the pairs of opposites and entrapment in the cycle of birth and rebirth. I know I will think about this again, and I will write about it in the fall of this year.

Later, Shawn comments about how powerful I am.

I look at her and say, "I reflect you." Again I am holding the mirror in front of Shawn so she can see.

I know that I came very close through this hour with Shawn to freeing myself of thought ties. An Intuitive Analysis I received years ago said that I was not particularly attached to things or people, but there was a tendency for me to be attached to ideas. I heard it in 1979 when it was first said to me, about me. I have been waking up, understanding that attachment ever since. Today in this moment, being with Shawn, the strings are being cut even amid tears and great sadness and despair.

This is the perceived loss of what could have been and indeed never was! All the learning from Christine and Paul's stillbirth fills me and understanding is born in my consciousness. The awesome power of imagination is mine.

Over the next few days I look back over that hour with Shawn and wonder if I talked too much. I know that's just a brain thought, a head thought, because my heart knows I said what was needed.

I remember sharing with her my concern about the reactions/ responses of others. This is both on her behalf and on theirs. "I didn't see people fighting for you," I told her. "I don't really know what to make of that." Someone had told me that when Shawn called Tina, her former college roommate and a longtime classmate, Tina was free with her anger and disagreement. She was the only one who I heard had given Shawn grief. I would understand some of this later this night during counseling class.

Before dinner, I learned that when Shawn told college graduate Greg Brown she was leaving studies at SOM because she wanted to be a midwife, his question to her was "Shawn, how many times do you think you've been a midwife?" The question is a reference to reincarnation, to the reality of previous existences before the present time.

I'm glad Greg thought to ask her. I understand the real value of this train of thought. It's the kind of question I have asked others before. My lack of asking it this time troubles me. The question remains, "Why didn't I think of this line of thought this time? I had time with Shawn, why didn't I ask her the question myself?"

Did I carry still mind too far? Should I have acted? Engaged my conscious mind more?

I don't know if it is a disorder, a "bad" thing, a harmful thing that more people weren't insisting that Shawn reconsider. I know certainly she had taken me out of that realm when I made my commitment to stilling my mind.

I marvel at all of this when I talk with Daniel later this night. Not fighting for someone in this way, particularly someone with the investment and the potential of this woman, was so out of character for me. It is when I am telling Daniel this that I begin to realize the reason I didn't fight for Shawn is simple: I *believed* her when she said she was quitting.

Perhaps this sounds too simple for you, dear reader. Simplistic even. Then I would ask you to consider, why shouldn't I believe her? Why shouldn't I accept her word? Until today, I would have answered, "because I am fully aware of what the person is leaving behind. I also know the future they will miss." Both thoughts take us out of present time, into a past that is gone and into a future that will never be. Today, I realize the full implication that all we have is now.

Now is the lesson of the still mind.

Today I have passed my final exam.

In a self counseling tape Shawn says early on, "I realize how I don't ask questions...because I don't want to know what the truth is. I want to maintain what my version of the truth is rather than asking questions and finding out what the real truth is. I want to maintain my version of the truth so I can hold onto my prejudices or my reactions or what I think I know."

Exactly a week ago Paul Blosser, who Shawn had met with at my request for counseling a week before, called to let me know that Shawn would probably be phoning Dr. Dan and I because she was thinking of quitting. This was the first time I heard "quitting" and "Shawn" together in the same sentence. When I reminded Paul of this on Thursday he didn't remember saying it. For a moment that threw me into another dimension and I wondered if Paul's call was a lucid dream. On second thought, I know better.

When I heard Paul say this on the phone, although I didn't realize it at the time, I accepted it. I believed it as truth. So when Shawn called on Wednesday afternoon, asking to talk to Dr. Dan and I together as soon as possible, then hesitating, the words were there – together – and I asked her, "Are you quitting?" The words came out of my mouth before I even thought. It is as if from that point forward it was done. Finished.

I've done a lot of thinking about how the mind works this way, a rush to judgement some call it. Or it is known as jumping to conclusions, or making assumptions. Such prejudices are most apparent with medical diagnosis where a label gets placed on a person – cancer, diabetes, ADD, and it is immediately accepted by the people. An awareness of this is what is behind Shawn S.'s fear of being gullible. Sometimes fears are useful and healthy. Sometimes they are a death knoll.

In light of these realizations, I know that part of why I didn't fight for Shawn was I believed her words and I respected her as a person. I know that she left because she needs to change. I know what she needs to change is her identity. Her ego. I also know that what she has produced is an external change. She does not have the mental strength or clarity to cause the mental change because she has not been faithful in her daily mental disciplines. I know this from Greg. He asked Shawn when she stopped practicing and she answered that she hadn't really been consistent with the exercises since she moved to Palatine. That was over a year ago.

It's difficult to live a lie. Sooner or later you have to come clean. In Shawn's own way that is what she is doing. Shawn is creating a new identity for herself, leaving this one, moving into another. She has to leave because of the prejudices she wants to maintain. In the new environment, she won't have any prejudices, not for a while. At the same time, any prejudice she wants to keep, the ones she would have changed had she stayed in this environment, she can save. Shawn's choice to leave our lives is a search for infancy, infancy in the physical world. Her need for change is manifesting as starting all over, like divorcing or quitting a job and getting a new one, or moving from one place to another.

While a self-counseling tape Shawn made this statement, *"I didn't want to deal with what thoughts you might say."* Upon first hearing this it cut to the quick, pricking an old wound. I think of others who have thought the same way, avoiding talking with me. I realize, in the light of my newfound Self appreciation, their avoidance was not because I was bad nor that I would say the wrong thing, that I might hurt them with what I said. Avoidance was not a manifestation of any fear I imagined in my head. *Reality is always the reflection of each individual's willingness to own their own thoughts.*

This concept came through most clearly when Shawn talked about something that happened at an annual SOM directors meeting a few weeks before. She said, *"During General Assembly when you first stood up, you said you wanted each of us to read what we had written* (about activities in each city for One Voice, the synchronized reading of the *Universal Peace Covenant* at midnight on New Year's Eve). *The first person was starting to talk and you got up a second time and said that you wanted us to understand why. The reason why was you wanted all of us to share with one another so we could all learn. It wasn't for some weird ego motivation or to make anybody feel bad if they hadn't written anything yet. I know I would have been sitting there thinking that's why you had done that, or at least part of the reason."*

Hearing this I know why – inasmuch as Shawn is concerned – it has been important for me to keep that still mind. Shawn has needed time and space to claim her own thoughts. I know that my thoughts have been directed elsewhere, leaving her with her own. What she says here is powerful Self realization. It is as if she is surfacing from being underwater, sometimes drowning, for a long time. I think about Plato's metaphor of the cave. It takes effort to be Self aware. It requires being in the present, fully. It demands honesty and decisiveness each moment. With these words, Shawn is coming up out of the water.

"I'm realizing that I short change myself so much," she continues, *"assuming I know what the truth is. Instead of asking to find out what the truth is. That's really sad to me because it keeps me from finding out who people really are, what they are really*

about, and why they do the things they do."

It is sad to me too. I feel like I have perceived the real Shawn all along. My failure has been disregarding the outer Shawn, the one who makes that "short change", the one who casts judgements that imprison self and others.

My outer self is never quite sure what the truth is. I think of myself often as not having a clue as to what the right thing to think, say or do is. This follows many lessons in humbleness and respect for the laws that govern our universe, those things beyond our control. What is the quote? Something like, "God grant me the serenity to accept what I cannot change, the courage to change what I can, and the wisdom to know the difference?" This concept is the reality of living beyond the pairs of opposites, of being neither-either, yet both.

As I think of this code to live by, it occurs to me that Shawn already does this in her dharma of serenity. I have admired her for that dharma, for how I and others feel in her presence. She goes on. *"With you at General Assembly I could have sat there and had this prejudice against you, thinking you were just trying to poke at people's conscious egos and maintain my prejudices about how that really doesn't motivate people in any way that is productive. I was so grateful that you got up there and said that in front of everybody. I was just (thinking), 'Shawn, this is not what you think it is.' I was grateful I had an understanding of what was going on."*

Shawn was meeting her own thoughts when she made that tape. They had little to do with me. I was a symbol for her.

Through Shawn, I am appreciating my insatiable curiosity. I have to know. It has been with me since I was born, this incessant urge to find answers. For years I described my choice to study journalism as a means to meet new people, to find out who they are and why they do what they do. I saw myself as a Charles Kuralt-type, traveling, interviewing people about their lives. In the early '70's, I hoped being a journalist would give me a way to learn all through my life. I now see my college experience as a head choice driven by the heart.

I have always wanted to know what the truth is. I learned while I was still in college that journalistic truth is often slanted, driven by material concerns more than enlightening ones, controlled by the ego more than the soul. *The desire for truth is what led me to the study in metaphysics.* I am becoming more conscious every day about just how much knowing and living by the truth is my number one priority in life. I choose Satyagraha – "holding onto Truth" – for it yields meaning and value to my life.

Saturday Evening Taraka Yoga Class

After dinner it is time for me to go to Moon Valley Ranch to teach the counseling class. Kie has done well all afternoon, spending time with Paul Blosser and with Greg, two of the best reasoners I know. He wants me to stay but in light of his increasing strength, I feel good about assuring him that he and daddy will have a great time until I get home.

Taraka Yoga is the preparatory work for Psi Counseling training. Taraka is Sanskrit for "causing to cross over", "rescuing". It is a most appropriate name for unifying consciousness from the bondage of the physical world. Taraka Yoga is the journey of harmonizing the conscious and subconscious minds in entrainment with the Highest Self. Some call it Self counseling and this is an apt description for union does bring the deepest insights. It also empowers its practitioner to entrain consciousness with another, a skill unique to Psi Counselors.

I have heard that the members of this class have already talked about Shawn's absence earlier this morning with Dr. Daniel Condron, their spiritual teacher in the SOM course of study. Since I was not present, I don't know the content in their minds, the opinions or conclusions they are drawing. I do however recognize this as the common, shared experience I have been looking for.

The Raja Yoga experience I lead the class through centers on death and immortality. In the future, these individuals will minister to others who have "lost" loved ones. This class will minister to them, revealing each one's level of awareness. They discover how open they are to grief or longing or thanksgiving. As each progressive step in the yoga unfolds it reveals the willingness toward Self counsel.

At one point class members draw a picture of death. This is followed later by a picture of immortality. At the completion of the entire yoga, we discuss the pictures. Each image is revelatory for all of us. We talk of finality and initiation, of the end and the beginning, of goings and comings. The pairs of opposites abound as our hearts and minds are being cleansed.

Here I share two student's drawings and the words that describe them. I found them particularly meaningful and relevant to the material included here.

Death

by Tina Coleman

Death is a constantly evolving process of change and evolution. The picture that I drew depicts this change as a quick process, one of chaos and confusion because at times in my life where I have been around death, there is so much emotion that it is overpowering and you don't really know what is going on. Being with loved ones at a funeral home was the scene that I had in mind when I added the black and blue in this picture. To me it represents the emotional state.

The pink on the outskirts of the picture represents love. There is usually a lot of love that is felt when someone passes. You remember all the good times that were shared, the accomplishments, hopes and dreams of the person. This can even elevate someone to sainthood if the death was seen to be 'untimely'.

The center of this picture is like the blades of a fan, quick moving tinted in red and blue ever spinning. It looks like it is moving towards you through the chaos of emotions, it's coming for you. Death cannot be escaped or avoided. It is the one constant in our lives. Death used to be a scary thing to me before I entered the School, now it is the next great adventure. What happens when you die? Will you be enlightened by then or will you come back or serve in another capacity? There are many questions that surround it, just like the black and blue clouds in the picture, what is really beyond it? Is there anything?

When we interpreted these pictures in class, Dr. Barbara said it was judgement and to read "Matthew", Chapter 7, which is a good Virgo chapter. It talks about judging others and having the plank in your eye while trying to remove the splinter in someone else's eye. Is it because the image is quick and final that it is about judgement, no room for questioning or debate? I don't think judgement is a "bad" thing, you have to stand firm in what you believe and teach what you believe in.

I know that I have been judgemental in the past and you're either with me or against me. This is right, that is wrong. If it doesn't fit in this box, it doesn't belong. These days, however, I look at things from different perspectives, or at least try to. To see things from a different angle. This picture can be viewed from many different angles, from the pink on the outside to the darkness surrounding the central image of a crosslike section waiting to be judged. It's all relative and open to many different interpretations.

In the Universal Language of Mind death signifies change. When we dream of someone dying, this symbolizes a part of ourselves that is undergoing a change. Tina's drawing depicts the pain she has associated with death throughout her life. They are "head" pictures reflecting a wounded "heart". It is a busy picture, dark and pointed as change in our lives can be.

Immortality

Tina Coleman

This picture is of the Earth drawn as a blue circle with green continents and rays of yellow light and pink radiating from it. This depicts what I think I could accomplish if I were immortal. Immortality seems like a bright, happy, shiny place where you could save the world. I figured if I were immortal, I would be able to 'save' the world, help everyone to be enlightened. And of course this would be done with lots of love, hence the pink interwoven with the gold emanating from the Earth.

To me this is a very uplifting image full of hope and light. When I originally drew this, the picture was perfectly centered in the middle of the page. When I copied it to an 8 1/2 by 11 sheet of paper, it became slightly askew, off to one side. At first I thought I would fix it to make it perfect, then as I thought about it, I realized I liked this bet-

ter. Life isn't perfect ,neither is artwork. It seemed more real and more balanced being slightly off balance. It gives the picture movement and more form.

This is very much a 'safe' picture, it doesn't really depict much of me in it, it was an automatic picture. We received the topic and this came to me, I didn't have to think about it, there was no extreme emotion attached to it which makes me think it's not a very 'deep' picture. Maybe it's more safe than true. I have a hard time drawing, even though I went to art school because I don't think I am a very good artist. I have a feeling that we are going to be doing a lot of drawing and that old image of me will be changing where I will actually enjoy drawing and look forward to showing my images to others. Right now, I don't.

This image also has a lot of space which is probably connected to the space that I feel between me and others. I'm realizing that even when you think you're close to people, you may not be as close to them as you think. Just like this image, it's of the Earth, but where are the people? If it's a picture of immortality, am I alone on a huge planet with no one to talk to? Am I it? Surely I would not be the only person left alive, to me that would be hell not immortality.

All of this makes me think of Shawn. Even though she's not here, I want to be close to her and connected and at the same time I don't. Space in my drawing, space between us. Space as a water sign, no space as an earth sign. This picture is actually kind of lonely, which is how I feel at times when there's no one else around. I don't want space in my life to pull away and be alone, I want to be connected. Forever and Always.

I have never thought of the element of earth as no space. It is a mind-expanding thought. In light of this I can see that a still mind is giving space. Her idea adds in every way to my understanding of still mind. What Tina saw as a safe picture, I see as one reflecting the simple Truth of the still mind. Calm, light, and clear, like that which is eternal. Perhaps that is why Tina describes it as safe. Safety breeds security so security must come from the still mind. How impressive this concept is in these days of terrorism when high levels of fear consciousness rule the heads and the hearts of the populace making for restless minds.

Death

by Ivy Norris

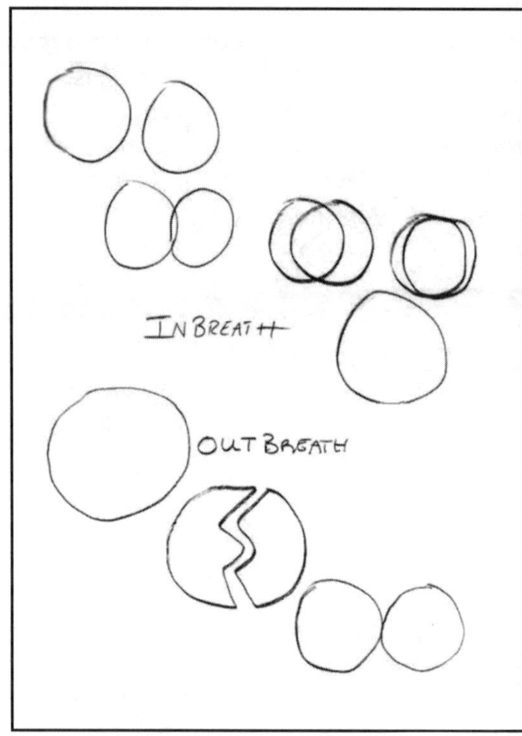

I drew my picture of death as an outbreath. I shortly realized that I was drawing my experience of Shawn, my classmate and friend, leaving the school. Her leaving was a form of death for many of us. When talking with her the day she was saying goodbye I said, "If you are the outbreath, it is going to be a mighty beautiful inbreath."

After getting honest with myself, I realized that I was a part of this inbreath. Even though I've been in the school for a few years, it feels like I am just beginning to wake up to my influence. Part of this influence I'm realizing is that of wonder and leadership.

The wonder I see in this picture is the everpresent Light radiating down from above that is in awe of the process, the observer. It is God's light. It is from where we came and to where we shall return, even more abundant. Even more abundant? That is a new thought to me.

Leadership shows up in this picture as conscious change because whatever our outer circumstances, it is us that has the opportunity to cause change, leading our own minds, and up to us to determine what we do with the changes that occur. I choose learning. I choose giving and receiving. What could I have given and received more from Shawn? Would it have helped?

The back of this picture follows with an inbreath. The nature of the physical is change and the nature of mind is motion. With the outbreath, space has been made to receive. This is certainly a different way to look at death. It is much more wholistic.

Ivy's outbreath illustrates the one becoming two, the coming into being of duality. The inbreath shows the two coming together, joining, merging into one. Death – change is a process of infinity, the coming and going, the past and the present, the lover and the beloved, separation and unity, the alpha and the omega.

Drawing of Immortality

by Ivy Norris

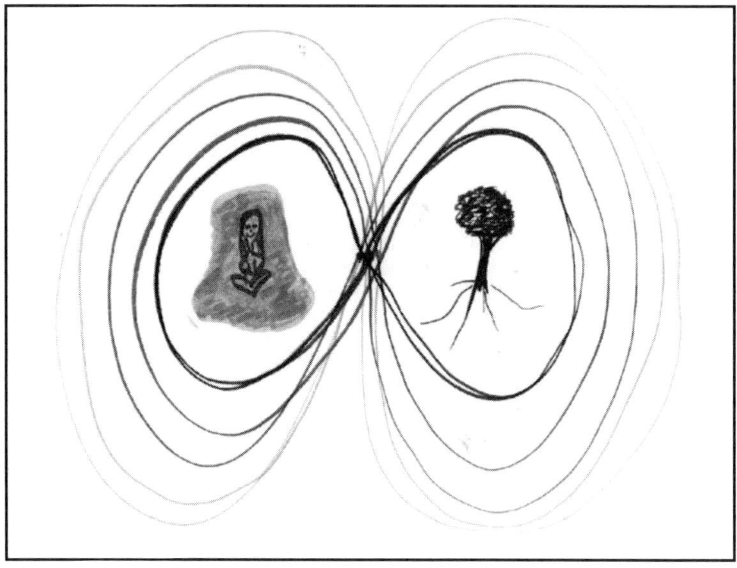

My first thought of immorality was actually Babaji, the Yogi-Christ of India. He is surrounded in this picture in the violet flame which represents utter purity. From what I've read, he has retained his physical form for centuries or more, making him an avatar or Divinity in the flesh. I see Babaji as a model of God-man. This state of consciousness is most likely unattainable for me this lifetime, though if we are going to attain greatness, we certainly need an image of it to hold in mind.

I also had a tree in the picture of immortality, the tree of life (right side up). This reminds me that if we produce seeds, we live forever. This is one of the reasons why teaching is so important. The giving and receiving of love and truth ensures forward motion and evolution. Ideally we teach teachers. From what I've read Babaji is an assistant of Prophets, helping them to fulfill their plan. Now we're talking!

Finally I drew a symbol of infinity. I love harmonizing with the Law of Infinity. The heart of it, I believe, has to do with connectedness and continual expansion of all space and time. It reflects our true nature that is completely free. One who is immortal is fully aware of the workings of this law and all the Laws of Creation. Life, I believe, is eternal. I am highly motivated to be a knower of this.

In Ivy's immortality picture, the duality meets, crossing, giving into the sign for infinity. It reminds me of a quote from Sri Chinmoy, "When the power of love supercedes the love of power man will have a new name – God." Who knows better about immortality than the Creator?

I appreciate this time of reflection with this group of people. They are amazing thinkers, people who spend time giving thought to people, God, and life. They do not take life for granted, and their thoughts and images this evening show this. Here are their hearts and their heads. Like Despereaux, they are beginning their own tales.

For the most part they are relunctant to go into the dungeon tonight. Shawn is mentioned few times. I wonder if this is because they lacked connection with her or because they deny the connection that is there. Experience tells me that time will give the answer. Tonight, they are more philosophical than spiritual, more head than heart. I understand their learning, and I am accepting my dharma in the world in new ways as they reveal to me who they are and who they want to become.

I am especially grateful for these people tonight in a way only human loss seems to stimulate. Tonight I realize how good gratitude is, and I can allow the stimulus to be what it is without wanting to change it. That is wisdom.

I get home late Saturday evening. Daniel says Kie has been fine all evening and went to sleep without any difficulty around 10. This is the first opportunity we've had to talk about Shawn since Wednesday night.

Daniel is a peer and a teacher as well as a husband and chancellor of the College. The ways we are related touch every area of our lives, and the learning and growth is rich because of that. With him I am free to discuss any aspect of my own experience with Shawn. I find myself saying, "My association with Shawn has not been as a teacher." This is highly significant for me since most of the people I know view me in this way.

In thinking over my time earlier that day with Shawn I realize I was thoroughly centered in the heart. I was in the moment completely. It was a multidimensional experience.

As time and space has moved me beyond those moments with her, my head has started to intervene. I am able to isolate thoughts, writing them has helped. Now I have the time and space to verbalize them.

"Had I been Shawn's teacher I would have had an entirely different meeting with her," I find myself telling Daniel. "I probably would have played the Self counseling tape she sent me. We would have listened to it together. I don't know where that would have led. Perhaps she would have gotten mad and left. Perhaps she would have had a change of heart. Maybe she would have felt pressured, or relieved. Embarrassed or cleansed. Bitter or resolved. I will never know.

"I would have asked, 'What is your influence?'

"But I didn't ask those questions and I didn't do those things. I was merely being who I am."

My head has since been trying to tell me that I was self-centered, focused on the personal lessons and losing sight of Shawn's need. I don't believe that's the truth because what is coming from this experience is an amazing growth of love and truth. I will keep Shawn in my heart, and I will learn more about how my head – the thoughts in my brain that limit my mind, disturb my emotions, cloud my vision, distract my attention – leads me astray, away from the truth.

I reflect upon something Shawn told me earlier. She said one of the people she started in the classes a couple years ago told her in reference to her dharma, "Shawn, what you bring to people is comfort." Shawn admitted that being comfortable is very important to her. She enjoys her freedom to come and go, her "Starbucks coffee" and time to herself.

Although this is not the way I thought of her, the idea comes back to me now as I realize my experience of Shawn has many times been one of comfort. It is easy to talk with Shawn, to make connections about people, places, and things. She often asks questions, thought-provoking questions, that I readily embrace and enjoy answering. I felt she understood my responses, and now I am finding that she rarely did.

I realize in my mind the pain I experience is in losing my comforter. The *Bible* verse *"I will send you a comforter,"* comes to mind as something from the distant past that I never believed I could have. Now the choice is mine, will I lose my comforter or will I understand what that passage means?

Shawn said on tape that she did not want to be uncomfortable. She wanted to be centered in what the truth is. She needed to be aware of what she needed to do to learn. She didn't want to be uncomfortable.

In leaving, she doesn't have to be.

As I talk with Dr. Dan I realize the responsibility of potential greatness. This is a thought that germinates in the back of my mind. It is a seed planted in 1977 in an intuitive report for the directors of the School of Metaphysics. The report addresses the reality of potential and seems to pose the question, "Who of you are prepared to meet greatness?" I secretly, in my heart of hearts wanted to be able to say I am, but my head was too filled with questions followed by doubts and fears and egotism. I knew at the time that responding to these was the work I needed to do. These distracting thoughts were the ones I needed to understand, to clean. Doing so was the way I could prepare.

Little did I expect part of this preparation to make sense in the way it does in this moment. I hadn't really put it together in that way, there have been so many compatible experiences between Daniel and I. We have come to understand that we experience the same energies in very different ways while coming to the same conclusions.

It is beyond being souls in a male body and a female body, although certainly this is a factor and part of our joy of sharing life. Our paths are very different. Astrologically our sun signs are square to one another, an aspect most astrologers warn couples against. The saying "being at cross purposes" comes into my mind. What that means is often what gives me the greatest joy, what thrills my soul, wounds Daniel. And vice versa. My relationship with my husband is a constant affirmation of the value of what we teach. It is a constant challenge to use what we learn, to bring forth understandings from our souls. It is a reminder to stay centered in our minds and hearts, instead of our heads and egos. We both know when either of us veer. Nothing is hidden long between us.

Our lives and therefore our relationship with one another is a testimony to polarity, to duality, to the ability to perceive the whole, to the understanding of the aggressive and receptive principles of creation. I realize in my constant battle of holding back because of my husband, from fear of hurting him unintentionally, there is an incredible self-denial that takes place in my mind. To come out of that denial is a recurring battle. It's like trying to free yourself from cobwebs.

This impinges upon my sense of wonder which is one of my inner strengths. The dis-appointment is palpable. It's like the little child who gathers flowers, takes them to the parent, who either doesn't acknowledge the gift or acknowledges it, then discards it where the child sees. The act of having been chosen and demoted – or having not been chosen in the first place – is a mind-altering element of learning in my relationship with Shawn. I was finally going to be able to give to Shawn in a teaching capacity. I had misgivings or anxieties about how – given the still mind state I had placed myself in. I was eager to move forward. I did know I had much to offer Shawn that she would find very useful in the life she dreamed for herself. I had faith I would draw to me the guidance to work it out in the best interest of all.

The element that I am dis-appointed from being her teacher is the biggest ego blow. I look at it and realize just how much work I have done on that part of me. Although the ego is there, it's motivating power is connected more and more through the heart.

In so many ways this entire initiation time is about motivation. Certainly it is for Dr. Sheila. Certainly it is for Shawn S. Certainly it is for female Shawn. And certainly it is for me. *"Who is the greatest,"* Jesus asks his disciples. *"The one who reclines at table or the one who serves?"* For many years I have known the answer is neither-either, yet both. In the interest of understanding this, I make sure my daily activities include humbling activities that serve the whole – teaching others, preparing food, cleaning and laundry, typesetting, proofreading and transcribing intuitive reports. This thought triggers a message I received long ago from an intuitive report, *"You'll have to appreciate Barbara"* it said.

I realize my motivation needs to change again. I need to stop being dependent upon the environment to stimulate me toward self appreciation.

Self appreciation is something I need to be willing to give myself.

I know this is my inner mind's message from this experience. I realize I am still very young at being able to manifest it.

My mind goes to Hezekiah. Before I go to bed I check on him. He is resting peacefully, and as time passes he sleeps throughout the night without waking.

Sunday

Sunday morning is another beautiful day. Hezekiah and I share the morning until it is time for our weekly PeaceMakers gathering in the Peace Dome. Many are present on this day which makes the room swell as we sing *"The Light of Creation"*.

"Let there be light! said the Lord of Creation.

So simple a statement, the start of our world.
Let there be light, brought the first manifestation,
Let there be light, and the Heavens unfurled.

Light, oh Light! I can see through the darkness.
A new day is dawning, the vision revealed.
Light, oh Light! How your beauty astounds me
I've made it my goal, to bring Light to the world!"

I think of Shawn's beautiful voice and wish she were here. I wonder if she has made it to Fayetteville, and if so where she stayed. I wish her well with a thought of love.

Today Dr. Dan has chosen a new way for us to explore universal truth. In place of improvising a holy scripture or morality tale, we are going to write our own. There are about 50 people present and we divide into four groups. Each group receives a piece of paper that reads, "The young boy went out to the orchard...." This is to be the first line of a story that we will create, right now, in our groups.

When we are finished, we perform our stories. Story one is a witty tale that takes us from *Genesis* to *Revelation* and beyond. Story two is about doubts and fears and dispelling these distractions for a happy ending. Story three is like a Zen Buddhist tale of light prevailing in the darkness. Story four, the group I was part of, tells about a talking tree that bears all kinds of fruit. This is the tree of life. Wisdom.

As the stories unfold I marvel at how they fit together reflecting the four stages of man: infancy, adolescence, adulthood, and wisdom.

I am so happy
I have made the choices
I have in my life.

Following PeaceMakers, I go to my office to get materials for the second part of Taraka Yoga class which is meeting this afternoon. As I pick up my notebook, I see the self counseling tape Shawn sent over a week before. In that moment I decide to take it with me. Last night I heard the confusion, the surprise, the shock from many of her classmates about her choice. "I had no idea she was going through this." "It was totally unexpected." I know I have the ability to shed light on what has occurred. I know some of the facts that became reasons in her head.

I also know for these people to learn how to use what they have been taught about the Mind, to develop the perception to use consciousness more fully, they need guidance and direction. Athough she is physically absent, Shawn continues (through her voice on a tape) to have a presence that benefits everyone.

The irony is the very class that Shawn could not abide finds insight through her choice to disconnect. I recognize this as another expression of head and heart coming together in an unexpected way.

The class learns the sequence of events over the past month that led to Shawn's quitting her studies. Beginning with leaving the College of Metaphysics the month before without turning in an assignment which those in the class had fulfilled. I inform them that I waited two weeks for some acknowledgement on her part of what had happened. I checked repeatedly in areas I thought she might have left the papers, believing she must have left it in my box in the office, or by the computer in the library, or even in my room. Finally I emailed her asking a very simple and clear question, "I have looked several times through the papers turned in during Counseling Class weekend and do not find one from you. Is this accurate?"

It took a few email exchanges before Shawn realized what she had done. I asked her to explore this in self-counseling, verbally talking it out, and send me the tape on it. My head knew, by her self-sabotage, that she was not prepared to be in this counseling class. I knew there would be another counseling class beginning, probably within six months. It was my hope that in working with her in this way she could better prepare herself.

 Shawn has an amazing ability for lucidity. She has a broad

command of describing thoughts and feelings. Insight comes easy to her. One thing I have been learning through all this is how people can make discipline unnecessarily difficult.

Everyone in the class has been making tapes each week and exchanging them as part of the learning process to become counselors. Before playing Shawn's tape I verbalize the reason for doing so: self counseling is the purpose of this class. I encourage them as they listen to take notes. This is unexpected because their practice for two months has been to give their complete and undivided attention to the person speaking. Complete listening. No notetaking. In this experience however remembering what draws their attention is important so I teach the value of time and place in recordkeeping. They note what they hear, and no two, I am certain, hear the same thing. I am equally certain each learned something new about their former classmate. It will now be my duty to counsel the class toward a deeper level of understanding of themselves in this experience. I can do so because I have been Self counseling all along.

Shawn did attend this class in a way none of us expected or wanted. Letting Shawn speak for herself is a way to keep our minds open, and our hearts.

Monday Morning

> *"How can I hope to make you understand*
> *Why I do, what I do?*
> *Why I must travel to a distant land*
> *Far from the home I love."*

The tune runs through my mind when I awaken and the words shortly follow. From the first time I heard it, I've always loved this song from "*Fiddler on the Roof.*" It's quality is haunting, longing. It is a song of desire. I know it is important to allow the words to come back into my consciousness now.

I've thought a great deal about heart this year. The Tale of Despereaux has put the open heart in perspective during these past two weeks in a most unexpected and illuminating way. Another song – *Hard-Hearted Hannah* – comes up out of memory. I think of all the Disney films that encourage you to "follow your heart."

When she is getting ready to leave with her Russian beau, the song Havilah sings to her papa says, *"Closing my heart to every hope but his, leaving the home I love*." It seems that this is what Shawn has done. She has closed her heart to everyone and everything but being a midwife. This is exactly what happens when one births anything new. What becomes most important in the moment is the desired image/object/circumstance. This principle can readily be seen physically,– once the human body becomes pregnant, it is no longer open to anything else. It is committed to producing a new human body.

John in the *Bible* represents in the Universal Language of Mind the one goal of believing that we can become like our Creator. Shawn has chosen her one goal. Her goal goes back to when her baby brother was born and her mother was attended by a midwife. She says she has known since she was 19 that she wanted to be a midwife, but didn't have the knowledge or courage or confidence to pursue it. What she learned at the School of Metaphysics has given her what she needs to pursue her life's passion.

I understand the mobilization of energy. Last year I experienced it on many levels with the construction and dedication of the world's Peace Dome. With devotion and dedication energy flows. Something Daniel asked me a while ago comes back to me: *"What makes you so sure you're right?"* I don't even remember what we were talking about at the time he said it. I do remember replying, "I don't know that I'm right. I do know what I perceive, think, and will do." To me, these words describe knowing yourself. When I know what I want and I am committed to doing what it takes to manifest that desire, my head and my heart align and magic happens. People on seven continents joining those of us at the Peace Dome in reading the *Universal Peace Covenant* at 1 pm October 11, 2003 is an example of this kind of magic.

For some this may sound egotistical. My attention can be distracted away from the awesome working of Universal Law toward self-doubt only when I am failing to be honest. A line often quoted to me from the *Bible* by my grandmother moves through my head like one of those banners on the bottom of a television screen: *"Trust in the Lord thy God and lean not to thine own understanding."* I rebelled against that statement for years. I heard it as don't trust yourself, don't think for yourself, don't be yourself. And I didn't like what I heard, so I pushed it away.

Through the years my mind has opened – a result of my metaphysical studies. I began understanding, in stages, the limits of the conscious mind and conscious ego. From the time I began this journey of Self awareness – 1975 – my sights were set very high, on I AM, the truest expression of identity. The closest to our common Source as spiritual creators. To "trust in the Lord" means to align with that I Am. To make every thought the highest I am capable of. To "lean not to thine own understanding" means to expand beyond what my conscious mind can see, hear, taste, smell, and feel.

Today this means experiencing joy and sorrow. It means accepting the presence of both in my life. I am happy that Shawn is pursuing her dream. I am sad that she will not complete the dream I am a part of. It means allowing both to be what they are. My heart grows to hold both. My conscious mind cannot function in this way. My conscious mind can hold only one or the other. I have to go into mind to perceive the wholeness and I experience this with a full illumination that is new for me.

Last evening, I came across an email I sent Shawn in early January. She had written, *"One of the things I am admitting about myself is that I often won't do things if it is just for me, it still takes something from outside to motivate me."*

The response I gave her: *"Have you considered that the idea that 'I won't do things just for me' may be an enlightened one? Just because 99% of the world doesn't get it or want it for that matter, does not make you bad, wrong, misguided, or underprivileged. It could make you enlightened. After all, all the great Masters didn't live for themselves. They seemed to live for others which is what dharma is all about. The illusion is thinking that we are separate when in reality we never are. I do understand the conflict, and I understand the resolve. It is in the present. Perhaps your 'external' motivation is the means by which you become connected to Self...."*

I heard that Shawn told one of the College students that she was quitting because she had been given a choice between being a field director and coming to the College. I now understood a conversation she had initiated with me a month earlier. She had asked what I thought was in her best interest. I told her "living at the College of Metaphysics." She said, "Dr. Dan told me he thought working with schools would offer me the greatest learning." From what she had heard, Shawn had chosen her fate.

Sometime during this long weekend, Greg Brown gives me an interview about her Creative Mind Report that Shawn completed before she left on Saturday. He says all the answers are there. I understand him to mean that the ways of thinking, the reasons Shawn is walking away are there. The answer to the following – *"You will also relate that which will foster a movement in the energy exchange between the ethereal and the material for the cultivation of genius within this one"* – is most helpful.

This would begin with Self respect. This one is aware of this and has been courting this. Building upon a sense of ability to see the self from many perspectives and in many different lights is a creative movement itself which requires a kind of constant motion in the thinking. It does not allow for there to be moments of retardation in the energies, but a constant moving and a constant moving forward. We see that there has been some resistance to this for varying different reasons within the past and they still do surface. This needs to be respected as well. There is a tendency for this one to become emotionally distraught, whether disappointed or fearful or doubtful when this arises. This one can change the way that this one responds to this movement in the consciousness and in doing so, through this one recognizing the respect, this one would be freed into a new avenue of creativity that this one has been wanting. It is a matter of this one respecting the need for this one to review and to assimilate and to adjust and to prepare to receive that which is about to be manifested.

This is a process of creativity. It is the process that occurs before the actual physical manifestation and this one needs to respect it and needs to respond to it in a way that reflects this ones desire, intelligence and creativity. There is a tendency for this one to allow what this one has been creating - to allow it to unravel when it reaches this point. This comes because this one, in essence, lets go of the direction. This is a time where direction is needed to an even keener degree from the outer mind. For it is the point where the creative energies are flowing from within the Self to a more physical manifestation. The key for this one is to remain mobile, adjustable in the thinking and this is much of what this one does learn in interaction with other people. This one needs to learn to internalize it. It is not because of other people that this one is cooperative and moldable. It is because this is a necessary part of creativity that this one has yet to make a part of the Self. This is all. (8-12-2001-BGC-1)

I too enjoy independent endeavors. Writing is certainly one of these. I also understand the need for follow-through to a point of completion. Completion is the means by which an experience can begin to become an understanding. I am seeing my drive for resolve in a new light. Resolve to me is the building and placing of an understanding into subconscious mind. Consciously.

Shawn's choice to study at the School of Metaphysics gave her information and practice to fully use five levels of consciousness, those comprising the conscious mind and subconscious mind, the creative faculties of consciousness. If used, she will become an outstanding midwife. Maybe someday she will attend ushering in an Einstein, a Mother Teresa, a Jesus, or even I AM. Certainly she will be witness to the miracle of creation again and again.

Since 1993 when I wrote Kundalini Rising, I have been pursuing deeper understanding of creation. I see everything I think and do from creating a meal to creating a Fibonacci film to mentoring a Spiritual Focus weekend as an act of creation. My powers of visualization improve daily and this is a cornerstone for Infinite Being.

When Shawn's report talks about respect, I fully grasp the practice. Sharing this writing is an example of *"this one recognizing the respect, this one would be freed into a new avenue of creativity that this one has been wanting. It is a matter of this one respecting the need for this one to review and to assimilate and to adjust and to prepare to receive that which is about to be manifested. This is a process of creativity."*

I am grateful once again. For it is in the stilling of the outer, conscious mind that what is manifesting can be received.

In the still mind,
all my thoughts go to God.

In the still mind, I am home.

A Week Later

Roads

Shawn comes with her dad to pick up the possessions she had stored at the Windyville Store. Teresa had left the keys with Dr. Dan.

When she returns the keys, she looks for me to give a hug and say goodbye. As we come into each other's arms, I say, "I'm going to start again," meaning crying. We both chuckle and hold onto each other for a while. "Love you forever," I say thinking of a wonderful children's book our midwife, Diane Barnes, gave us when Kie was born.

When we part we hold onto each other. I look Shawn in the eyes and say, "After you become a midwife. You can come back. We will need a midwife here." She already knows this. We spoke of it several times over the years. She doesn't say yes. She doesn't say no. It doesn't matter.

I laugh. "I feel like you're our kid going off to college!" Daniel is standing nearby and I hear him laugh, too. If he and I had met when we were students at the University of Missouri, we might have gotten married and had a child who would now be close to Shawn's age. I realize quite fully that the experience is the same as what I am experiencing now. It is finite and I can see many more possibilities today than I would have had I had children at 18.

It's funny because I thought I was so open-minded at 18. I thought most adults close their minds to possibilities. In time I learned that is the norm. I have come to know reality as a constant unfolding of what can be. It is an inward journey we are about all along.

The thought of choices comes to me this morning. Life is the moment to moment choices we make. Will power is making more correct decisions than incorrect, so our lessons say. This rang true the first time I read the words. I wanted to know how.

"Trust in the Lord and lean not to thine own understanding," comes into my mind again. When I am attached to outcomes I have placed limits on my conscious mind. This is reality. Life.

Our lives are combinations of two factors: Choice in the moment and the result of past choices echoed back to us in the present through Universal Law. God brought Shawn into my life for Godly reasons and I know how to meet God face to face so my life may be spared.

Eternal life. That is what ministry in the Interfaith Church of Metaphysics conveys. Living fully in the now, aware and wake, connected to past and present. The right choice is the one that feeds your soul. Even today, in this moment, I make choices concerning Shawn.

I want you to know what a privilege it is to know her. How calming it is to be in her presence. How fortunate all those women will be to have her at the moment new souls enter the world. Choices.

When I was 17, I wanted to give an address to my peers at graduation. To be considered, we were asked to give an audition speech. I chose to create mine around the final stanza of Robert Frost's poem *"The Road Less Traveled"* for it expressed a sentiment deep in my heart that I now understand as Infinite Being.

"I will be telling this with a sigh
Somewhere ages and ages hence:
Two roads diverged in a wood, and I–
I took the one less traveled by
And that has made all the difference."

I value choice highly while understanding that there is a destiny for each of us to fulfill.

Like Despereaux on the quest to save the Princess from a life in the darkness of the dungeon, we each are free to choose our quest.

It is the head that makes such a choice.

And like Despereaux when he loses the thread that will lead him back through the maze of the dungeon, we realize we cannot go back. "I don't have a choice," says Despereaux. "I have no choice." It is his heart that beats the words, "no choice, no choice, no choice."

Head and heart. Conscious and subconscious. Karma and Dharma. Light and Dark. Each of us has every available opportunity for a fulfilling existence whenever we choose. Infinite possibilities are before us when, like Despereaux, we are in love with light.

Infinite Being is about the space to exist.

Infinite Being is about the freedom to burst into song because your heart is filled with It. Feeling like you can walk into the orchard, and fill the air with joy. The orchard is so beautiful that the memory images of Julie Andrews on the top of the Alps singing "The hills are alive with the sound of music" surface.

So much of human man's life is filled with people living on top of other people. Image apartment buildings in cities. The only hope we have that we can learn to live in harmony like that is to understand that we are Infinite Beings, that there are infinite possibilities, infinite choices in every finite experience.

Before my husband read what I'd written for this book he asked if I was going to get Shawn's permission to write about her. I told him when Shawn and I sat in the library that day for almost an hour, one of the things I said inbetween the silences – the space that existed between us yet did not separate us – was "I will probably write about this." Then I looked at her and she nodded.

I asked, "Is that okay? Is that all right with you?"

"Yes," Shawn replied. "I would expect you to."

There is a level in multidimensional consciousness where Shawn and I are One. There is no space and no time. That is how she has helped me to understand Infinite Being, in ways that are very real to me. It is the way that all of the people I've known, who have touched my heart and opened my mind, enabled the highest energies known to man to be alive within me. It is in the way I experience each one of those people that I know the reality of Infinite Being.

An associated memory thought from New Year's comes. Our dedicated effort to read the *Universal Peace Covenant* with people all over the world as they welcomed the new year, was a multidimensional experience for all of us. It was an amazing experience of the reality of Infinite Being, the reality of all of the Infinities we have talked about here.

In the Peace Dome there is a book, like a joint diary from all of us, that tells about our experiences of coming together, in different formations, time after time over a 24 hour period for the purpose of reciting the *Covenant*. One of the entries I made in the early morning hours after it had already become the new year in Windyville, Missouri, was this one:

4:15 am
Barbara Condron -- Again I find I do not want to leave the Peace Dome although fatigue is settling into the body. After 24 hours (2 – 4) the Spirit is willing but the flesh is weak and I accept it for what it is. As I enter the crisp morning air, the stars greet me again, just as they did the morning before when this journey began. The words of "*Desiderata*" written in 1927 by Max Ehrman come to me....

"*You are a child of the universe no less than the trees and the stars.*
You have a right to be here.
And whether it is clear to you or not,
no doubt the universe is unfolding as it should.
Therefore be at peace with God,
whatever you conceive him to be,
and whatever your labours and aspirations in the noisy confusion of life,
keep peace with your soul.
With all its sham and drudgery and broken dreams
it is still a beautiful world.
Be cheerful. Strive to be happy."

I smile the smile of gratitude for having others in my life who share a vision of living peaceably. I smile the smile of equanimity for having the grace to know when to stay and when to leave. I smile the smile of fulfillment born from a privilege eagerly received and a duty well served. I smile because this day peace has been with us all ways.

Today we helped peace prevail on Earth.

I remember reading "*Desiderata*" on a poster in a head shop when I was studying at the University of Missouri in Columia. I remember part of me soared when I read it. Part of me was quite cynical. There was a huge separation, a gulf, inside of me between my heart and my head. I had yet to awaken and begin my conscious journey toward infinity. Yet a part of me was there, and that girl never could have fathomed that 30 years later she would be looking up at the stars just yards from the world's first Peace Dome.

This morning as I prepared for the day, I asked Daniel – after he read what I have written here – "Do you still think the book is about Shawn?"

He looked at me and replied, "I think it's about you."

I nodded, receiving his realization from experience. He told me he thought people would derive three things from it, at least these were the first three thoughts that came to his mind. The first was that there are two different things going on at the same time in the story, like in *Star Trek* stories of multiple universes or time lines. I am pleased this has come across for this is the multidimensional quality that I experience as "Infinite Being."

The second neither of us can recall.

The third is the humanity. He says what I've written is laden with emotions that many people experience and it will give them a way to see something different. I had expected people would see alternatives to their usual ways of thinking in what I have described.

When Daniel says the book is about me, I receive this thought more completely than ever before. The temptation that is always present within me is that piecemeal judgement I spoke of earlier. The tendency to be sensitive to others' conclusions about who I am, what I intend and understand, is a constant learning for my conscious mind. Daniel's first comment gives me an opportunity to evaluate where I am presently with that thought. There remains a need to shed more light here. The tendency to interpret the thought of others' judgement with fear is much less than ever before but I feel it tug at me. It is still here. And I will still share with whoever is drawn to this book the fullness of my experiences over five days in multidimensional consciousness.

I'm coming to realize that much of my mission on Earth concerns emotional honesty. There is a reason why my soul chose a Sagittarius moon. There is a reason why it is the sole and hardly existent connection in my astrological makeup to my sun sign, the universe's door to who I really am beyond this life. On one level, my raisin d'etre is the Karma of the need to do the kind of thinking I hope I've illustrated well here. On another level, it is to bring emotional truth to the experience. Over and over I help people unravel, update, transform debilitating attitudes and emotions toward the self, attitudes that are often lumped by their owner into bad versus good.

I hope in some way, dear reader, that you look at what you have read and in some way realize in a new light that there is only good, that we do have choice, and that it is the choice, especially when it is not apparent to us immediately, that is our journey to light. The journey gives you the ability to know your Self as Infinite Being. There are no beginnings without ends and no ends without beginnings. This is not double-speak. It is the nature of existence. Neither-either, yet both.

As I was dressing this morning, a thought occurred to me. It is so perfect that Christine chose to tell her story of love and loss and redemption in *Book Three* of *Infinite Possibilities in Finite Experiences*. I realize that what I was doing with Shawn, and the lessons in the still mind I was learning because of it, is parallel to what Christine was doing during the first eight months of her second pregnancy. Christine was forcing her mind to be still. She didn't dare dream for fear that the dream might be stolen from her, again. Only in the moments after Shawn told me that she would no longer be in my life did I deal with thoughts of a dream being stolen. Before then, my still mind had calmed my fertile imagination.

The stillness I experienced was dual. It had come from my love for her and from my need to be able to achieve it. That did not in any way spare me the pain of farewell. What it gave me was the equanimity to experience the pain fully without losing who I am or why I exist in a bitter past, in an imagined pretense, in the cold loneliness of denial.

I love life and I love people. I have found because I do, the world is good. There is light and it is good. The opening verses of the Bible float through my mind. "And God said, 'Let there be light, and there was light'." Morning comes, evening follows, each day. This is what it means to resonate with Infinite Being. This is what it means to reach to become like God.

Infinite Being is what it means for your life to be spared. The Biblical image of Jacob wrestling with the man/angel until the break of day is before my mind's eye. Jacob contends with divine and human beings and prevails. For this his name is changed to Israel. I remember the first time I heard this passage with more than physical ears and brain. I heard it with my inner sense, with clairaudience. Until that day in the late 1970s. I thought Israel was a country that had been created after W.W. II for the Jewish people to have a home. My heart was happy for others, "how wonderful they at last have a home!" The way war atrocities were taught in school fed my head. "The world owes them this!" I thought. It was years before I realized how what was in my head – what I had been led to believe – stirred my emotions to one side, the side of the one portrayed as the underdog, the victim. It was decades before my still mind could receive the image beyond good guy/bad guy. The mental eye of perception enabled me to hold a more complete picture of those who lost their homeland so others could gain. With the whole picture in mind I understood how the pain and associated darkness fuels the bone of contention between people that continues on and on half a century later.

Human Beings made Israel a country.

In holy scripture, Israel is a new name given to the man whose 12 sons (historically speaking) sire a dynasty that will eventually lead to Jesus. Linguistically speaking, the first part of the Hebrew name *Yisrael* is given a popular explanation in the word *sarita* which means "you contended." The second part is the first syllable of *elohim* meaning "divine beings." In the Univeral Language of Mind, this passage symbolizes a change in identity. The change has everything to do with what nowadays we call enlightenment. I see it in my life every time I struggle with bringing light to dark thoughts. Each time I hold onto truth. *"I will not let go until you bless me,"* Jacob tells the man/angel. Blessing lifts you from the pairs of opposites, the taking sides and everything that comes with it. The blessing is seeing the whole.

Infinite Being gives us the power to perceive the whole. Infinite Being encompasses all that comes before it – Intelligence, Energy, and Manifestation, the whole Self.

Jacob names the place where all this takes place – Penuel, *"because I have seen God face to face, yet my life has been spared."* The name means "the face of God". It is where the smallest endocrine gland in the body derives its name – the pineal gland. Far from being coincidental, this gland resonates with the Crown Chakra in man, the highest of all energies.

I think of contending with divine and human beings and prevailing often when I am troubled. It inspires me to reach up toward the light when I am experiencing moments of darkness. In this way contending means building a bridge, allowing my humanness to evolve, to be a stepping stone toward Spiritual Being. *"Love ye one another,"* Jesus' second commandment enters my mind. Love is the lesson for human man. Love is present in Infinite Being.

Then I think of contending as the struggle between good and evil. The heady pursuit for truth. Who will win, the good guys or the bad? The light forces or the dark? Who prevails is always up to me. Jacob prevails. His life is spared.

When my struggle is with the divine, there is light. There is goodness. My grasp of Truth moves from head to heart. I no longer take sides. The inner and outer selves are entrained, in synchronization. Through the open mind, I experience the whole. I experience grace.

A line from one of the lessons in the School of Metaphysics course comes to mind,

"Grace
is the power and energy of Infinite Being.

Grace
is realizing God is always present
in the space between our thoughts
as well as in our thoughts."

Legend has it that King Solomon's captain was a man named Benaiah. A loyal servant, Benaiah prided himself on his faithfulness and obedience to his king.

One day Solomon heard Benaiah boast to his men, "I can accomplish anything King Solomon asks of me!" The remark did not find favor with the king who had known his captain as a thoughtful, quiet man not a self-seeking egotistical one.

Wanting to teach Benaiah a lesson in humility, King Solomon was determined to give Benaiah an impossible task. Then he will no longer have cause to brag, the King reasoned.

"Benaiah!" Solomon summoned his guard. "My heart longs to own a particular magical ring and I want you to procure it for me."

Benaiah bowed low saying, "Anything, your majesty! I am eager to do your bidding, and will act on your will. Describe this ring so I will recognize it."

King Solomon's eyes twinkled mischievously for the ring he wanted did not exist! "Within a year, bring me a ring that can make a happy man sad and a sad man happy."

Benaiah was astounded, for he had never heard of such a ring. Honoring his master he replied, "I will search the world if I must to serve you. I will bring you the ring you request." With that Benaiah left the palace for the marketplace. He talked to goldsmiths and silversmiths. None in Jerusalem had even heard of such a ring.

How strange, Benaiah thought, that not one would have knowledge of such a ring. "It must be very rare! And obviously from some distant land." He set out to meet the caravans that traveled long distances. Surely one of them would have heard of the ring. Through desert sun and cold nights he asked every trader of stones, "Have you ever seen a ring that can make a sad man happy and a happy man sad?" Neither traders nor camel herders knew of such a ring.

Undaunted, Benaiah sought the seaports, asking every sea captain of such a ring. His efforts were of no avail. Distraught, Benaiah feared he would not be able to accomplish the task for his king.

Months passed until the appointed time drew close. Returning home, dejected and ashamed that he had failed in his mission, Benaiah still held hope in his heart. On the roadside he passed a beggar boy selling crude rings and bracelets. At first he passed the boy, thinking if those of greater means knew nothing, surely this boy would give no answers.

"I must not leave any stone upturned," Benaiah thought and he asked the question to the boy.

"I know of no such ring," replied the boy.

Benaiah's eyes welled up in tears.

"Perhaps I have just the ring for you," said a voice from the shadows. The boy's grandfather stepped forward and handed Benaiah a simple gold band with engraved words on it. Benaiah looked at the ring and his sad face was transformed by a long sigh of relief. Instantly the frustration and sadness was gone. "This is the ring I have searched for all this time!" he cried joyfully. "Thank you, thank you!"

The next day Benaiah entered King Solomon's palace where a feast was prepared for his return. Solomon did not know how much he had missed his trusted servant until he saw him that day. His heart was moved, and Solomon thought, "I will not let him suffer long in his humiliation. After he admits that he was unable to complete the task given, I will tell him I gave him an impossible task as a lesson."

Benaiah came forward and bowed, presenting the ring to King Solomon. As Solomon examined the ring, his smile vanished from his face. The simple gold band was inscribed with the Hebrew letters gimmel, zayin and yud, "Gam Zeh Ya-avor" meaning *this too shall pass.*

Solomon knew this ring would bring comfort and relief to anyone consumed with grief or misfortune as equally it would temper and humble anyone lost in the pleasure of the moment. He embraced Benaiah, asking his forgiveness. Giving the captain his own ring, Solomon placed the magic ring of truth on his hand as a reminder of the lesson he had learned from his loyal and faithful servant.

King Solomon asked for a ring that could make a sad man happy and a happy man sad. In the Universal Language of Mind a ring symbolizes completion, a cycle. Completion indicates the ending of one movement and the beginning of another. Certainly we can experience mental and emotional extremes concerning these. What experience teaches us is the temporary nature of our physical situations.

The faithfulness and obedience displayed by Benaiah are universal qualities that support and foster the commitment completing something requires. Being willing to do whatever it takes can be an expression of love. By doing so, Benaiah embodies the reality of "do unto others as you would have them do unto you." To continue giving even when others do not do as we might want or expect, is to understand love. Understanding love brings forth a discerning heart – the quest of Solomon.

Solomon's captain symbolizes self discipline. Self discipline makes us honest for it gives us the power of the present moment. When the attention is fully in the now, we can experience the still mind. The still mind accepts the temporary nature of the finite experience. It frees us by opening what the Tibetan Buddhists call the wisdom eye, the mental eye of perception.

Attention and will are tools employed by every Psi counselor. Being a counselor means being wise enough to give someone guidance. Psi indicates the whole mind, beyond the physical part of Self. To be in the company of a Psi counselor is to be in the presence of a metaphysician, one versed in spiritual, mental, emotional, and physical healing.

Universal Truths arising in physical life beckon us to move beyond the pairs of opposites into worlds where head and heart can be entrained. A Psi counselor reaches to open the door to your whole Mind where infinite possibilities exist.

I see life as dancing.

I see it as giving and receiving, as breathing in and breathing out. Sometimes it's time to consciously figure it out with reasoning. Sometimes it's time to still the conscious mind and let the intuition work and come through. Consciousness is a complete movement."

–from Q&A session with Drs. Barbara and Daniel Condron during Genius! Spiritual Focus Weekend

Dreams

PERSONAL EXPERIENCES IN

Infinite Being

Oh can you come!
Taste the Truth
in the still forest rain
Hear the One inner voice
Speak your name.

-from the song "One Inner Voice"
(Dreams are Doorways)

Like consciousness itself, dreams are dual in nature. They are universal and they are personally relevant to the dreamer. In the hands of a skilled Psi counselor, your dreams can resolve, create, predict, energize, restore, heal, inspire, entertain and enlighten.

When you begin to seriously investigate dreams, you learn dreaming is as old as mankind. As long as man has had a soul and has been able to think and to reason, dreams have come to him.

In the Orient, it is a widespread belief that dreams are a communication from God. Now this is not so far from how Western people approach dreams, especially Western religious leaders. They also tend to think that dreams are messages from God, either as a personal revelation or as one to give to the masses.

The American Indian, throughout history, has used dreams in religious rites. The Greeks thought that dreams were a way to be receptive to thought, a way to be telepathic, or to send and receive thoughts. They also thought that perhaps dreams were ways of communicating with spirits or with ghosts.

The father of metaphysics, a Greek philosopher named Aristotle, living around 350 BC, determined that dreams come from within the self. That was a fairly revolutionary belief or idea, because up until that time, most thought dreams came from outside of you somewhere, instead of welling up from within you. Aristotle's teacher Plato heeded an inner voice that guided him toward considering others and away from selfishness. He believed dreams were communications from the soul of man.

Two thousand years later, an Austrian Sigmund Freud, who is revered as the father of modern psychoanalysis, determined that dreams are about the dreamer. Research through the School of Metaphysics over the past forty years, supports what Freud discovered in terms of the dreams being about the dreamer. In fact, that's one of two universal principles in discerning the meaning and benefit of dreams. The first principle in dreaming is that every dream is about the dreamer. School of Metaphysics research takes this a bit farther in recognizing that everyone and everything in the dream is the dreamer. This is where the way that we view the messages from the inner self to the outer self in what we call dreams differs from what you may be familiar with.

Probably the most cliched type example of a Freudian idea is that if you dream you want to kill your mother, that's what you really want to do. That never made any sense to me because if you want to kill your mother, if you really want that, then you'll think about that when you're awake. You won't need to go to sleep in order to think that.

The sleeping state is different from the awake state. *We spend a third of our lives sleeping.* You figure, if you're 60 years old, or if you live to be that old, then you've spent about twenty years of that time sleeping. Your sleeping time is very important to you. Moreso for what it has to say to you than as a time of escape for your outer, waking consciousness. For most people sleep is passive access to the inner self, what we term Subconscious Mind. I say passive because most people don't really have knowledge or expertise in drawing on inner, subconscious abilities. Yet each time you bring a dream forward from your sleeping experience, you are drawing on information that is of a subconscious nature.

A couple centuries ago a woman named Mary Shelly had a dream. When she awoke from that dream, it was so vivid and so alive in her mind that she took the images which originated in the inner levels of her own subconscious mind, and turned them into a novel. In case you haven't guessed already, that novel is Frankenstein. Robert Louis Stevenson's Dr. Jekyll and Mr. Hyde, Coleridge's "*Kubla Khan*", and the final measures of Handel's "*The Messiah*" each owe their existence to their maker's dreams.

Your ability to create and to bring out creative genius is very much linked to how much attention you pay to your dreams. Your subconscious mind is a part of you, it's an essential part of your creativity. When you can learn to draw on that inner subconscious mind, you can use it in your every day life to produce wonderful works of creativity that benefit not only you but all of mankind.

Albert Einstein is another relevant dreamer. He was furiously deliberating an idea for some time, arriving at an intellectual dead end. In exhaustion, he went to sleep. A dream gave him the missing piece he was seeking that empowered his waking mind to describe what he is most remembered for – the law of relativity.

Abraham Lincoln gives another glimpse of the subconscious abilities that we have. Before he became president, he had a dream which he was convinced showed that his death would be impending, untimely and very early. He told others about this dream. This dream ended up coming true, it is what we call a precognitive dream. It illustrates a subconscious mind ability for clairvoyance. Clairvoyance is a French word, which means "clear seeing". This is your ability to perceive beyond the five physical senses with your subconscious mind, to see clearly the past, the present, and the probabilities of the future.

There are other subconscious abilities that can also happen when your conscious mind is asleep. Telepathy is one. A little bit over ten years ago I had a memory of a dream experience, an experience that happened while I was asleep. My grandmother, who I rarely dreamed of, came to me in a dream. We were in a very beautiful place, in a place filled with flowers and woods, and we communicated for some time. The communication was not verbal. It was a mental understanding. She could project to me or think to me certain thoughts that I would hear and then I would think my response and send it back to her. We had the deepest conversation about the nature of life and death, and things that we had never talked about when we were together physically. When I awoke from that experience I remembered it because it was so unique, it was different from anything that we had experienced together before.

A couple days later my dad called and said, "Barbara, I have some bad news for you." I said, "What?" And he said, "Your grandmother died last night in her sleep." When he told me that, immediately I knew what that dream experience two nights before had been about. I knew it had been a way that we could communicate, because she was getting ready to withdraw from the physical, to die.

Subconscious Mind possesses many abilities. Often we draw upon these through the sleep state, and we remember them as dreams. A Psi counselor can assist you in learning how to interpret your dreams for soul progression as well as good health, well being. Dreams are doorways to awareness shedding light where there was darkness, security where there once was fear.

Dreams tell you about every part of Self – conscious aspects, subconscious aspects, superconscious aspects, the ego. For this reason they reflect your understanding of Infinite Being, at the same time they illuminate new areas for understanding. They are a miraculous, Self reflective and Self instructive phenomenon.

Dream Interpretation as Self Respect

by Dr. Teresa Padilla

An important tool of counseling is self-respect. An individual having counseling can begin the session any place they desire, go any place they desire during the session and end up where they desire. There is no interference upon the counselor. Early on in Psi counseling training we learned that it is *their* counseling session. They determine what takes place and where they go with it. This has been illustrated in each counseling session I've given. The individual opening up and revealing themselves is like a flower in full bloom or an orchestra that is in the midst of a performance. Counseling aids anyone to look at something differently, to be able to see a situation and Self in a new light, to evaluate and continue to correct themselves and to know how to look in the mirror and move forward with new awareness.

Self-respect was illustrated in a counseling session I did with Dan. He was a student in the School of Metaphysics. He was born under the astrological influence of Sagittarius. Dan knew that I am married to a man who was also born under the astrological influence of Sagittarius. He thought that I would have some insight that was based upon experience. Dan shared that he was not in a good place and he thought that I could help him. So I asked him about a recent dream. He shared his dream.

"I was crouching over. I could not take a step forward until I picked up all these little pieces of paper in front of me. I was up close and looking at each piece of paper."

This dream was symbolic of examining and looking at what was ahead of him on his path in life. He would not let himself take a step until he had looked at what was in front of him. Everything in front of him. In listening to him, he was talking about all the thoughts and attitudes he had. He was very focused on each and every thought. There was a kind of restriction in this. He wasn't allowing himself to move forward without full examination of these little tiny pieces of paper, which were all his thoughts and information that he had. Almost every thought he shared, he viewed as negative about himself. I realized that he needed to give himself credit for what he was doing. I asked him about what he had accomplished.

His whole attitude changed. He had a different perspective about his life and his thinking. It was immediate. This was a good example of self-respect. I knew he had practiced interpretation of his dreams. So I asked him to interpret his dreams daily and write out what he was going to apply from his dreams. I wanted him to come up with goals and a clear plan of action based on the feedback from his dreams. I also wanted him to give himself credit at the end of each day for what he had accomplished.

The next time I saw him, he had manifested many desires in his life that previously he couldn't figure out what to do with. Heeding the message from his dreams and applying it in his life helped him to harmonize his inner and outer life. Thus, his dreams were manifesting in front of his face. He was out of the way. His thoughts and perspective was aligned and positive. He is a wonderful artist and painter. He had been trying to get work as an artist. The next time I saw him, he had been hired to paint a mural for someone. This was one of his first professional jobs to paint a mural. He was literally creating his dreams!

Teresa's experience reminds me of a dream

I interpreted for a 51-year-old woman who emailed into our website www.dreamschool.org a few years ago. A medical professor, she stated she had had many dreams over the past 25 years with the same theme.

She wrote, "*I am supposed to be somewhere such as work, at the airport to catch a flight, or similar obligation. I either forget to start preparing for departure on time or repeated obstacles and barriers occur which prevent me from being prepared or arriving on time. In the dream, I am constantly thinking oh no, I'll never make it, why didn't I plan for this. I awaken with feelings of extreme frustration that I am feeling in the dream.*"

On the surface this dream does not seem related to Dan's picking up pieces of paper dream. However, both dreams reflect the restriction produced by placing limitations on self. Dan could not move forward in his dream until he accomplished his task. This lady professor was feeling held back by repeated obstacles. This is the response I gave to this dreamer:

"When you have this dream, you are finding it difficult to respond to the unexpected factor that other people bring into your life. It's like having a long awaited vacation where nothing turns out the way you wanted (flights are canceled, it rains the entire time you are gone, and so forth).

"When you have this dream your subconscious is encouraging you to be more knowledgeable, reminding you to be willing to learn from every experience. The repetitious nature of the dreams indicate your need to be attentive to what you are deriving from the choices in your life. You experience frustration when you lose sight of the benefit to you of the people, places, or things in your life.

"It is easy for us to put others first. Were you taught that others are more important and valuable than self? Many times people are taught this as children. If this is true for you, these dreams can serve as your reminder to make time for self reflection."

For anyone who values their dreams, these night time messages become a stimulus for deepening Self awareness. Dreams are doorways into inner worlds, offering access to areas of consciousness far beyond the physical realm. In dreams we find the fulfillment of our most heart-felt desires. Sometimes dreams shock us or scare us into new ways of thinking. Other times they are the answer we have been seeking. Always dreams tell us the state of our conscious awareness. Interpreting your dreams is a remarkable tool for self counseling.

Dreams are Doorways to Infinity

Communicating with others is a way to expand our understanding of Self and our world. Throughout my adult years, I have had the good fortune to travel throughout the U.S., meeting people of all ages, cultures, and religions. In the past decade, the internet has given me the means to correspond with people from from North Dakota to South Africa to the Philippines. Many of these people I have met because they had a dream they wanted interpreted.

The Q&A section of dreamschool.org is where we post people's dreams and our interpretations in the Universal Language of Mind. Each week we receive dreams, and each week we select around 20 to interpret in detail and post on our site. Current and past dreams are available for home study. Our goal at dreamschool is to interpret one dream for every man, woman, and child on the planet. We know that giving real attention to your dreams opens your mind to infinite possibilities and we want to contribute to the awareness of humanity in this way.

Dream messages are the most readily available and reliable feedback concerning the content and state of your consciousness. The more you understand your dreams, the more you understand the different divisions of mind, levels of consciousness, and aspects of Self. By interpreting a dream, you can identify what you are doing that produces what you desire or what is getting in your way. You can learn how to communicate mind to mind or how to stop procrastinating in a dream. You can remember other existences, other lives, in a dream, or see probable future events. When understood, dreams can be a key for good health and spiritual growth.

The questions our dreamers ask range from content dreams like "the red snake in the middle of the kitchen floor" dreams to inner level projections such as flying dreams to inner level experiences like dream-visitations with loved ones who have passed on. Increasing numbers of people are experiencing lucid dreams where they know they are dreaming. More of us are becoming conscious in the dreamstate. This means we are awakening to more of our consciousness than what exists in the physical world. Through remembering these experiences we expand the limits of our knowledge and that redefines who we are.

The following are dreams of this nature. They come from dreamers from around the world who sent their questions to our dreamschool website. First you will read what the dreamer emailed to us. This is followed by our response. These entries offer you insight, understanding, and direction in your own exploration of dreams and I know they reflect the infinite possibilities in one of our finite experiences. The one we call dreaming.

INTERPRETING OBE's

Hello,

I've recently purchased your books The Dreamer's Dictionary and Interpreting Dreams for Self Discovery, and have found them extremely helpful and have enjoyed learning to interpret my dreams.

However, I have a question about interpreting OBE's and/or astral projections. I've been able to have conscious OBE's for the past 2 years and have always taken them literally. I assume a real-time OBE would be taken literally, but what about astral projections? I haven't been able to find anything on your website or in your books about interpreting conscious OBE's where I am projecting into the astral plane. Is it your school's philosophy to use the same symbology for projections as you do for dreams?

Thank you for your time and thank you in advance for your reply. With Love & Light,

SM/female

Response

Thanks so much for your questions. It is always gratifying when people find what we have learned to be useful in their lives. For anyone who is not familiar with the acronym, OBE is the abbreviation for **o**ut of **b**ody **e**xperiences.

There is a book in the works that is actually linked to many of the dreams that we have received from all over the world and interpreted right here at dreamschool that will address your question and many others. The phenomenon of dreaming is the means by which human man becomes aware of the infinite potential of his own intelligence. It's kind of like the picture books we might read to a small child. We understand that the scope of reading, of communicating thought, is very expansive. We introduce the child to this wonderful world in steps which he or she can receive, digest, and understand. You might look at dreams as the picture books the subconscious mind gives to you.

Since you are becoming aware of the abilities in subconscious mind, it's like you have grown from childhood into adolescence. Adolescence we understand as a time of experimentation, a kind of "let's try this and see what happens." There is significant research based upon personal experiences that have been verified in a number of ways that inner level experiences (like your projections and OBE's) are as real and significant as sensory experiences in the physical waking world. This area of exploring human potential is what the School of Metaphysics pursues.

What we have found thus far is that even with actual inner level experience (OBE's, visitations, telepathy, projections, precognition, retrocognition, and a host of other intuitive abilities) what the conscious mind receives as a dream is still in the Universal Language of Mind and can be interpreted for its message value to the dreamer. Therefore, even in the case of your projection dreams these would be talking about your developing ability to function and move in the inner levels of mind.

There are many varied accounts here at dreamschool of out-of-body experiences and other inner level experiences that it would be worth your time to investigate. We are in the process now of further cataloging the dreams we have received over the last few years so that this kind of research can more easily be accomplished.

We anticipate this to be available around the first of the year. Until then, the wealth available here is waiting for you to explore.•

RETURN OF HER FATHER

After a difficult break up with my husband of 28 years my father who died when I was 4 years old came to me and stood by my bed and said not to worry that everything was going to be okay.

What does this mean?

N female*

Response

As we discuss often here at dreamschool (see visitations) these dreams can be dual experiences. Dreams are always about the dreamer and his/her state of awareness. They can also be inner level experiences. In your case, the soul who was your father could have come to comfort you.

This visitation is possible but unlikely for two reasons. One, he talked to you in the dream. When experiencing and communicating in the inner levels, talking as we do in the physical world is not needed. Subconsciously we are all connected and therefore can immediately, at will, know each others thoughts.

Second, your father left the physical world decades ago. This is a fairly lengthy time to assimilate his previous life. In our extensive research into consciousness, we have found there to be no set lengths of time between death and rebirth. What we have discovered is this growth process like all others is responsive to universal law. This means the individual entity progresses at their own rate of speed — your father could have reincarnated in a matter of physical years or may still be assimilating his previous lifetime. If the latter is true, he could still identify as being your father and appear to you. These are possibilities to consider.

What is more certain is that this dream is about you. At the time of the dream you were drawing on superconsciousness to give you strength and perspective.•

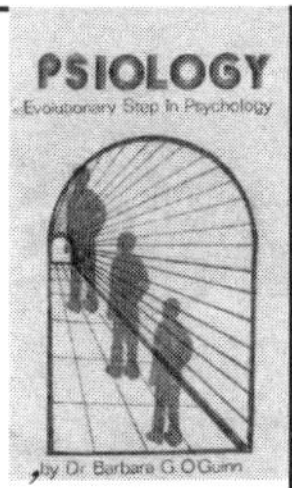

Behavior considered abnormal in todays society will eventually, to the psiologist displaying a fuller understanding of the mind and how it functions, no longer be considered aberrant or deviant. Recalling the case of Joan of Arc, the behaviorist would view her insistence on hearing voices as definite signs of abnormal behavior. To the psiologist who understands the function of the subconscious mind, this will be taken into account as possibly not a conscious imagining or daydreaming but a subconscious reality. Since the conscious mind works directly with information in the brain, there is distance between conscious minds. In other words, there is a difference in the information each brain stores depending on what each person has been exposed to throughout life. This creates distance between conscious minds; however, in subconscious minds there exists no distance. Jung called it the collective unconscious, however the psiologist of the future will recognize that this is a function not of the unconscious mind but the subconscious mind.

We have said that the subconscious mind holds all understood experiences. These experiences are of great benefit to the individual as well as others since they have been earned through trial and error and perhaps many mistakes. When speaking of hypnotism, we mentioned past life profiles. A past life intuitive report is merely information gained between the fourth and fifth levels of consciousness in the subconscious mind. This in some ways could be termed the collective subconscious. The term Akashic Record refers to that place in mind where events, people, places and actions are recorded from the present time throughout the past. It is comparable to a library or volumes of history books where information on anything or anyone could be obtained. This is available for anyone to tap at anytime if they have the degree of concentration and a mode of getting to this place.

In this way, with significant study and practice, one can tap within their own subconscious understandings stored there. Many of the current "psychic" happenings are still disregarded by psychologists, primarily because there is not the understanding of the individual as a whole functioning Self. "Psychic" happenings are a function of the subconscious mind whether out of the body experiences, experiences catalogued by Dr. Elizabeth Kubler-Ross or near death patients, or such psychic happenings as telepathy, clairvoyance or clairaudience. Joan of Arc probably was experiencing clairaudience, or hearing with the subconscious mind. This could have been listening to her own subconscious or to another entity since there is no distance in subconscious minds--a type of telepathy. To most psychologists the behavior she displayed would definitely have been viewed as aberrant. The diagnosis would probably have been schizophrenia or psychosis. However, the psiologist will view these behaviors according to his own understanding of mind and how it functions so that indeed many of the behaviors individuals display will no longer be termed abnormal or aberrant but will be seen as significant tools to be used to better understand the full functioning Self.

–from *Psiology: Evolutionary Step in Psychology,* ©1977, School of Metaphysics

LUCID DREAMING

Hi,
I would like to get more information on the Lucid Dreaming. I've done this when I was (15-20 yrs. old) and find that I lack the ability to do this now (36yrs. old). It seemed very difficult when I had done it in the past and have grown too tired to get anywhere now.
Thanks

Response

What you describe is the result of continued interaction between consciousness and the finite material world. Unfortunately this happens with most people. We won't change this in a couple of minutes conversing on the internet but we hope the ideas we will give you will shine a light on your experiences and maybe even spark a desire on your part to start learning again.

Consider this, you, the real you that thinks and creates and feels, exists beyond the physical body and the physical world. This real you is talked about in every culture on the planet. It is often described in different words more because of the differences in languages than the difference in the idea which the words describe. If you can go there in your thinking, then you can probably also accept our use of the word soul or subconscious mind as a means to identify this real you.

Now consider that the soul enters into the physical world for the purpose of gaining understanding. The veracious appetite of babies and toddlers and children for learning is very apparent. It continues until the environment shows us one way or another that there is something not quite right about innocence and openness and purity and trust.

From what you describe you were a pioneer in consciousness because you kept the sense of wonder that is so much a part of that first stage of growth (we call it infancy) alive even through your teenage (the next stage which is adolescence) years. Most of your peers were busy becoming distracted by adolescence, making outward appearances more important to their identity than inward realities. This is the difference between who you are with, what your body looks like, are you on the winning team, do you have the best friends, are you gonna make it to that college, kind of consciousness and the kind of deep thinking, heart centered, serious minded, helpful, imaginative, consciousness that keeps the communication lines open between the subconscious mind and conscious mind. In your adolescence years you tended toward the latter.

This gave you the ability to remain conscious during the dream state. Remaining conscious is the definition of lucid dreaming. This ability was natural for you at the time and you probably enjoyed it. Now it is time to rekindle the ability and to learn the skill.

People lose the ability for lucid dreaming when the people, places, and things in their physical waking life become more important than the purposes, intent, and discoveries available in the inner mind. Between the ages of 20 and 36 what was occurring in your physical life overtook your desire to know yourself. One of the results of this was losing your ability for lucid dreaming.

The beauty of it is the memory of your experiences during your early life. This has stayed with you and can now serve as a stimulus to once again become conscious about your learning and soul progression. The course in mastering consciousness available at the School of Metaphysics teaches what you need to know to initiate and sustain lucid dreaming states of mind. More than this it will give you the tools to become increasingly conscious of both your inner and outer life.•

5 OR 6 DREAMLESS YEARS

Can you please tell me why I don't remember my dreams anymore. I used to have such vivid dreams and have had some psychic dreams and recurring dreams. I am on anti-depressants. I haven't remembered but a couple of dreams in the last 5-6 years. I would appreciate any insight you have on this.

Sincerely,
L R, female

Response

There are several reasons why people will forget dreams. Happily you have given us enough of a description of your situation to very quickly identify what is blocking your memory recall: the culprit is the anti-depressants that you are taking. Whatever has occurred in your life and in your consciousness that has led you to the belief that you need to chemically alter your body in order to have mental equilibrium and emotional calmness and happiness has produced limitations inherent in chemical remedies. In this case one of the limitations is an interference in the communication between the inner and outer selves commonly referred to as dreams.

When students begin studying with the School of Metaphysics there are three will busters that they are discouraged from pursuing. One of these is drugs. The mind and body has a very delicate chemistry of its own that is attuned to your consciousness. When we alter that chemistry artificially we interrupt the communication between the mind and the body. Failing to remember dreams is only one manifestation of this kind of interruption. Other kinds of manifestations can be read in the warning label section of possible "side effects" included with every man made drug on the market.

Depression is a common condition of the mind. Although it has been labeled an illness and as such can be medicated, a metaphysician seeks to understand why the depression exists and what causes it to arise so that it can be cured from a point of cause. In his book Permanent Healing, Dr. Daniel Condron sites the mental attitude disorder for depression as **"all of the attention on what is not had for the self without creating goals or desires. Suppression of goals and desires."** The cure for depression is to stimulate the mind's creativity through setting goals of what you desire to accomplish and being purposeful with those goals. This means claiming those desires. For instance, the goals you image you are invested in. You can see yourself and the kind of person you will be when you can give that lecture or win that medal or earn that raise or walk down that aisle in wedding attire or whatever it is you desire.

Depression is so subtle and is so poorly understood in the academic and professional fields that it is easy for well-intended and caring medical experts to offer a quick fix in the form of drugs. You do not have to be a slave to a pill. You can learn the necessary mental and emotional skills that will free you from this addiction. There's a great story about a student who did this with Prozac that is now available at our renovated website www.som.org . The book What Will I Do Tomorrow: Probing Depression is available at the same website. If you live near a School of Metaphysics location please call them and ask about classes. You will be very glad you did.•

COMIC BOOK WRITER LOOKS FOR STORYLINES

Dear Sir/ Madam

First of all, let me introduce myself: I am a comic book artist/ writer researching for a new story (English is not my first language, so I apologize for the mistakes). In this story dreams have a vital role, for they are our only way of knowing what the characters really feel. Before writing/drawing about something I always like investigating about it, and that is how I came across your webpage, which I found to be one of the most interesting sources on the net. You have transmitted me an until now unknown interest and hunger for dream knowledge.

There are some questions (some more specific than others) I would like to ask, and I would really appreciate it if you could answer them, or at least suggest where I could find the answers myself.

My first question is: What would happen if for some reason (maybe mystical) a person would start dreaming someone else's dreams?

Is it possible to 'encode' dreams? I mean, to start with the raw emotions and messages I want to get through and then translate them into a dream sequence?

I would be very grateful if you could guide me with some of this matters. Thanks in advance,

GB

Response

You already have a kind of brilliance working within you because you are wise enough to realize the inspiration your dreams can afford. It is particularly affirming that you value dreams as a tool for your writing for as you understand more about dreams this understanding could be conveyed through your artistic endeavors. So on that level keep up the good work. Also there is an article about creative-genius types who have used or responded to their own dreams for insight, inventiveness, inspiration, and altered states that you might want to take a moment or two to read. It was just posted on our renovated site at the School of Metaphysics and to read it click here.

Now on to your questions. There have been many documentations of what you ask about in your first question actually occurring. Some can even be found at this website. The phenomena of people dreaming the same dream is more common than realized. It is becoming a realm of discussion because people are more frequently remembering their dreams. Many of these kinds of occurrences come in the form of visitations with loved ones who have passed on and most of these are experiences in the inner levels. Other occurrences involve people who know each other usually well who through talking with each other discover that they had the same dream. Enterprising couples will follow up on these kinds of dreams, recording them, discussing them, and studying them. Some of our advanced students find this occurring with classmates and begin to induce these kinds of experiences as a prelude to becoming more conscious in non-physical levels of reality.

Just as there can be communication through words physically there is also communication on a subconscious level through images and thought-form projections. Therefore it is just as natural to believe that we can transfer thoughts whether awake or asleep in a very similar way as we do when we interject a new idea in words in a conversation. When you understand how the mind works you realize that there is very little difference between suggesting that your friend stop at the next coffee house on your way to the movie in real life (as we call it) and staying up at two o'clock at night thinking about your friend and you talking at that coffee house and your sleeping friend dreaming about it. What difference lies in the different situations is a matter of how conscious we are willing to be.

This ties in with your second question about encoding dreams. This happens all the time. How many times did your mom or dad say "turn off that TV. It will give you nightmares." And lo and behold your dreams are filled with monsters from outer space and giant tarantulas and boogie men lurking in dark closets. This is a function of how the mind works whether awake or asleep. Seed ideas are planted and when the mind substance is fertile they grow. Whether awake or asleep, the ideas we accept into our consciousness grow to become the reality of what we experience. If as a child you were told you were beautiful/handsome smart capable responsible trustworthy and all other sorts of admirable human traits those seeds have sprouted and grown making the foundation for the productive person you now are. If seeds were planted of limitation and doubt and fear those seeds may also have grown. You will find that it is not the quality of the seed that determines the growth but rather your ability to nurture it through attention, concentration, memory, visualization, desire and will. This is why pursuing self awareness in a disciplined fashion is so incredibly valuable.•

CAN'T MOVE, CAN'T BREATHE

I have this recurring lucid dream.

I am aware that I am on my bed sleeping but I cannot move and I have trouble breathing. I will be aware of sounds around me and hear my mother saying go and wake her up. Even when I am being shaken it has to be very vigorous shake before I can snap out of it. But the urge to go back to sleep is so strong that I have drag myself out of the bed or I will go back into the same dream again.

I have been to a parapsychology meeting and was relieved to hear that there are others with this problem. Do you know of this kind of dream and are there are cures for it.?

Thank you. S/female

Response

The kind of experience you describe is a problem to someone who doesn't understand what is happening. Think of it this way, if you see a little boy in a store who seems visibly shaken and can't seem to catch his breath you can interpret this in a number of ways. One person might think the boy is lost and therefore frightened. Another person might think the boy was having an asthma attack. Another might wonder if he is disappointed because he can't get what he came for, while another might interpret the emotion as anger or a temper tantrum. A concerned person who would ask, "Can I help?" would be the one who would discover that none of these imagined scenarios match the experience. The person who asks learns that the boy is experiencing the effects of running too hard too fast and is actually caught between trying to catch his breath and keep from laughing at his own state of affairs.

Experiences that happen when the outer conscious mind is asleep are often left open to these types of conjecturing. This is why we at the School of Metaphysics have been studying and researching dreams and human potential for almost three decades. What we have learned explains experiences like yours and we can say with the authority that comes from experience that there are answers to your "problem".

You are experiencing the difficulty in moving and breathing when you are in the in between state of dreaming and conscious alertness because you have yet to learn how to keep these two parts of mind separate. The mystery teachings throughout the ages have conveyed the vision of superconsciousness and oneness of spirit. This is our inner urge and it is growing stronger in our universe. Not everyone is experiencing this change in the way that you are but all of us are feeling the affects of the shifting of energies. Your "symptoms" are not of a physical disorder but are the means by which you can be taught your need to heed this inner urge.

Once you become attentive and determine that you want to respond, the course in Mastering Consciousness taught at Schools of Metaphysics throughout the Midwest will become more valuable to you. This course teaches the disciplines and practices, of a mental, emotional, and spiritual nature, that have been long kept from the masses. These are the secret teachings previously available only to those of fortunate birth, wealth and position, or those willing to renounce physical life. We believe it is now time for these teachings to be made openly available. The teaching is in the practice and our teachings offer instruction and guidance in the cause, the meaning, and the relativity of lucid dreaming. By practicing specific breathing exercises during your waking hours you can gain the self control needed to ease the breathing difficulties you describe. By practicing Stillpoint Focus you would empower yourself to be able to move in the inner levels of consciousness as well as the outer.

It has been said that with knowledge comes power. As metaphysicians we would more aptly describe this as with reasoning comes power. Making the choice to cease reacting to your own experiences (with fear, doubt, panic, or even the other extreme of pride because your experience makes you special) will free your mind to learn. Learning stimulates the reasoning power in your conscious mind which, when brought to full fruition becomes intuition.•

WHISPERS from the INNER VOICE

I was just visiting your website and I would like to share this dream with you and see what you think about it.

I have had this recurring dream since I was a small child. It only happens a few times each year. I am in my grandparents' bedroom in my Grandmother's old house, my grandfather is dead, and I have this Dove soap. I can clearly smell it and I am very happy about it. Then my parents begin whispering my name. My grandparents join in, none of them are actually in the room with me, I can just hear their voices. So they're all chanting my name and I see their faces in my mind and can distinctly make out their individual voices even though they're mostly in sync. They continue to get louder and louder until they are yelling my name. I get so sad and I feel as though my heart is broken and I'm all alone. Then I usually wake up.

Please let me know what you think of this or if I should send it to someone else. To me it is kind of a nightmare. I wake up feeling kind of scared and sad and alone. Again, please let me know what you think!

Thank you

Response

There are several dimensions to your dream experience. The recurring element says that the same subconscious message is pertinent to you each time you have the dream. It is also significant that the dream began when you were a child. This is a very important element because it puts the dream in context.

This is a frame of mind dream. In the universal language of mind it is telling you to be centered in a higher purpose for your existence and to let go of what ever distracts you.

What was happening in your life the first time you had this dream was the beginning of moving away from connection with your own inner authority and becoming increasingly caught up in the outer physical world. This is symbolized by your parents whispers turning into louder and louder voices. This symbolizes your superconscious mind's efforts to draw your attention inward again. In School of Metaphysics studies we often refer to this as the inner urge toward enlightenment.

Your inner urge is very strong. This is a very clear message because you continue to have this dream even now in your life. It makes a good deal of sense that you feel scared, sad and alone when you wake because when we fail to heed, understand, and respond to our inner urge we cut off the sense of inner connectedness with our own superconsciousness. Any time you have this dream you will want to still your conscious mind and enter into a peaceful state of prayer and meditation so you might become more receptive and attentive to the inner part of you.

You might also explore your thinking and actions on the previous day to see how you may have become overwhelmed--lost in the emotions and experiences in your waking life. If your subconscious mind is needing to yell in order to get your attention then this is a good indicator that you need to balance your inner and outer life. Daily meditation would help considerably.•

Every one of us has a whole functioning mind. I think it is our responsibility and duty to ourselves to understand that mind and to endeavor to use it with the highest ideals. Dreams are a way that the inner self is trying to talk with each one of us. So by responding to the dreams and saying, "Hey, I'm listening" you'll have access to a personal "therapist" any time, anywhere. If you've been prone to nightmares and fears, these will cease. Recurring dreams will cease or you will understand their function in your life. You will establish a rapport between the outer you and your soul.

The best way to begin using this inner Self counseling tool is to begin a dream journal. Record your dreams immediately upon awakening. Writing what you remember as soon as you awake gives you the details of your dream experience that will fade as you bring more of your attention into the physical body. Every detail is an important part of the dream's message.

The who, what, where, and how of your dream message conveys the state of your awareness at the time the dream occurred. You can explore this in a number of ways.

For those who want a concentrated study we offer **Spiritual Focus Sessions** seven weekends of each year. Psi counselors who hold doctorates in metaphysics serve as your mentor during the weekend, leading you through a personal journey of Self realization using many of the modalities discussed in this book. Each session focuses on a particular subject (influence, genius, dharma, etc.). Intuitive Reports have been developed for each session. The personal insight each offers is life-changing.

When your focus is understanding your dreams, the **Dream of the Month Club** fills this need. This innovative educational service is conducted over the internet. Each week, members receive educational materials through email. The first week of the month you receive a detailed dream analysis including all symbols and their meanings, the interpretation of the dream, and how the dream fit into the dreamer's life. The third week a mentor from the College of Metaphysics provides this kind of analysis for one of your dreams. This gives you a model to strive for in interpreting your own dreams. The second week articles on recurring dreams, nightmares, health dreams, and the like are mailed to you, and the fourth week an in-depth look at a Creative Mind Report will be mailed to you. Detailing how the individual utilizes the conscious and subconscious minds, the information revealed in these intuitive analyses is a window into how thinking occurs. The Creative Mind Report is given for SOM students studying in the third cycle of lessons and for those attending the ***Genius! Develop the Power Within You*** Spiritual Focus Session.

For those wanting to become Psi counselors, the School of Metaphyics course of study is offered in cities throughout the Midwest United States. This course teaches how to use the whole mind in harmony with the laws of creation. Entrainment of head and heart through daily disciplines opens the mind. Infinite Intelligence, Infinite Energy, and Infinite Manifestation become much more than intriguing words. They become the means through which you master and develop your whole Self. The first cycle (1-24) of lessons are offered through correspondence with a teacher at the College of Metaphysics. Psi counseling training begins with Taraka Yoga in the latter half of the third cycle of study.

Infinite Being gives each of us the freedom to interpret the relevance of our situations. Too few people respond to this freedom. I trust reading these words will empower you to think differently about yourself, your life and the people in it. Each of us are multidimensional beings. Infinite Beings experiencing finite situations.

Dreams as States of Awareness

by Dr. Paul Blosser

Dreams are an excellent method of working with the form of Infinite Being because dreams always relate truth about the seeker's current state of awareness. I use dreams and dream experiences as a Self-counseling method so I can know where I am in the development of my consciousness. I have also used dream interpretation as a counselor to clearly identify the seeker's thoughts and attitudes. This is illustrated in the following story.

Dreams offer the counselor of Taraka yoga a grasp of truth from the subconscious mind of the dreamer that may not be available in any other immediate way such as an intuitive report. For example, John, who is a college student, sought counsel with a dream he had. Here is the dream:

"I was walking out the east door of the main building on campus. The sun was setting and Tad came up. He was really excited about something he had to do. Both of us went around to the back of the building. Through the back gate there was an obstacle course. It was like construction with different kinds of obstacles to get through. So we just started on it and then Tina and Stacy joined us. We started discussing the different options we had to move through it. We were looking to where we could go and talking about it. Dr. Dan, my teacher, was observing us."

John is experienced with dream interpretation so he interpreted the dream. He identified the major symbols in the dream. Tad represents a conscious quality of dedication and determination. Tina and Stacy both represent subconscious qualities. John described Tina as aggressive and Stacy as expressive. His teacher, Dr. Dan, represents John's connection with God and his higher Self. John described the obstacle course as a way to increase his capability to think, to become mentally stronger and agile, a way to exercise the mind. John had a very good understanding of the dream.

I added that the goal of an obstacle course is to complete it, usually with some form of competition such as a time limit or team competition. The course itself is like a path or road in a dream, symbolizing a path toward a goal. The obstacles symbolize limiting thoughts that must be 'overcome' such as doubts and fears. I explained to John that he was aware of the path he needed to follow to achieve a goal, but in order to achieve the goal, there are things to do to get there, particularly there are limiting ways of thinking that need to be changed. In his dream, John was using all parts of mind, conscious (Tad), subconscious (Tina and Stacy) and superconscious (Dr. Dan) to explore his options. All parts of self are being incorporated to look at everything, both conscious and subconsciously, also the perspective of superconscious mind to determine what tact, what perspective to accomplish the goal.

John had this dream two nights before we counseled. The day of the dream, he said he and another college student named Greg had been working together and spent a great deal of their time talking about their ideals about being world servers. They were talking about what they were learning as spiritual students and creating a vision for themselves about the differences they could each make in the world.

John said "What came to me was the different challenges that would occur and the things I just want to move through because I have fears about being a spiritual leader. It still is something I am wanting to achieve. And just how we (Greg and John) can both be magnetic. I can see things that are holding me back and there are also just a lot of desires too."

John could see the connection between his day with Greg and his dream. He understood that his thoughts of fear and self-doubt were the obstacles in his dream. John is self-aware so he could begin to identify " Yeah I've got this fear here about public speaking and this is what I can do about this or a fear of having to be responsible for this or that."

I counseled John that he was really assessing his thoughts. I told him the way he could make the most of this dream is to have a definite goal of who he wants to be and how he wants to influence the world. I said he needed to work with the thoughts he has that gets in the way of him accomplishing this. John admitted having fears of being a public speaker and doubts about himself as a spiritual leader.

"Have you given any thought about how you can begin working with this today?" I asked. "How can you start working on being a better public speaker today? Or how can you work on this fear of being a leader for humanity today?" I asked him if he knew people he would describe as spiritual leaders, people he sees as role models. He named four people, two who he knew personally, as well as Gandhi and Martin Luther King Jr. I had John write these names in four columns at the top of a sheet of paper. Next, I instructed him to write down what he thought were the qualities of a spiritual leader, either based on his personal experiences or what he had read or heard about these people. Under each heading, John wrote down specific qualities about each. Some of the qualities he listed were loving, caring, compassionate, motivational, wise, strong-willed, dedicated, directed, expanded consciousness, expressive, visionary, honest, intuitive and persistent.

I instructed John to look at the list and place a check mark by the qualities which he had some experience with and a star by the qualities he had a great deal of experience with.

I asked him which qualities he had a little experience with and which he had a great deal of experience with. Remarkably, out of all the qualities he had listed as the qualities of a spiritual leader, he either had some experience with that quality or a great deal of experience. There were no qualities with no check mark or star. I asked him, "Would you say that you have the makings of being a spiritual leader?" John replied "Yes."

John's dream offered an open and honest exclamation of his thoughts; his ideals and goals as well as his doubts and fears. The dream gave John a way to open himself up and admit his fear of public speaking and his doubts about being a spiritual leader. From that point, then I could help him begin to become objective with himself. By asking him to list the qualities of various spiritual leaders, and to examine his experience with each of those, he was able to assess where he was with each of those qualities. He could separate, identify and admit about himself. He had the foundation about who he was as a spiritual leader. His list also gave him a self-evaluation he can use to gain more experience with compassion and other qualities he had only some experience with.

As a counselor, I was able to offer guidance about how to apply the message of the dream to specific situations in his life.

Around the same time Paul counseled John, Stacy – one of the subconscious aspect "stars" in John's dream – wrote the following about experiencing herself as an infinite being. She calls her story "Getting out of my Room of Limitation".

Getting out of my Room of Limitation

by Stacy Ann Ferguson

Dream from September 18, 2002

I am at the College of Metaphysics and Dr. Dan gets sick of me and kicks me out of my room and puts my bed propped up in the corner to prepare it for a new college student (Nicholas from Dallas). I go to Dr. Barbara crying very hard and tell her what happened. She said it didn't make sense because I need a place to sleep. I tell her that I don't want to change what happened. I just want to understand. Later I am in the upstairs of the old building and I overhear Dr. Dan explaining to another student that he no longer wished to align himself with fulfilling our desires. He uses the word "our" because he also kicked Lisa Bold out of her room. Later I am at a big picnic and the new college students, Chris Sheehan and Nicholas Zajac, have arrived. I am not sure if I want any of the food. None of it looks very good. I finally get something small--fruit, I think. Then I walk along and talk with John M. about what happened. He had also gotten the same treatment. We talk about how it is a good learning opportunity because we can use it to learn about appreciating Dr. Dan and our teachers more.

The next dream I remember I was looking for a job. I was getting ready to start a semester at a university. I was nervous looking for a job because I had no idea what times I would have classes and I was thinking about rushing a sorority and I didn't know how my job would work into that. I then thought that I could change my schedule when I found out what times I would be working and rushing a sorority.

Then I had a dream where I was outside a house that looked run down. The dream had lots of brown colors. I was not supposed to be in the house. I was outside the house and I was taking care of this little girl who lived there. I ended up going inside the house because I was with her and taking care of her. Then once I was in the house I noticed that the little girl had bugs in her mouth. They were the yellow and black polka dotted bugs from the garden. I took about five of them out of her mouth and when I looked in her mouth to find more I saw that the whole back of her throat was lined with them. I had no idea how to get all of those bugs out of there. Then the little girl wasn't really in the picture anymore and I was going in different rooms trying to take a shower and change my clothes and stuff and I was afraid of being found because I was not supposed to be in the house. I kept being found, however, I did not get in trouble by anyone who found me. In the dream my mom and dad were combined with Dr. Barbara and Dr. Dan so it was my mom/Dr. Barbara and my dad/Dr. Dan.

When I woke up from having these dreams and remembered that Dr. Dan had kicked me out of my room and how upset it had made me I wondered what I had done wrong the day before that my superconscious mind would kick me out. I had a really productive day the day before and the dream was a pretty big deal so I had a feeling that it was about something core within me. I was going to do Intuitive Breathing with Dr. Barbara that morning so I knew I could ask her about it and maybe the breathing session would tell me more about it.

When Dr. Barbara and I began our walk over to the Moon Valley Ranch where the Intuitive Breathing session would take place, I began telling her my dream and how I was being kicked out. She said that was "Great!" I was shocked at first. Why was it so great?! Then she told me that I was finally getting out of "that room." The room she was talking about was a mental room or headspace I would go in whenever I thought someone was saying that there was something wrong with me. The room became a part of my brain when I was little and my dad would yell at me and I would go to my room, shut the door and cry. I have been working my way out of this room ever since I began studying in the School of Metaphysics and especially since I became a College of Metaphysics student.

What she said made sense. My superconscious mind was no longer going to support me using that old brain pathway that no longer served me. When looking at the dream from this perspective I was glad that in the dream I did not want to undo what had happened. I only wanted to understand. This shows that I really am consciously ready to change. Dr. Barbara also explained to me that it was significant that in my third dream my mom and dad and my teachers were blending because it shows an updating of the way I see my superconscious mind.

When I looked back over the previous day to see how this dream fit in, it made a lot of sense, especially with my experience that morning. My plan was to get up in the morning around 6:00am and come over to the main building and begin making cheese so that when Laurie, my classmate, got done with 4th Root Race Lab she could begin her cheese. When I woke up that morning and looked at the clock it read 7:00am. I jumped out of bed, grabbed my stuff, and took off for the main building. I didn't even go to the bathroom or change out of my pajamas.

When I got over to the college Laurie was already starting my cheese for me. I thanked her, told her what had happened and took over the process. Waking up the way that I did had created a lot of scatteredness in my mind. I probably spilled at least 6 different things that morning. I could have felt really bad about myself for waking up late and then each time I spilled something, but for some reason I just didn't go to that place of feeling bad. Every time I spilled something I reminded myself to still my mind and be in the moment. I also thought about how my thoughts of today create my reality tomorrow and I thought positive thoughts so I would have a positive experience the next day. Another thought I had about how I was using my mind in response to the experiences I was having was that I was setting a really good example for everyone around me because all the other college students know how to feel bad about themselves when something goes wrong or they do not live up to their full potential. What I was teaching them through my example was that they could do something different. They could have love and compassion for themselves even when they make mistakes. I felt pretty good about this realization.

I told Dr. Barbara about all this and about all the serious work I have been doing this last month with learning to still my mind. With all of this in mind, she and I both wondered what kind of breathing session I would have.

Intuitive Breathing -- Session #11

At first I was in and out. Very relaxed. None of the thoughts I had moved through my emotions which is what usually happens. Finally, Dr. Barbara told me that maybe there didn't need to be an obstacle. Maybe there was something I needed to give to myself. She told me to ask my highest Self what it wanted to give me. The answer I received was Clarity. I experienced it almost like a window in my mind. I told Dr. Barbara what I received and that I did not know what to do with it. She told me to receive and experience it fully. I did and I felt very quiet and peaceful. At first when I received "clarity" I thought I needed to bring it out here in the physical and start looking at my life and experiences and figure out how I should use the new insight. Then I realized it's okay to be still. This is a reflection of my thought that my mind needed to be active to be productive and that stillness = stopping forward motion. I realized, however, that this was not the time for thinking and figuring things out.

When I was done breathing I felt like I was centered within and with stillness. I think this is a reflection of the work I have been doing to still my mind. Dr. Barbara said I am learning to separate my mind from my brain and also my conscious mind from my Self. This directly reflects my dream and that it showed that I was no longer going to live within the limitations of that room, and my whole mind (conscious mind aspect represented in the dream by Lisa, subconscious mind aspect represented by John M., and superconscious mind aspect represented in the dream by Dr. Dan) is aligned with this change in how I use my mind and how I see myself and my experiences.

Stacy's story conveys the remarkable benefits of pursuing Self awareness through Essential Life Skills. Through the combination of dream interpretation, pranayama (breathing) practices, memory, and listening, remarkable Self respect is achieved. Hers is a story of Self realization from applying the mind's potential. It is a story that – through studying and developing your whole Self – can be yours.

Evolution

In this basic review of the major approaches to dealing with individuals, whether the Freudian, the Behaviorist, the Humanist or the Existentialist, we have attempted to show how the psiologist of the future will integrate each of these, recognizing value in what has been previously discovered as theories that will work. These theories lay an important foundation for the future of psiology. However, in no way will these limit the psiologist. He will deal with the individual as just that--a person with mind to use. He will aid that person in understanding his conscious behavior and reactions, his emotions, his mental attitudes, as well as the spiritual part of himself. Working systematically with the levels and divisions of mind briefly discussed earlier, he will encompass the total individual.

This vantage point will release many of the anxieties, tensions and misunderstandings that have occurred in the past through various different theories and treatments. The psiologist will be working toward understanding his own whole functioning Self. In this way there will not be the problems or pitfalls in becoming emotionally involved with his patients or in storing emotional energy that will work against him. As earlier stated, as a profession psychiatry has a high degree of suicide. This will not be a fact with the psiologist for as he continually learns, observes and applies his understandings he will become of more benefit to those seeking his assistance. As opposed to many psychologists who get trapped in their own theory of dealing with abnormal behavior, the psiologist will be open in his own life to learning and understanding. As he improves and gains more, so his understanding and effectiveness to aid others will improve.

Exploring Anxiety Neurosis, or, I'm Afraid-- I'm just not sure what's scaring me.

In an attempt to show or illustrate what the psiologist will do with present clinical disorders, we will briefly look at neurosis. In general psychology today, neuroses are viewed as mental disturbances characterized by severe discomfort from which the patient seeks relief. This discomfort may take many forms--exaggerated fears, overwhelming feelings of anxiety or fright, loss of memory, physical lethargy, debilitating tension, shyness and so forth. The various symptoms are divided by psychologists into a number of subclassifications. It is important to remember that no neurotic patient restricts his behavior to only the symptoms listed to each subclassification designed. There are overlapping symptoms.

To get an overview of all neuroses. we should note that the patient feels he has lost control of himself and that the world is going to crash in on him. More than anything he is overly sensitive to what is going on around him. As opposed to psychoses, the neurotic may feel threatened and his world may be turned upside down, but he is still able to see more or less what it is without grossly misrepresenting or distorting what is going on. The neurotic is at least still oriented to a physical reality, as most of us view it, even though this reality may seem intolerable most of the time.

In order to effectively aid and help an individual suffering from any neurosis, the psiologist will have to be familiar with what the patient is experiencing in his own mind. What many psychologists or psychiatrists tend to think of as another world created by a psychotic person or experienced periodically by the neurotic person is in actuality a reality. From the outside looking in (from the conscious mind looking into the subconscious mind) these experiences will often appear as another world or reality. Where the mentally ill or disoriented patient loses his effective control is in not understanding his experiences while in the subconscious mind. The irony is that most psychologists do not recognize that these levels of inner consciousness of the subconscious exist in their own mind and can be utilized at any time. The mentally ill patient experiences these levels and their qualities, however, has no sense of reference or stability in using those experiences to create a whole, functioning self. Their major problem is relating their experiences to physical reality. Since psychologists rarely recognize or understand the totality of their own minds, it is difficult to aid someone who is functioning in those levels with no balance, control or stability. A good case in point is dealing with a psychotic or schizophrenic who, to the outside world, has created a world of his own--not only individuals or creatures, but perhaps his own language. A psychiatrist who tries to aid this individual from the conscious mind by breaking into this world will find himself rejected at every turn. The patient will delve deeper into his mind because he feels threatened.

An excellent example of this is in the 1977 movie, *"I Never Promised You a Rose Garden".* In this movie, the attempt by one psychiatrist to "break into" the world of the schizophrenic patient is immediately met with distrust and ambivalence. The psychiatrist in this case is trying to relate to the subconscious mind of the patient through his own conscious lack of understanding. There is not the least consideration on the part of the psychiatrist that he could indeed communicate with the patient if he were to use his own subconscious mind and meet the patient on his own ground. In this way the therapist could interpret what is occurring and benefit the patient through understanding and guidance. This would not only speed therapy but pose no threat to the patient, building trust rather than alienation. The psiologist will first place his attention upon the development and understanding of his own mind in order to aid other individuals.

The most predominant problem recognized today for the neurotic is overcoming his fear of the reactions to him of others. To simplify matters even more I would specifically like to explore anxiety neurosis. First it would be helpful to discuss what anxiety actually is. Some theorists believe that anxiety is at least in part responsible for all neuroses; however, in the subclassification devised by psychiatrists anxiety rates an entire classification itself. Anxiety basically is a generalized feeling of apprehension affecting the emotions. Often a distinction is made between anxiety and fear, because with fear there is a specific threat to you but with anxiety you may not be sure what it is you fear. Both however stem from a fear.

For instance, if you are attending a speech class, designed in theory to provide all of us with self confidence in public, there might be a sinking feeling when you must present a lecture to the class. With the looming of ridicule and smirks, or the possibilities of saying something that inadvertently becomes obscene, or of not being able to speak at all, you might find your palms sweating, your hands trembling and a queasy feeling at the pit of your stomach. These are all symptoms of anxiety. You know you have it, but it's hard at surface value to pinpoint why. In this case you're afraid, but you're not exactly sure what you're afraid of, so we are dealing definitely with an emotional response with no apparent reason behind it.

The psychologist will recognize that this basically stems from a lack of self confidence and a fear of others not giving their approval or outwardly rejecting the person. The Freudian view of anxiety is that the neurotic is "infinitely expressive although often reluctantly communicative." This means that we may develop all manners of psychological disturbances, but even if we choose not to talk about them or act them out, they will be expressed into the physical through physical symptoms or diseases. Thus the strange or unusual behavior of the neurotic is nothing more than the physical expressions of energy forces that are inside us and about to burst open. Abnormal behavior; therefore, is symbolic because it represents what is going on beneath the surface. It is an external manifestation of a seething cauldron of unacceptable energy impulses trying to free themselves.

Freud believed a neurotic behaves as he does because the pressures of society, relationships or people around him create stress in the individual trying to express himself. For Freud, the central problem in the development of neurosis is the accentuation of anxiety beneath the surface of consciousness as a result of unacceptable desires which create a moral conflict. The psiologist will agree with this viewpoint to the extent that external stimuli or the rejection or approval by others, govern our expression through the emotions or the conscious mind. When the demands of those around us do not meet with our own perceptions--conflict often results. The psiologist will see this as potential for change, a very beneficial aspect rather than a detriment. He will attempt to point out to the individual that he is responsible for his decisions whether correct or incorrect, and that incorrect decisions are merely stepping stones to greater understandings. The psiologist will also realize that what Freud saw as an energy force of the body giving protection from symptoms, was indeed the basic workings of any physical disorder or disease.

In our discussion of abnormal behavior we have found that we could fit into some of these categories if not most of them. Is it so outrageous to consider that our thoughts and our attitudes do indeed influence the state of our physical health?

There is probably not one person who at one time has not thought himself ill, so it would stand to reason that if we can think ourselves ill we can also think ourselves well. Through constant information gained through experiencing, observing and utilizing the subconscious mind one can readily see that all attitudes, if not expressed into the physical and conscious mind, will seek outlets in the physical system manifesting eventually as a physical disease or disorder. Physicians claim they have been trying for years to find a cure for the common cold by eliminating the symptoms of the cold rather than finding the source or cause. Physically speaking, the psiologist will recognize that a cold involving the respiratory system is actually the result of a mental attitude of restriction, that there are decisions which need to be made and expressed containing several emotional factors. A person who manifests a cold would be the one that is indecisive about something in his life;however, he is not expressing his viewpoint or lack of decision to anyone, choosing to hold this to the Self. Such could be the case with someone trying to decide whether to change physical locations due to his occupation or end a marriage. However, this consideration and indecision is never expressed to the present boss or spouse. This conflict and turmoil remain in the Self creating more related thoughts which also seek expression. If no other avenue is open or used, then you will manifest a cold. The severity of that cold will depend upon the individual, his receptivity to the virus which he attracts to himself, the degree of emotional turmoil called into action, as well as the weight the decision carries.

To illustrate how receptivity comes into play, visualize a room of ten people. Now imagine that someone enters this room displaying all the outward symptoms of a chest cold. Of those ten people present only one catches the cold so to speak. What would cause one person to "catch" the virus when the other nine are left unaffected? Consider the importance of your thoughts and attitudes. Remember the last time you had a cold, recall your mental and emotional state. I think you will begin to see there is a definite connection between certain attitudes and their manifestations and specific diseases. [A comprehensive list of disorders and their mental and emotional cause can be found in Permanent Healing by Dr. Daniel R. Condron.]

Neo-Freudians agreed with Freud's emphasis on the importance of early conflict between the ages of one and seven as was discussed earlier, (when) information is placed in our unconscious mind. This is the source in most cases of inexplicable fears. If you will consider your own fears, hesitations, or doubts you will begin to see that they are not the same as those around you. Some may have common ground but many are different. What causes one person to fear, for example flying, while another never travels unless by plane. We are individuals and have mind to work with in creating our desires and fears. If a fear exists it is merely that we know enough about a situation or incident but do not have a complete understanding of this. Our reaction is to eliminate the possibility of having to experience this, so we continue to illogically fear the unknown whereas the personal experience would relieve this feeling of not knowing.

A further assumption by Neo-Freudians is explained in the

definition of one who finds himself in an intolerable job. Yet this occupation is one which satisfied the requirements of society or perhaps his spouse or family. This individual feels he has the potential to move onto better positions but is afraid of failure which society condemns. This fear probably is the result of frustration and earlier attempts to break away from his hamstrung condition originally instilled by his parents. This could indeed have stemmed from interactions with the parents, however the individual is still an adult reacting to external stimulus or the demands of others rather than the demands of the total Self.

Another Neo-Freudian viewpoint of the same dilemma suggests that at a very early age we develop an idealized image of ourselves. Our ego, in Freudian terms, thinks of us as something we are not, thereby creating a large gap between reality and fantasy. Neurosis strikes because we are unable to live up to the expectations we've set for ourselves. We then have the choice of facing reality that we are not fulfilling our wishes, needs and desires or we have to admit defeat in order to satisfy ourselves, an anxiety provoking conflict. However, this is often a limited viewpoint on the part of psychologists or psychiatrists. Not recognizing the full workings of the mind themselves, they do not recognize that imagination and fantasy, or dreams do create what a physical reality is. The problem with the neurotic is very similar to the psychotic or schizophrenic. They do not know how to relate what they perceive as imagination or dreams into a physical reality integrating the total Self in what they see themselves as being and what they can become. An excellent example of this is someone raised in a ghetto area who through consistent dreaming, effort and imagining ultimately builds and wills himself into a situation of becoming successful and wealthy. This potential within mind is available to anyone who integrates and uses it. Each individual will use mind each day, but how often do we place attention upon exactly what is happening and how the mind works. If we understand the answer to the questions we begin to gain understanding about abnormal or neurotic behavior.

The major evolving step the psiologist will take will be not to view the person as abnormal or something to be changed, but will see them as a total individual, not suffering from a mental disease but merely lacking the mental tools to gain a better understanding of mind and how he can best use it to suit his desires and needs within his physical life.

The humanist basically sees the neurotic as deficient in the art of enjoying himself and the world around him much like the phobic who fears elevators or closed places, the anxious neurotic places himself in such a restrictive environment that he cannot enjoy what the world and others have to offer. Most of the neurotic's problems are located in the belongingness and esteem areas according to the humanist. Because of early blocking of his potential, the neurotic is not able to share love with others and because he is deficient in this expression he lacks self esteem. One who lacks self esteem is so inwardly grown he becomes a neurotic mass of confusion rather than an orderly creation working toward a worthwhile end with others. This will be an important perspective for the psiologist, seeing this concept as implying a lack of goals and purposes to the activities in a day. Confusion will always indicate some form of indecision, that a decision has not been made to travel one route or another. Once a decision has been made a goal is in mind. The ideal, what you picture in your mind, and purposes, why this is so important to you, so that you are stimulated to put forth the activity to make the mental concept a physical reality. Whether this is a quality within yourself, obtaining a job, or accomplishing everyday tasks in this way you can create your life to be well-ordered with you as the intelligent director. As the director you can channel and direct your thoughts, words and actions in the ways that will benefit yourself as well as others.

From the existential point of view, neurotics (have) distinct behavior patterns. Intellectually they express feelings of meaninglessness and uselessness and emotionally they rarely get farther than to express blandness, boredom and depression. Behaviorally they fail to get involved with others and spend only a minimum amount of effort in everyday life. Underlying the existential point of view you may recall is the need that each of us has (while we can) while still accepting our finiteness. A fear of nothingness can ironically freeze a person, so that rather than do something with the time one has, it is spent in a continued state of anxiety. To the existentialist many neurotics seem to be caught in this bind. The neurotic is bound within himself, the only escape is to become more external and find a deeper meaning in life. In essence, the psiologist will use this point of view for it integrates well with the others, unconscious fears related to how others will react often seem to force the individual into himself, not relating to an individual. Therapy will definitely include an inventory of self, honestly evaluating and exploring things in the unconscious mind achieving understandings that can be used and applied towards not only the dealings with self but the environment as well. The major point of difference for the psiologist will be the fatalism or finiteness expressed by the existentialist.

The psiologist will explore and make usable concepts of the continuity of existence, thought and the total self. Death will cease to be an unknown creating fear in the individual, but will be understood as withdrawing the attention from the conscious mind, retreating into the subconscious. A process undergone each night when you sleep. If you can understand the sleep state or your subconscious mind, you will realize what death is and place it in its proper perspective as merely a change--an indication of growth and accomplishment.

The behaviorist's viewpoint is that anxiety and any other manifestations of the neurotic is that they are learned, just as anything else is learned, through association. Undoubtedly as a child if you are continuously and severely punished for a certain behavior you will as an adult have a tendency to ignore, reject, or avoid anything related to that particular stimulus which at one time resulted in great pain being experienced. However, this is not to say that we are robots not having the intelligence to think and choose how we will act or react. Once again this is external stimulus; is there a reward or is there negative reinforcement?

If one can learn to respond from Self then each action will be fulfilling within the self and more fulfilling to those around the self as well. In essence, the psiologist will be open to and draw upon psychological, philosophical, and metaphysical theories which have to the present time been acknowledged as beneficial and acceptable. The difference with the psiologist is he or she will be tying the loose ends together.

In recognizing the individual as total mind, understanding the functions and workings of each part of mind, the psiologist will better be able to integrate and aid the individual in understanding his own situations and circumstances, then giving that person mental tools so that he may become the director of any of those, fulfilling his life as he would choose and therefore becoming much more fulfilling to those around the self. As is acknowledged by most psychology texts today, inevitably the thing the Greeks called soul, the philosophers called mind, and psychologists call psyche will come into prominence even though at this time, from that point of view, most people do not know what it is.

The psiologists will integrate the soul, mind, or psyche into the person's concept and perception of himself, enabling that individual to see himself with greater appreciation and respect. Once this is understood within a general context and better accepted by the majority of therapists today we will see the evolution of psychology into an integrated workable system to help develop the total individual not dependent upon any other person, place or thing for their peace, contentment, or happiness. From this vantage point each person will truly be an individual with the highest ideal and purpose to each activity he chooses.

As this is fostered and recognized in the individual the effects will be widespread and long range to humanity as a whole. Just consider how such an individual would raise his own children. If indeed information is stored in the unconscious primarily from external stimulus between the ages of one and seven, just think of the lessened amount of unconscious attitudes that will be created by the environment of a child who is born to parents who recognize who they are, what they are and where they are going. The world will change considerably.

This is what we can create and anticipate with a fulfilling sense of respect, pride and accomplishment.

–from ***Psiology: Evolutionary Step in Psychology***
© 1977, School of Metaphysics

9-11-01
A Child's Perspective

I turned on the television in the bedroom a couple minutes before eight in the morning. I had made this a practice, my time to check in with the world for a few moments before rousing Kiah for the start of our day.

Live footage of a smoking World Trade Center Building in Manhattan, NY, filled the screen. As the story progressed it captured my attention. I watched as the second plane circled the second building exploding into it. The commentators were unaware until the flames burst forth. Another man-created disaster was unfolding.

After a while Kiah stirred and began listening. Then he wanted to see. He came over to the bed. "Wow!" he said, impressed by the fire display.

"It's really happening Kiah," I said gently. "It's not a video. The building is really on fire."

"What happened?" his big eyes held the question more than his words.

I explained how one plane had flown into one building, then a second plane into the second building. I paused, and his silence told me that was as far as he could go with it for now.

We continued to watch for a few more minutes. Kiah grew restless and moved to play. My attention moved to what was happening. All we didn't know yet. Memories of 1993 bombing of this same building. Oklahoma City's Murrah Building bombing. Waco. Columbine. All the acts of violence and harm that had left their imprints on American consciousness in the last decade.
My thoughts moved to the increasing energy levels in our universe, the shift of the ages, occurring in our world. I thought of forgiveness and allowing, and knew this to be another test of the collective consciousness of Americans and of the world. Teaching my child, leading our community, required an alignment of consciousness.

News of another plane crashing into the U.S. Pentagon shook me and I recognized the testing of my reasoning skills. It was the uncertainty of where this might lead, how long it might continue that entered into my mind for a moment. Hezekiah responded to this shift in energy with "Come on, let's go! I want to go downstairs."

We proceeded in the morning ritual and Dad came inviting Kiah to go out to the orchard to take part in the cider making. He happily went off with his dad.

Christine would later tell me, when she was at the sandbox with Kiah that afternoon, he had wanted to build dams to keep the Pakistanis out. No one living here had talked about Pakistan. Even the television coverage we had watched had yet to bring up the country. Kiah knew his continents and some countries where we have friends, but as far as I knew he didn't even know where Pakistan was. It was a direct reception of thought foreshadowing what would occur several hours later.

At dinner Kiah announced, like some of the people interviewed on TV, that he wanted to get whoever did this. I understood his pain, his instinct to lash out when hurt, to protect in human fashion. I also knew what I had learned about forgiveness and repentance and grace, and I want to teach this to my son.

I told him we would find out who did this. I asked him what he wanted to do with the people when he got them. "Stop them. Kill them so they can't do it again," his reply seared my heart. I understood his words were a reflection more of our frustration, collectively, than his own personal opinion. I was becoming more and more aware of how to describe what I know.

"That won't stop it, Kiah." I replied.

"What will?" he asked.

"Love." It was an answer I would have thought terribly sappy and idealistic ten years before, but I knew love's power increasingly every day. It has been demonstrated over and over, through Gandhi and the British soldiers, through Jesus and the Jews, through every mother and father and their newborns.

The destruction of the World Trade Center was an opportunity for us to be who we imagine ourselves to be at our best. *A collective learning experience.* And the focus of the media was fear. The real lesson of all of these recent tragedies played out on satellite tv around the world was not fear, nor was it the shattering of pride or the evil of humanity. The lesson I can see is about who we are. This lesson is a test of what we believe individually and collectively. And more importantly what we want to know. Every "disaster" has shaken beliefs, all for the purpose of separating beliefs from what is known through experience. By knowing the truth of our experience we can love one another. We can allow the physical world to be what it is without reaction that leads to our own darkness. We can learn to be in the world but not of it.

Certainly our individual mastery of self affects, directly and by example, the pattern we give to our children.

Kiah finally settled into bed shortly after 10 p.m. I was transcribing an intuitive report across the hall and Dad was putting him to bed. It didn't take long for him to fall asleep.

About an hour later I came in and quietly turned on the television. I had wanted to watch President Bush's remarks I had taped earlier that evening. Kiah began to stir. Then cried out, "No!" I knelt by his bedside comforting him with soothing words and a caress. He moved around under the covers, at first quieter then agitated again.

He sat up, then turned around, eyes wide open. "Kiah, it's okay, mommy and daddy are here," I said with directed thought. I had seen him do this several times before. The pop term for it is night terrors. Having researched the mind for years, including dream phenomenon, I understood what he was experiencing.

He alternately calmed and reared. I gave him water. He relaxed for a few minutes then cried out again.

Dan came in offering his comfort, and a drink of water, which Kiah again accepted. He knew we were both there and laid back down. In a few moments he was back up and I offered to hold him. He came into my arms and I endeavored to lift him. Being dead weight I sat in a nearby chair and he stood up, still not conscious with eyes wide with expression, trapped in the emotional level. I expanded my mind to be where he was, a familiar presence for him. It was the way I had learned to lull him to sleep in the first few months of his life.

Dan picked him up and carried him up and down the hall. He laid Kiah on our bed and we both soothed him. He settled in under the covers. It was like swimming underwater. He would fade and begin to drift, then cry either aloud or in muffled whimpers. I knew I was hearing the sounds of those who had died so quickly in the past twenty four hours as well as those who were still alive. Emotions, raw, confused, distorted.

At one point Kiah sat up, looked toward the door of the bedroom and yelled, "Stop!" He was obviously afraid.

"What do you see Kiah?" I asked. He looked at me, then back to the door. "What do you see, tell mommy and daddy, we can help you understand." He relaxed, laying back down, saying "I don't want to tell you." I had learned this meant he didn't know how to talk about it. I did not ask again, and for the most part he was calmer and able in minutes to move into a deeper level of sleep.

He slept through the night between his father and me.

The next morning when he awoke the television was again filled with information. Kiah came over so he could see it and said, "Again. They're still talking about that?" I explained there were still many questions everyone wanted to know the answers to and so they would continue talking about it for a while.

Later some of the teachers at the College and I would talk about the difference in the energy as experience moved forward. Yesterday was a shock for just about everyone. Collectively that instinctual pulse that aligns the mind to do what it must because of crisis was felt. It seems ironic when you realize that same alignment is what we inwardly crave, and can attain at will, at any time, through meditation. Because most remain in human consciousness, they are buffeted by their experiences, sometimes rudely forced to experience repercussions of what their thoughts cause. The way they experience is emotionally. This second day was a day the emotions became pronounced.

One of the teachers had awakened and cried for an hour. Some were feeling out of sorts, upset stomachs, turned solar plexuses. Others were channeling the energy into their work, cleansing and aligning their minds through concentration, prayer, and meditation. For them, this was a day for living meditatively.

Throughout this aftermath day, Kiah stayed close. Even before getting dressed for the day he took off downstairs to find daddy. He wanted to know where we both were. After lunch, I passed his room heading downstairs and he came running out to tell me to "Stay up here, Mommy. Don't go." I reassured him I would stay. He just wanted us near.

For a young child, being present is everything. It makes me realize anew just how close we are as children to the Truth.

*(reprinted from **How to Raise an Indigo Child** ©2002, School of Metaphysics)*

What to do when your child experiences

night terrors

1) Know the external stimuli your child has received during his/her waking hours. When you are not with your child, talk with those who are. When you are knowledgeable concerning what your child has heard, seen, felt, tasted, and smelled, you can better identify what his emotional experience is.

2) Remove stimuli that is upsetting, especially in the hours before the child sleeps.

3) Know your own mind. Be constantly learning about yourself and creation. The more conscious you are, the better parent you are both as an example and in the guidance, love and teaching you offer your child.

4) **Admit emotional conditions present** around the child. If they are yours, seek ways to resolve them. Take classes, read HeartMath by Childres or Walking Between the Worlds by Greg Braden, pray and meditate. Learn how to admit your emotions so you can learn and evolve your awareness. Stuffed emotions find a great outlet through young children, often to their detriment.

5) **Trust yourself.** The love you have for your child need to guide you when your child does not understand the world he finds himself in. Do what your heart says is right. Hold your child, let him sleep with you, talk about difficult subjects (the bombing, people dying, loss, anger, whatever). The more open you are to listening to your child, the greater your knowledge and understanding of him/her.

6) **Always tell the truth** to your ability to discern it. Do what your head says makes sense. Know your priorities. Your child comes first. Sometimes that means missing a lot of sleep and being late to work. We need to all grow a heart that understands priorities in life and mature our head to respond to it. You can help others in growing theirs as well as your own.

7) When in the middle of the "night terror" **holding your child** can be the best thing for you and for her/him. The giving and receiving of love is a great healer.

8) **Talk to your child about your dreams.** Then ask about theirs. Keep a journal until they are old enough to keep one themselves. Someday this will be an invaluable record of this soul's awareness. Honor your place as custodian of those subconscious messages.

9) **Learn to interpret dreams** so you can better teach your child, responding to where they are and what they are learning as they mature. Interpreting your dreams is a skill to learn. It's like learning English or Spanish or Japanese, but a lot more fun because it is universal. And what you will learn about communication will serve you and your child in ways you can't even imagine until you get there. Get started today.•

Studying Your Dreams

We stand to gain in awareness by giving attention to our dreams. In fact there are six other worlds waiting to be explored and our dream experiences tell us of these. They are doorways beyond human consciousness, into the realms of intuition and superconscious awareness.

Every one of us has a whole functioning mind. I think it is our responsibility and duty to ourselves to understand that mind and to endeavor to use it with the highest ideals. Dreams are a way that the inner self is trying to talk with each one of us. So by responding to the dreams and saying, "Hey, I'm listening" you'll have access to a personal "therapist" any time, anywhere. If you've been prone to nightmares and fears, these will cease. Recurring dreams will cease or you will understand their function in your life. You will establish a rapport between the outer you and your soul.

The best way to begin using this inner Self counseling tool is to begin a dream journal. Record your dreams immediately upon awakening. Writing what you remember as soon as you awake gives you the details of your dream experience that will fade as you bring more of your attention into the physical body. Every detail is an important part of the dream's message.

The who, what, where, and how of your dream message conveys the state of your awareness at the time the dream occurred. You can explore this in a number of ways.

Δ For those who want a concentrated study we offer Spiritual Focus Sessions seven weekends of each year. Psi counselors who hold doctorates in metaphysics serve as your mentors during the weekend, leading you through a personal journey of Self realization using many of the modalities discussed in this book. Each session focuses on a particular subject (influence, genius, dharma, etc.). Intuitive Reports have been developed for each session. The personal insight each offers is life-changing.

Δ When your focus is understanding your dreams, the Dream of the Month Club fills this need. This innovative educational service is conducted over the internet. Each week, members receive educational materials through email. One of these is a monthly in-depth look at a Creative Mind Report. Information revealed in these intuitive analyses is a window into how thinking occurs. The Creative Mind Report is given for SOM students studying in the third cycle of lessons and for those attending the Genius Spiritual Focus Session.

Δ For those wanting to become Psi counselors, the School of Metaphyics course of study is offered in cities throughout the Midwest United States. This course teaches how to use the whole mind in harmony with the laws of creation. Entrainment of head and heart through daily disciplines opens the mind. Infinite Intelligence, Infinite Energy, and Infinite Manifestation become much more than intriguing words. They become the means through which you master and develop your whole Self. The first cycle (1-24) of lessons is offered through correspondence with a teacher at the College of Metaphysics. Psi counseling training begins with Taraka Yoga in the latter half of the third cycle of study.

Dr. Daniel Condron: "Giving and receiving is a cycle. The cycle's always completed. So you look at what you've received in your life and what you received has built a foundation that you've moved in some direction towards learning and growth and fulfillment. Then at some point it's always important to give that back out. If you think of it physically, people are raised by their parents and then at some point they get married and raise their kids. When they become grandparents, they teach the grandkids. Usually they don't teach the grandkids quite the way they taught their own kids 'cause they've learned some things along the way. That's the process of maturity that people go through when they teach others what they know. In the School of Metaphysics we call it teaching teachers and it's akin to parents teaching children and their children coming up and becoming parents and then teaching their children what they've learned, adding to the whole.

To complete anything, you have to give back what you received. To move to the next level, it's important to even give back more or on a higher level so that then you can receive more. For instance, with spiritual growth you give completely and then you can receive completely on a higher level. The wonderful thing about teaching and sharing is you realize how much you know. I do it every day, all the time when I'm teaching the students here at the College of Metaphysics. It's from the alignment that I practice of inner and outer minds so more of my soul, more of my understandings, more of my awareness is coming forth. Each of you need that too because you have it to give and you have it to offer the world and it will help you progress also. That will move you from the third stage of growth to the fourth stage. The four stages are: infancy, adolescence, adulthood, and wisdom."

–from Q&A session with Drs. Barbara and Daniel Condron during the Power of Influence Spiritual Focus Weekend

Reconciliation

Creating the Infinite Self

Everything happens for a reason, and it's time for us to know why.

"Think about it. The Dalai Lama travels the world forgiving China for killing thousands of his countrymen and attempting to destroy his culture yet there is no hatred in the man's heart. He even said, "Give the 2008 Olympics to Bejing" when all these other people were saying, "No, they're inhumane; undeserving." When you listen to what His Holiness says, you have to begin wondering how you or anyone can still hate their own brother. From where does this power of forgiveness originate? How can someone allow such atrocities to continue, not seeking revenge? Such a voice of compassion upsets the apple cart of many beliefs. It brings us into a whole new realm of thinking, which is really good. This is the process of entraining the minds, aligning consciousness with Superconsciousness. I like what I see happening in our world. We are becoming the change!"

–from Q&A session with Drs. Barbara and Daniel Condron during Your Soul's Purpose (Dharma) Session

Many times in a lifetime, situations will arise that we did not expect. Sometimes we view them as pleasant surprises: news of a potential grandchild, a promotion at work, a chance meeting with an old acquaintance, even a book or movie that comes at the right time. Usually we take these happenings in stride. Hopefully with a healthy dose of gratitude, a thanksgiving for our good fortune. A Psi counselor can help you receive these events in life with grace and alertness. Knowing how and what you are doing with your thinking that contributes to bringing about such good fortune insures that it will come again.

I look at this as a personal responsibility. To be the best that I can be, and to initiate change, a bettering of Self each day. This is the reality of Infinite Being. It opens the door to immortality. Each day becomes a fresh opportunity for my soul to move in the world. When you know how you bring about the good things in your life, you can teach others to do the same.

Sometimes the unexpected is at first seen as unwanted, undesirable. Deaths have this stigma, as do losses of any kind – job, home, reputation. Christine wrote about one kind of loss in Infinite Manifestation in Book Three of *Infinite Possibilities in Finite Experiences*. I write here about another. The truth is most of us do not receive the unexpected with grace or equanimity. The unexpected quickly becomes the unwanted and we become emotionally reactive. Our heads and hearts are out of sync. We allow the situation to become a crises. There are individual crises – health, divorce, and so forth. Then there are shared crises.

In the minds of many, the events in New York City of September 11, 2001 are an example of shared crises. Not since the Civil War in the United States had the consciousness of this nation been so stirred. At the time, Psi counselors aided themselves and others toward the light of understanding during a very dark time. Some of what they wrote at the time is included here to illustrate the essence of Infinite Being.

As I review the ideas, I realize how timeless they are, how what is written can be applied to situations today in our lives wherever we may live on the planet. That in itself connects us with Infinite Being. We begin with some of my thoughts immediately following the tragedy that shook New York City, the United States, and the world.

The Universal Lesson of September 11, 2001*

This event was foreshadowed eight years earlier in the bombing of the very same building that now no longer exists. The perpetrators had reasoned well in those years, and this time they succeeded in their mission. This is more on the physical and psychological level, the combative arguments and actions of judging right and wrong.

The much greater foreshadowing was in consciousness. This was a test, so we could evaluate how much we had learned with each lesson presented. For Americans, we had seen several such incidents in the last decade – the WTC bombing, the Waco, Texas attack, the OKC federal building bombing, the Columbine (Colorado) school shooting. These acts of senseless violence were causing us to think, to come out of too often drug-induced mental stupors of denial and into a lucidity that admits and forgives and accepts and allows. The kind of thoughts that bring insight and illumination, that lead their owner to go beyond the goodness for self and align with the goodness for all.

One woman interviewed said she told her child "something good will come from this." The sentiment was echoed by many in the aftermath of the tragedy. The older among us had seen another day that lived in infamy and what it had brought. Now the lesson was being presented to a new generation. "Let us pull together" became the refrain. Let us care and love and do better.

The woman's words stuck with me. I knew them to be true, and I knew they were incomplete. Too much was left to the great cosmic forces in that word "something." The reasoner in me was pressing to know, what good and how? I thought about it for hours, meditated and prayed. Then it came to me, quite clearly: for something good to come from this, we must learn the lesson.

Being at School of Metaphysics world headquarters during this time, I was abreast of thoughts and opinions in a wide berth. Telephone calls from around the country and emails from around the world flowed in. Universal Peace Covenants were our first response. The Multidimensional Experience concerning the events of September 11th was the second.

Initially I created this experience with those on campus in mind. The Saturday following the attack, a group of teachers and students gathered in the College chapel. The experience was designed to stimulate awareness throughout the levels of conscious and subconscious mind. The purpose was to bring resolution in a way that would entrain the minds toward productive action now. The experience was poignant for each one present. Placing the basic experience on the internet became a natural response to the many requests we were receiving asking what the School of Metaphysics' viewpoint of the attack was. It was not that we had an official stand on the tragedy. What we did have were viewpoints of thoughtful metaphysicians from many backgrounds and an example of what we teach that could assist anyone in putting their own experience into perspective.

Multidimensional experience assists in the movement of consciousness from a state of believing into knowing. I could see more clearly how this is the universal lesson in September 11th. The lesson received by each of us is unique, accepted or rejected according to our own understandings or need. To learn our lesson requires reasoning.

It requires that our hearts remain open as well as our minds. *We must learn to think with our hearts and feel with our heads.* Multidimensional experiences are designed to stimulate this entrainment.

The "Multidimensional Experience from September 11th" which appears on our website is presented in this book beginning on page 237. If you have found it impossible to forgive the events of that time and want to reconcile your thoughts and feelings, please give yourself an hour or more to move through the instructions. Then tell others about it.

When undesirable and unwanted situations arise in our lives, we can choose our response. Rather than a cause for tethering our consciousness with blame, guilt, regret, revenge and other forms of suffering, we can choose to learn from each experience. We can embrace even unwelcomed experiences because our minds are opened to the infinite possibilities that at first, because of our sorrow, we could not perceive. In the following, Dr. Laurel Clark describes the opening of her mind in the 9-11-01 experience.

The Lesson I Am Learning

by Dr. Laurel Clark

Early in my School of Metaphysics studies, I was introduced to the concept that the subconscious mind views all experiences as learning for the soul. The conscious mind judges them as good or bad, pleasant or unpleasant. We can elevate our thinking to see things more wholistically, to function as a soul using our physical experiences for growth. Recent events have given us the opportunity to examine ourselves and our world from the soul's perspective. Reasoning enables us to learn, to change, to discover the good in our experience.

The attacks on September 11, 2001 stimulated all of us to ask, "why?" "Why did it happen?" "What are the lessons we need to learn from this?" The urge to make sense of an event that seems so horrible, painful, and evil is the urge within us to know the mind of God. If we can understand how all of this aligns with Universal Law and what our soul needs to learn, then we can take steps to build understanding. With understanding comes peace.

There are collective lessons, group karma, for all of us. There are also individual lessons for each person. The Saturday evening following the attack, Dr. Barbara Condron led a group of us at the College of Metaphysics through a Multi-Dimensional Experience to learn and come to some resolution concerning our own thoughts, feelings, and reactions to the event. Going through this experience helped me to clarify the many thoughts that had been flying through my mind.

The lesson that came into focus for me is that God exists and there is life beyond the physical body. This is a lesson that has been the theme of much of my life for the past year. For me, the timing of September 11th was especially significant. On September 10, 2000, my husband John died. Before the catastrophic attack occurred, I had planned to do a kind of commemorative ceremony on September 11th to celebrate my love for John and to pray for guidance to give my energy to God in the highest way I can. Little did I know the form that this would take!

When John was alive, we were mentally connected, energetically connected. We often communicated telepathically when we were in different cities. We could feel each other's emotions. John's death brought to me many experiences to understand that we are still connected and that his spirit still exists even though it is no longer incarned in that body.

My mother had a massive stroke a few months after John's death and died two weeks later. That experience furthered my lesson in "life beyond the physical body." I was able to use the telepathy I have developed through my SOM studies to communicate with my mother when her brain was damaged by the stroke. Knowing how to go into the inner levels with awareness helped me to know that she was doing well after her death.

My good friend Dr. Sheila Benjamin's mother died a week later. Although I did not know her mother very well, I bolted awake at 5 a.m. (the exact time she died), from a dream indicating that she was moving on. I immediately started to pray for her and Dr. Sheila and her family. I knew that they needed support and that I could offer it through prayer and projection of love. All of these experiences were connected. They all called me to move from believing to knowing that God exists and life exists beyond the physical body.

Tuesday morning, September 11th, I was driving from Windyville to Lebanon, MO (25 miles from the College) when I heard the news on the radio. The first plane had struck the World Trade Center Tower and, as I listened, the news reporter suddenly exclaimed, "Oh my God, the second tower has been hit!" Seconds later he announced that the second tower had burst into flames. I immediately wondered, "what can I do?"

Images of New York City flashed through my mind. I thought about the people I know who live in New York, my sister-in-law and 10-year-old nephew, some friends who work not far from the World Trade Center. I thought about my father who used to commute there every day and what it would be like for me if this had happened then. I imagined all the people rushing to work, concentrated in that small area, and how dramatic the impact must be. Physically far away, I knew there had to be some way that I could help.

The thought came to me right away, "pray." I started to pray. I prayed to God to help and protect and comfort all of the souls who were involved. I prayed for everyone in New York, for those who were alive, for those who had been killed, for those who were helping, for the families and friends who had lost loved ones, for the hijackers. I prayed for understanding, for all of us to understand the lessons our souls need to learn from this. I continued to pray all day long as I drove from place to place taking care of mundane errands.

At one point I saw a vision of the earth, with points of light, like candle flames, all over the globe. I saw points of light everywhere, floating in space. In my mind, I heard this thought, "We are all in this together." I felt comforted, and knew that God was with us. I could feel all of us in the arms of God. I could feel the energy of those who had died going up to God in a great sacrifice. I knew that all souls, whether incarned or disincarned, were reaching out to help one another.

I asked to be filled with the spirit of God and to be a

loving presence. I gave my love and light to everyone I met that day. Most of the people in the stores moved as if like robots, on automatic pilot, riveted to the sound of the radio broadcasting the horrible news. I imagined my light embracing each person I encountered, enfolding them with love, brightening their light.

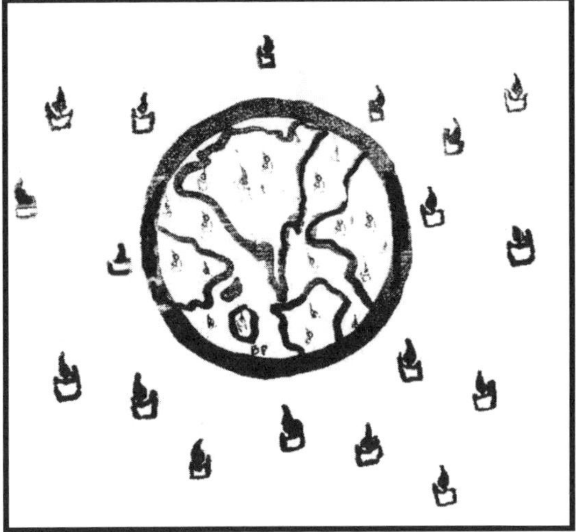

Tuesday night, the evening of the attack, I had a dream in which my husband John appeared. He was helping all the people who were killed. I asked him, "are they all right?" He smiled and said (telepathically), "yes, once they are out [of the flesh] they are fine." It was clear to me that those on the inner levels are helping one another with kindness and generosity just as people are here in the physical existence. It proved to me that love is eternal. It showed me that life exists beyond the physical body. Once souls are released from the body, they are fine.

The beauty of this experience was manyfold. At first, when I heard the news, I felt powerless. My physical power was limited — I could give blood, I could give money, I could even drive to the East Coast to help. But that would help only a few. I needed a Greater Power. Prayer helped me to connect my mind and my spirit to God. Invoking God's presence centered me in the real power I had. It helped me to be calm and loving, and to connect with people who were shocked and afraid to bring them warmth.

Prayer also helped me to link the personal lesson I was learning this past year to a universal need that I can fulfill through teaching and sharing my own growth. "We're all in this together," I heard in my prayer-vision. Those "candle flames" I saw were souls, all connected in a great web of creation. My need to know God's love and eternal existence was stimulated by the loss of loved ones close to me. Now, many people, all at the same time, are experiencing loss — the death of people they know, uprooted beliefs, sudden insecurity — it takes many forms. Asking myself, "What can I do? What can I give? How can I help? How will I learn? How can I be in greater harmony with Universal Law?" it has become clear to me that the next step in my own learning is to be a guiding light for others.

My primary lesson in this is that God is with us and that we must live with God's presence and love in our hearts. Instead of being afraid of loss, to give completely. To be grateful for what I have. To thank God for all of the blessings in my life and show respect by giving and teaching what I know. To claim the importance of my influence. We bring about change with each moment, each thought, each deed. One person makes a huge difference. When we each accept that, we all make a difference.•

A Psi counselor, Dr. Laurel Clark is on the faculty of the College of Metaphysics and is an ordained minister in the Interfaith Church of Metaphysics. She was reared in a suburb of New York City. (Thresholds Quarterly, November 2001, ©School of Metaphysics.)

For others, the events of 9-11-01 served to connect them with their life purpose. How they chose to respond forged new bonds of friendship while strengthening old ones. From tragedy came personal revelation, great insight, and leadership as we sought to redeem value from something that at first seemed senseless and unnecessary. Many may think they are far from the level of awareness of the Dalai Lama, yet the truth is in this day of telecommunication increasing numbers of people are awakening to infinity every day.

Multi-Dimensional Living Experience

by Dr. Paul Blosser

Infinite Being entrains the conscious and subconscious minds so the seeker can connect the inner and the outer, using a particular experience to cause a shift in consciousness. The idea of Infinite Being is for the seeker to learn from the life experiences, by integrating the conscious thoughts and elevating some experience for example, to a higher plane of consciousness.

Following the September 11 terrorist attacks on the World Trade Center and the Pentagon, I attended a multi-dimensional experience conducted at the College of Metaphysics by Dr. Barbara Condron. This experience awakened me to a broader perspective on these attacks so that I could understand how such an attack could move my consciousness ahead and how this can benefit the spiritual growth and progression of all of humanity.

After my experience I recognized the importance of my calling as a spiritual teacher and the need in the world for teachers and students of great strength and determination. What a new perspective.

Just two weeks later, I led a group of people through the same multi-dimensional experience. About 10 people gathered at the School of Metaphysics in Palatine, Illinois on a Friday evening. We talked about what had happened. We wrote down our conscious thoughts. We moved our minds inward to look at our place within the scheme of the events. We drew pictures to remind us of what was being built within ourselves and the people of New York. All walked away with a deeper understanding of these tragic events and a renewed sense of self and humanity as a result of the multi-dimensional experience.•

Dr. Paul Blosser was among the first counselors trained in Taraka Yoga. His stories are recorded in "Infinite Intelligence" in Book One of Infinite Possibilities in Finite Experiences.

9-11

THE *Reconcile* *Experience*

The following pages give the steps in the multidimensional experience Laurel, Paul, and I reference in the preceding pages. It is described as an experience in Reconciliation. The impetus for its creation was the aftermath of the destruction of the Twin Towers in NYC, however its potential value to us in any situation of similar impact is limitless. This is why I have chosen to include it here.

Reconciliation can easily be adapted to personal experiences. Where you find a reference to the Twin Towers' destruction, substitute what is troubling you – betrayal by a friend, loss of property or job, separation from a loved one.

Give yourself at least an hour to move through the steps given here. For the deepest insight, do not even read the pages until you are ready to give this kind of attention to what is offered here. I trust these focusing exercises will be useful to you – and to those you care for – many times in the days ahead.

Reconcile

Lead yourself through a multidimensional experience. The following pages are step-by-step instructions designed to lead you through your own multidimensional experience.

This multidimensional experience is based upon a modality offered on September 15th at the College of Metaphysics to help students and faculty assimilate their mind experiences since the attack on the World Trade Center in New York. We offer the following in the hope that it will initiate, assist, accelerate your healing also.

As you move from one page to the next, you will be guided through a series of movements in thinking. Hold in mind your purpose for responding to the direction of each page...your own healing, assimilation, and growth process.

Each movement is designed to aid you in admitting, allowing, accessing, and accepting your thoughts and feelings in five separate and connected dimensions of experience.

May peace be with you all ways.

∞∞∞∞∞∞∞∞∞∞∞∞∞∞∞∞∞∞

To begin....

Prepare yourself by setting aside at least one hour. Make sure your physical needs have been met and will not be a distraction during the course of this experience.

For the full effect of what this can bring to you, you will want to complete what you start once you begin. Therefore, make sure you will not be interrupted or pulled away.

You can join with others if you so desire, experiencing this sequence together.
There are points where talking with another can be most helpful
in elucidating your thoughts and feelings.

You will want paper and a pen for writing.
You will want five index size papers or cards (about 4x6).

When you are ready to begin, turn the page.

∞∞∞∞∞∞∞∞∞∞∞∞∞∞

Dimension 1

Write your dreams since the destruction of the NYC World Trade Center.

Explore the meaning in these dreams by noting..

..who appears in the dream...
..what are they doing...
..what are they feeling.....
what is the overall theme of the dream..
...what is its tone...
...what is expected or unexpected......

Consider the following universal truths

Every dream is about the dreamer.

Everyone in the dream represents an aspect of the dreamer.

Each dream is a message from the inner self, the subconscious mind, the soul,
concerning the state of the dreamer's conscious awareness.

[access www.dreamschool.org for further insights into what these images mean]

then

If you have a partner, spend 10 minutes discussing

"What I find hard to believe"

If you are alone, write your thoughts.

BREATHE

[deeply in and out three times
then turn the page]

∞∞∞∞∞∞∞∞∞∞∞

Dimension 2

Write down this question then answer it:

What made me most angry about this happening in my life?

BREATHE

∞∞∞∞∞∞∞∞∞∞∞∞∞∞

On your file card write the answer to

...what I want to know...

Fill the card with your thoughts.

then

Study what you have written.
Think about this for a moment.
Breathing in and breathing out in rhythm
for 3 minutes.

BREATHE

∞∞∞∞∞∞∞∞∞∞∞∞∞∞

On a sheet of paper, write in a stream of consciousness

(constantly writing whatever thoughts come to you)

How have I felt helpless?

When you have exhausted your thoughts

BREATHE

∞∞∞∞∞∞∞∞∞∞∞∞

Look for the **most repeated word** in what you have just written.

Think about this word.

What does it mean to you? Why does it echo in your mind?

Breathe in the word, breathe out the word

Rest for a moment then

BREATHE

∞∞∞∞∞∞∞∞∞∞∞∞∞∞

On a new card, write the letters

P

Write

what the letters stand for that reflect what you stand for

BREATHE

Dimension 3

What if.....

If with a partner talk about your thoughts and feelings concerning What If..

If on your own, write your thoughts in prose or verse.

When you have exhausted your thoughts

Breathe in, breathe out. Create a rhythm.

Breathe in and breathe out until your thoughts and feelings become one.

Then write your new thoughts on a new card.

BREATHE

∞∞∞∞∞∞∞∞∞∞∞∞∞∞

Dimension 4

Fill one side of a new card with....

Who Do I Feel For?

BREATHE

∞∞∞∞∞∞∞∞∞∞∞∞∞

On the opposite side of this card write

GOODNESS FOR ALL CONCERNED

Breathe in and breathe out
listen to the flow of your breathing

Breathe in and breathe out

until you identify how what you feel is
good

B R E A T H E

∞∞∞∞∞∞∞∞∞∞∞

Dimension 5

On your final card draw a picture of what it means to be

A FORCE FOR GOOD

Talk about your picture with your partner or to yourself. Verbalizing your thought completely.

Breathe in and breathe out
who you are
Breathe in and breathe out
who you are becoming
Breathe in and breathe out
in tranquility
Breathe in and breathe out
light and love

B R E A T H E

∞∞∞∞∞∞∞∞∞∞∞

Unification

The Multidimensional Experience

Universal Peace Covenant

Peace is the breath of our spirit.
It wells up from within the depths of our being to refresh, to heal, to inspire.

Peace is our birthright.
Its eternal presence exists within us as a memory of where we have come from and as a vision of where we yearn to go.

Our world is in the midst of change.
For millennia, we have contemplated, reasoned, and practiced the idea of peace. Yet the capacity to sustain peace eludes us. To transcend the limits of our own thinking we must acknowledge that peace is more than the cessation of conflict. For peace to move across the face of the earth we must realize, as the great philosophers and leaders before us, that all people desire peace. We hereby acknowledge this truth that is universal. Now humanity must desire those things that make for peace.

We affirm that peace is an idea whose time has come. We call upon humanity to stand united, responding to the need for peace. We call upon each individual to create and foster a personal vision for peace. We call upon each family to generate and nurture peace within the home. We call upon each nation to encourage and support peace among its citizens. We call upon each leader, be they in the private home, house of worship or place of labor, to be a living example of peace for only in this way can we expect peace to move across the face of the earth.

World Peace begins within ourselves.
Arising from the spirit peace seeks expression through the mind, heart, and body of each individual. Government and laws cannot heal the heart. We must transcend whatever separates us. Through giving love and respect, dignity and comfort, we come to know peace. We learn to love our neighbors as we love ourselves bringing peace into the world. We hereby commit ourselves to this noble endeavor.

Peace is first a state of mind.
Peace affords the greatest opportunity for growth and learning which leads to personal happiness. Self-direction promotes inner peace and therefore leads to outer peace. We vow to heal ourselves through forgiveness, gratitude, and prayer. We commit to causing each and every day to be a fulfillment of our potential, both human and divine.

Peace is active, the motion of silence, of faith, of accord, of service. It is not made in documents but in the minds and hearts of men and women. Peace is built through communication. The open exchange of ideas is necessary for discovery, for well-being, for growth, for progress whether within one person or among many. We vow to speak with sagacity, listen with equanimity, both free of prejudice, thus we will come to know that peace is liberty in tranquility.

Peace is achieved by those who fulfill their part of a greater plan. Peace and security are attained by those societies where the individuals work closely to serve the common good of the whole. Peaceful coexistence between nations is the reflection of man's inner tranquility magnified. Enlightened service to our fellowman brings peace to the one serving, and to the one receiving. We vow to live in peace by embracing truths that apply to us all.

Living peaceably begins by thinking peacefully.
We stand on the threshold of peace-filled understanding. We come together, all of humanity, young and old of all cultures from all nations. We vow to stand together as citizens of the Earth knowing that every question has an answer, every issue a resolution. As we stand, united in common purpose, we hereby commit ourselves in thought and action so we might know the power of peace in our lifetimes.

Peace be with us all ways. May Peace Prevail On Earth.

Created from October 1996 to April 1997, the Universal Peace Covenant is the result of spiritual collaboration. People from all walks of life, several religious beliefs and nationalities, diverse occupations, all races, as young as seventeen and as old as seventy-five, came together with the intention of creating a timeless document that would accurately reflect humanity's hope, challenge, and destiny.

BREATHE

∞∞∞∞∞∞∞∞∞∞

Remember, then record, your dream this night.

This is your soul's feedback to the work you have done consciously.

∞∞∞∞∞∞∞∞∞∞

We hope this is helpful in your search to know yourself during a time of trial and testing. Multidimensional experiences continue to reveal themselves for days and even weeks. They are opportunities for us to focus our energies for deeper understanding. They can free us from self-imposed limitations we had not recognized, thus quicken healing. They can accelerate soul progression. They can teach us about our Self in ways available to us only now, at this time of the shifting of the Ages.

MultiDimensional Living is a bridge to higher consciousness. Like an artist who wields brushes filled with color as though they are an extension of his own hand, knowing what mind tools are available and how to use them enables you to create life. Multidimensional experiences, like the one you have just experienced, strengthen your inner resources. They enable you to know your Self mentally, emotionally, physically, and spiritually.

The Reconcile Experience can help you sort out your thoughts and feelings following any trauma. When something unexpected comes into your life, make the time to take yourself through these dimensional steps. From missing out on a much desired opportunity to an argument with a loved one, anytime there is a need for perspective, forgiveness, and tolerance, Reconcile can give you what you need. Each step is designed to move your consciousness to a new place. You can transform what at first was an unwanted and rejected experience into one of acceptance, love, and enlightenment.

By synchronizing head intelligence and heart intelligence the soul is reunited, giving you incredible insight, energy, and love. This is the reality of entrainment. Entrainment is a scientific term that was created by Christiann Huygens, a pendulum clock maker in the 1800's. He noticed when he would hang a new clock on the wall that no matter where it started its movement, eventually it would move in sync with the other clocks. No matter how long or how short the pendulums, they eventually all came to move at that same vibration. That's entrainment, when everything is moving together. This phenomena is prevalent in nature. It is breathing in and breathing out. Together.

There is a pulse to the universe. Each one of us is either in alignment with that pulse or we are not. You know when you are and when you aren't. When you are, things are going great. Everything works out. When you're not in alignment with pulse, you have troubles. Everything you touch turns to ashes. Entrainment is being able to cause universal rhythm within your being of who you are.

One of the ways I'm becoming more conscious with entrainment is through MultiDimensional Living, a development we are bringing into the world. MultiDimensional Living describes well the movement of uniting the conscious mind and the subconscious mind to ultimately reunite what is the soul. Instead of being two halves of a whole, they are one entity that works together.

MultiDimensional Living is the ability to be conscious in more than one level of existence at one time. It's being able to function in all seven levels of consciousness simultaneously. This idea has been part of the School of Metaphysics since the early years, at least as far back as 1975 which is the year I entered the study. *Ascended masters function in all levels of mind simultaneously, with awareness.* This has been part of the ideal that I've had in mind ever since I heard this idea at the age of 22. "What is that like? I wanted to know, and I still want to know.

MultiDimensional Living are the steps that you can take to have experiences that are on more than just one level so that you can experience your Self and existence, life, more fully. This may come in a counseling venue. It may come from a healing experience. It may come from a Spiritual Focus Session weekend at the College of Metaphysics. It may come through receiving an Intuitive Report from the School of Metaphysics. The reality of MultiDimensional Living is taught at Schools throughout the Midwest U.S. and through correspondence with a teacher who lives on the college campus in Missouri.

I was counseling one of the students not long ago. Music is where his heart is and he is potentially a musical genius. The talents are there but he hasn't been able to find a focus, consciously, for bringing them out in such a way that feeds him while helping others. Yesterday I listened to his compositions relating to him what I sensed and what I heard. Some pieces were intrinsically

about reincarnation. The vibrations carried you to different places and lifetimes or time periods. They opened inner doors if you would allow it. He could create a whole album of songs conveying either his journey or a universal journey.

Then we spoke of Atlantis, something he is fascinated with, and the power of the dulcimer to rekindle memory. We spoke of aligning with Holy scriptures and allowing them to move through you into music. Then I told him one day he would create a piece of music that is the same forward and backward. This idea ignited him. His kundalini rose.

When I get connect creatively with somebody like this, my mind soars to the possibilities. I see command of music, of vibration, as the essence of healing. I know there are such realities, and he does too. There's a woman that he knows of, who people come to, and while in her presence she makes a vibration with her voice and the people are instantaneously healed of whatever affliction. I have never heard of this woman yet I know this is possible. Intuitive Health Analyses have addressed epilepsy and other nerve disorders by offering specific notes on the musical scale to sound in mind or audibly when certain conditions start approaching. This is the essence of the sustaining power of chanting for centuries. Mantras entrain and cause the mind to move at a certain vibratory rate.

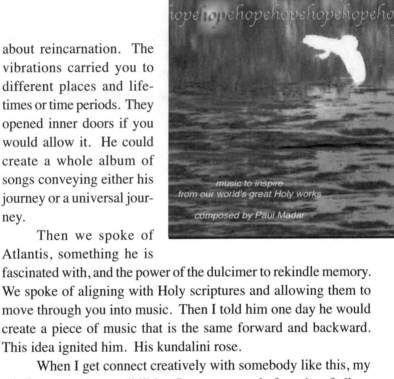

The challenge is to produce the entrained state of mind any time, anywhere, with anyone.

Multidimensional experience enables us to create through the power of visualization instead of the toil of our body. It frees us into a balance that brings peace of mind because it centers us in Infinite Being. Like a teacher, or world leader, or yogi who inspires greatness in others through his or her presence, disciplining mind and body make you a channel for universal wisdom. Inviting Infinite Intelligence, Infinite Energy, Infinite Manifestation into your consciousness illuminates each thought.

In most, the crown chakra, the highest of energies flowing through human beings, is turned downward, engrossed in the finite, physical world. Multidimensional Living is realizing the multi-faceted nature of the whole Self.

Within each of us are seven distinct worlds, levels of consciousness that empower us as mental creators. To enter into these worlds is like being awake in your dreams traveling to known and never before discovered lands, conversing with people you believed you would not have the opportunity to meet. Multidimensional Living is the world of inner consciousness where every dream brings insight, masters teach the initiated, and life unfolds according to your most heartfelt desires. It is the freedom to explore who you are and who you can become; the power to remember, and to imagine.

Being familiar with the seven levels of consciousness is the difference between eating bread and water every day and having a banquet of fresh, organic fare to choose from each day. It is the difference between doing the same work every day and being fluid in tasks that challenge your creativity and ability. It is the difference between reacting the same way in similar situations year after year and realizing you can view the experience in seven distinctly different ways. It is the difference between planning your life largely around its end when you could be experiencing eternal life, right now.

Multidimensional Living brings out the best in you. It stimulates your understandings aiding you to experience the wisdom of Solomon.

CHRIS' DIAGRAM OF
CAUSING INTENTIONAL CRISES

Perpetual Motion & Continual Growth

by Chris Sheehan

As I remember, it all started when I was a child, at about age eleven or twelve. It was at that time in my life that I began to more keenly notice the difference between how I thought and the reality of the world around me. The further along I progressed in school, the more I experienced the structure of life primarily based in physical security. My life up until that point had been in large part rooted around my love of creating. This love often expressed itself in the various forms of art, music, and play. In many ways my imagination was my best friend. In my mind, I saw infinite possibilities where most often others did not.

In hindsight, I would come to recognize that within me was unfolding a vision of what could be. This connection within me painted the picture of potential. I would describe this as wanting us all to be free, aware of our divine, our roots, and open to the discovery of our true natures as creators. At times in my adolescent years, this was cause for great frustration as I felt overwhelmed by the magnitude of the gap between where I could imagine humanity being and where we were. I also felt restricted within myself in that what I could imagine was different than what I was living. For years I waited, unaware of how to begin to match my inner vision with my outer life. Nevertheless my urge to know myself and to change the

In my mind,
I saw infinite possibilities
where most often others did
not.

In hindsight, I would
come to recognize that
within me was unfolding
a vision of what could be.

world remained strong within me.

When the Universal Laws drew me to the School of Metaphysics, my inner vision began to grow even stronger. As a student in the classes, I came to recognize the depth of the opportunity I have been given through the school. I experienced a harmonious resonance with this school almost immediately due to the compatibility of common purpose and the love I received from my teacher. This resonance fostered an intense desire to give. Through the School of Metaphysics I found what I had been looking for, what I needed in order to bring out the vision within. The school's purpose is to accelerate the evolution of humanity by ushering in Intuitive, Spiritual man. I felt as though I'd found home. I could learn how to become what before was only a vision. Now I could live it with others!

Daily concentration and meditation practices, over the past two years, have encouraged me to be aware of the ways I move towards my ideals and the ways I limit myself, impeding my development. With my sun and moon in the astological influence of Scorpio, I have a tendency to create and destroy. This often has made it difficult to sustain forward motion in myself, my relationships with others, and in my goals. As an effect, this cycle of create-destroy has led to a mistrust within myself. The cause of this self-sabotage was mostly unconscious within me until I became a student at the College of Metaphysics.

My Dharma is described in an intuitive report as *steadfastness* and at its very essence includes the qualities of loyalty, devotion, motion, and tenacity. Throughout my life this has afforded me the ability to hold an image in my mind and to stick with it until it becomes a reality. My personal life challenge has been to bring forth my Dharma so I can overcome the limitations that cause me to separate from others, myself and my dreams. The College has provided me with an environment for meeting this challenge.

I am reminded of an experience that afforded me exactly that opportunity. It was December here at the College of Metaphysics and traditionally a time for making bread. As a new student this would be my first opportunity to be a part of this activity. I was pretty excited. Every year the residents of the College of Metaphysics bake hundreds of homemade rolls and personally deliver them to the neighbors in the surrounding community. On the morning of the second day I was given the opportunity to knead the dough. This was new to me and at about five to ten minutes into the kneading I wanted to quit. I wasn't giving it my all and was starting to feel withdrawn. The familiar pain was right there, interwoven into my growing separation. I continued to knead the dough half-heartedly, until the pain got to be too much. I started to leave when Dr. Pam Blosser called out "Don't you leave, you stay right here!" It took everything I had inside me to keep from just walking out. I stayed, and from that point on Dr. Barbara Condron stayed with me, giving me her love and attention. I soon discovered a new application of my dharma as I chose to stay with the dough. I was steadfast with my desire to change. It seemed like a lifetime but eventually the dough transformed and I was done. Later I realized the power of the choice I had made in that moment. It was a demonstration of my growing consciousness and a testament to the transformational nature of life at the College.

Through my experiences at the College of Metaphysics I have come to discover some of the key factors that help align me with my Dharma. In addition I have uncovered some of the causes for what I and others refer to as "funks." I see these times of shutting myself down and shutting others out as excursions into the depths of self-consumption. The stimulus for changing this form of polarity is quite pronounced here due to the wonderful examples of my teachers and the love of those I live with.

It was always the little things that did it. Like a permanant loop in my head. This would best describe the action and quality of what causes a "funk". For instance, there was a time when I was invited to participate in a workshop on intuitive reports here at the College. This was during a General Assembly weekend (a special weekend for the directors of the schools) and I and my classmates had the privilege of attending. To fulfill our college responsbilities we would need to leave halfway through the workshop. As the workshop started I didn't have a notebook for notes, I just didn't have it in my thoughts when I came out. When it came time to leave Dr. Barbara asked me how come it was I didn't have anything for notes. I really didn't have an answer. She firmly and directly told me why I needed to bring one and described the consciousness of the person who is prepared. I listened as she talked. Her tone told me that what she was teaching me was important but a part of me was hurt and angry.

When I left I just couldn't understand why she talked to me like that. The hurt I felt was deep and I couldn't ignore it. Slowly, my thoughts became reruns of the event and the experience, including the hurt. The more I thought the more separate and hurt I felt. As a type of protection mechanism I started to shut down from my inner self and my environment. This is a mental disconnection and is pretty intense. Like a snowball it builds and eventually I ended up isolating myself with a constant pull to go unconscious in sleep. Eventually Talina, my classmate, found me and we talked. I realized that Dr. Barbara was not the cause of my hurt. How I interpreted the experience and how I felt about it, was. I was grateful for her teaching and I knew I would do something different next time.

I am grateful for people who care. They've helped me change through their love. My wrong thinking is that by shutting pepole out I am protecting myself from hurt. In reality, the funkiness, of being seperate from people is more painful than the memory stimulus of the past. This I wouldn't fully understand until many "funks" later.

At the college my spirit has had the freedom to soar. I have discovered the heights of my passion, devotion, and caring about life, love and creation are matched by an equal depth of experience in apathy, separation and the resulting pain.

I am reminded of an example of this I experienced around Christmas while preparing for a special musical performance I was a part of. It was called *"Christmas in the Peace Dome"* and consisted of both traditional Christmas songs as well as SOM songs. As one of the musicians in the performance I was responsible for learning the songs, several of which I was leading. In addition I also memorized a stanza from the *Universal Peace Covenant* that I recited during one of the songs. Each song we sang had a section of the *Universal Peace Covenant* that was read along with it.

In preparation for this musical journey we would practice quite often. Through Dr. Barbara's elevated coordination of these songs it was turning out to be a truly brilliant movement in consciouness. I loved the connection, the intimacy and the expansiveness of what we were creating. As much as I loved what these experiences were giving me I would often times feel an anxiety about what I had to offer. Sometimes my mind would go to fear thoughts of not being able to live up to the expectations of what I thought Dr. Barbara or the group had about the music. This insecurity would paralyze me to the point of extreme sensitivity. My whole experience up until the actual performance was a shifting back and forth between elation and condemnation, each self-induced. In the end, it was great.

I was connected because I stuck with it. I trudged through the akwardness of my new experience to become a little closer to seeing that I am the cause of my feelings, my experiences and my life. It was the qualities of allowance, acceptance, openess and love that once again aided in my transforamtion, expanding my options.

About a month ago I committed to changing this unpredictable roller coaster by practicing something different. This image is the result of close to a year's worth of work in understanding how I can embody the quality of consciousness described as steadfastness. It was first sketched out upon hearing the words of Dr. Barbara at the end of our Intuitive reports class here on campus. Her thoughts that night seemed to bring it all together for me, culminating the different pieces of an inner puzzle.

This image that I have drawn is a symbolic representation of a growing awareness that I have recently begun to see with newfound clarity and simplicity. In addition to this it is also a pictorial reflection of a state of consciousness that I would best describe as *perpetual motion in the ability to sustain continual spiritual growth.*

In the center of the image is a heart with the words **"Causing Intentional Crisis."** These were the words used by Dr. Barbara to describe the action of open-hearted giving demonstrated by a person who chooses to go beyond what they think they are capable of. Oftentimes this can be stimulated by a need in another person. For instance, say you have planned out your entire day and it is full with activities that need your attention. Then somewhere in your day an opportunity arises to respond to something that was not in your plan. Perhaps a friend needs a ride to the airport or your boss calls and needs you to come in. When these opportunities are embraced it causes *intentional* crisis. This crisis is not unbidden or even unwanted. This kind of crisis is a conscious choice. This only comes from an open heart that cares about the needs of others.

The benefit is that this action of love and generosity creates the space to truly utilize more of our minds. Memory, attention and imagination – all the ingredients of reasoning – are all required to find a solution as to how to integrate the greater stretch into your day. From these choices a shift is made from brain to heart and into Mind. Through this movement, we can come to know more of ourselves.

Causing intentional crisis can also arise when we surrender to accepting greater responsibility. When opportunity knocks and our decision to invite her in is based on our old memory thoughts then most likely we end up rejecting growth. Our failure to stretch denies ourselves fulfillment, thus we (and situations) stay the same.

When I have a commitment to stretch beyond my limitations then I am the one directing the change in my life.

I have recognized that by continually giving of myself in the present moment to a greater vision of what I and humanity are becoming I can infuse each activity with a higher purpose that has a global, beneficial influence for all. This state of being connects the reality of the present moment with the image held within my mind of where I am going. It is truly in the choices made within each moment that create the manifestation of a dream. This I also received from Dr. Barbara, one morning at the brunch table. She helped us see the reality of what is required for the kinds of global change we desire. This was stimulated by the question: ***What do you think the world will be like in twenty years?*** I see that as choices are made which embody the consciousness of the vision desired, real change is occurring. When I have been in alignment with causing real change, I have found that I am truly creating and have all the energy that I need in the moment. I have had experiences here at the College where I am so involved with what I am creating that I end staying up until three o' clock in the morning or sometimes all night. The only other times I've experienced this infinite energy was when I would create artwork all night long.

The love and fulfillment inherent in causing forward motion is tremendous. Knowing its essence as it flows through mind is like riding the crest of a wave bound for the shores of my highest ideals, dreams and visions of what can be. By choosing to live with my mind, heart, and body on the outstretched bridge that spans what I have known and where I am going, I experience an intimacy with the grand plan of creation.

I am very grateful for the awareness that I have gained regarding sustaining perpetual spiritual growth and for all of the people who continue to love me when I really need it.

I am thankful for knowledge of how I can cause my inner vision to match my outer life. This has been one of the greatest gifts I have ever received. It is my hope that this image aids many others in making similar connections.

on Discernment

"....We see that there is a strong proclivity for the capacity to hold within the thinking many different trains of thought simultaneously. As this is an urge and is responded to, there is the capacity for this one to reveal a kind of illumination of connected energies amongst seemingly variant thoughts or substances. This has been cultivated within this one for much time and we see that there is the capacity within the present for this one to bring this to a point of fruition.

"There have been times when this one would investigate, in past lifetimes, particular avenues of expression. There were times when this one was a botanist, there were times when this one was a zoologist, there were times when this one was an architect. There has always been present within this one the tendency and therefore the urge within any physical endeavor or avenue of expression, any career as it were, to cause there to be an exhaustion of experience with it and we see that it has brought to this one particular understandings of cause and effect. There has been some difficulty at times in being able to understand the organic wholeness of all things because there was attachment to the physical expression themselves." (11400BGC1)

It's All about Choices

It is all about choices – in the moment.

The funny thing about choices is they are all in the present. You have to be in the now to make a choice. The past is a web of choices already made, experiences that have come and gone. The future is a projection of choices made today and yesterday, a web made of lines of probabilities, experiences that could happen.

One of my favorite poems is this four line thought inspirer:

Yesterday's history
Tomorrow's a mystery
Today's God's gift
That's why we call it the present.

Modern life endeavors to teach us to value choice. How many times did grownups ask you as a child, "What do you want to be when you grow up?" Imagine their response if you said, "I want Infinite Being!" This is the answer of every soul. Yet we teach our children to answer in physical terms – an astronaut, president, musician, computer programmer – largely because we lack the ability to see with the wisdom eye.

I continue to learn through and in life, reaching for wisdom in every experience, in my own way praying Solomon's prayer. Along the way I have learned more of Solomon's story, how he squandered his inheritance and according to some historians was a tragic figure. These scholars say Solomon never realized his potential. The physical evidence supports their conclusion. In the Universal Language of Mind, I see Solomon's life a bit differently.

In symbolic terms, what Solomon became aware of, Jesus realizes. What to Solomon is the ability to direct the full attention of the Mind toward gaining from each experience – be it good or bad, win or lose, physical or spiritual. Solomon is discernment, the ability to know the difference and make a choice based upon that knowing. The maturity in consciousness discernment produces is reflected through Jesus's exhortation to

"Seek ye first the kingdom of Heaven,
and all else will be added unto you."

From understanding the consciousness that Solomon represents we can hope to become an enlightened being, to in effect bring into existence the consciousness of one who will become a Christ.

True riches begin within the mind, in the spirit. The physical world, the pleasures of the flesh, are temporary. Every culture of spirituality, every religion, teaches this Truth for it is Universal. A Universal Truth describes a Universal Law. "*Seek ye first...*" is a whole Truth describing the employing of many Universal Laws. This is why as teachers in the School of Metaphysics we often call "*Seek ye first...*" the complete law.

A student argued, when he didn't approve of something I had said or done, "It's all about perception." He meant that people judge appearances. The comment stuck with me for some months, reverberating because I wanted to understand it fully. It opened a Pandora's box of childhood memories of people who talked one way and lived another. Symbolically, these are the Biblical Pharisees, aspects of self who fail to practice what they preach, aspects settling for pretending when they are actually one of many steps on the road to Being.

Intuitively I knew "It's" all about Truth, and perception is about our individual capability to grasp that Truth. I learned I needed to mature my outer, conscious mind. Like Solomon, who appeared to have everything, I needed to grow beyond wisdom. Materially abundant, Solomon was head smart. Yet Solomon is another step in a long series symbolized by a lineage which begins with God through generations: from Adam through to David on until it finds fruition in Jesus. I don't intend to preach to you here, rather I hope to open your eyes to what a wonderful manual for Intuitive, Spiritual Man the Bible is. That is the book's beauty and value, and the secret to its longevity and worldwide appeal.

The people in the Bible represent parts of Self in the journey to become compatible to our Maker. King Solomon represents permanent results, the benefit of reasoning. Solomon is the son of King David the controlling consciousness that learns the relationship between cause and effect. It is David who symbolizes the ability to reason. His offspring, Solomon, symbolizes the product of reasoning which is intuition.

Just as living by appearances is not enough to produce enlightenment, so being head smart is not enough. All the material possessions in the world do not bring happiness, enlightenment, or peace of mind. In "*The Invitation*", an innovative and unique presentation in the Peace Dome, His Holiness the Dalai Lama expresses this idea very well: *"Peace, in the sense of the absence of war, is of little value to someone who is dying of hunger or cold. It will not remove the pain of torture inflicted on a prisoner of conscience. It does not comfort those who have lost their loved ones in floods caused by senseless deforestation in a neighbouring country. Peace can only last where human rights are respected, where the people are fed, and where individuals and nations are free.*

"True happiness comes from a sense of inner peace and contentment, which in turn must be achieved through the cultivation of altruism, of love and compassion and elimination of ignorance, selfishness and greed."

As I read these words, I remember that it is Bathsheba who gives her son the name Solomon. Solomon means *peaceful*. Solomon wants wisdom and what the Lord gives him is a discerning heart. Solomon's incredible insight and understanding of human and animal nature is abundantly clear. He is ostentatious, showy in his wealth, egotistical we might call him. Hence the "big head" overshadows his heart, bringing the two out of balance.

Solomon is much like us when we want to be spiritual yet our hearts are divided by a head populated with many wives, children, possessions – both figuratively and quite literally. We cling to something else. We are like the young Christian who loves the Lord – but he is mesmerized by internet porn. Or like the businessman who sees himself as doing good – yet he tolerates unethical practices in his business. Or like a country that wages war because it desires security. Or like any one of us, when we say we are doing the best we can, knowing we are not.

We can cling desperately to something in our lives which we know is not in our best interest. It might be a relationship we know is wrong. Perhaps it is some practice we know is wrong. Yet we refuse to change. We insist we cannot choose. This was Solomon's problem. He had a divided heart. He loved the Lord, but he loved his foreign wives. And he loved his own wisdom. He felt that he had more insight into ruling people and lands than God did. His heart was not loyal like his father David's. So although the kingdom looked secure, internally it began to erode away.

Life is all about choices. In the present. It is making choices whose effects we willingly want to live with. Solomon asked for wisdom to rule God's people. What the Lord gave him was a discerning heart. Thus he learned how to heed his conscience. When he did, he came to understand polarity, the pairs of opposites in the physical world.

The challenge of Solomon is admitting what is most important to you and choosing accordingly. When you do, you know every experience counts. Every experience produces something. The choice we make determines what is produced.

Discerning choices contribute to the consciousness that culminates in Jesus, the knower who becomes the Christ. I believe this is the destiny of every human being: to become a spiritually enlightened Being knowing where she came from and where he is going. Being illumined in the moment is being fully conscious of your thoughts. When you know your thoughts, you can entrain head and heart bringing light into your world.

Wise choices in the now make Light for us all and I trust reading these words have done so for you.

from a Dharma Profile on

Discernment

"....As this one becomes more self accepting there are open to this one opportunities to perceive in different levels of consciousness or different expressions of creative thought. As this would be understood by the self, there could be the opening to release attachments to how the thought is constructed or what it contains. It is through the cultivation of knowing the self as being that will afford this one the freedom, for it will aid this one to separate the thinking consciousness from that which is thought of. When this occurs, then there will be the viewpoint needed for there to be the discernment through all expressions of thought, be they refined or more gross." (11400BGC1)

Barbara Condron teaches the unfolding of consciousness, including Taraka Yoga and Psi Counseling, at the College of Metaphysics. She lives on campus with her husband Daniel and their son Hezekiah, and is currently writing books on the mystic children, the chakras and Kundalini.

Additional titles available from SOM Publishing include:

Every Dream is about the Dreamer by Dr. Barbara Condron
ISBN: 0944386-27-X $13.00

Peacemaking: 9 Lessons for Changing Yourself, Relationships, & World
Dr. Barbara Condron ISBN: 0944386-31-8 $12.00

The Tao Te Ching Interpreted & Explained
Dr. Daniel R. Condron ISBN: 0944385-30-x $15.00

How to Raise an Indigo Child
Dr. Barbara Condron ISBN: 0944386-29-6 $14.00

Atlantis: The History of the World Vol. 1
Drs. Daniel & Barbara Condron ISBN: 0944386-28-8 $15.00

Karmic Healing by Dr. Laurel Clark ISBN: 0944386-26-1 $15.00

The Bible Interpreted in Dream Symbols - Drs. Condron, Condron, Matthes, Rothermel ISBN: 0944386-23-7 $18.00

Spiritual Renaissance– Elevating Your Conciousness for the Common Good
Dr. Barbara Condron ISBN: 0944386-22-9 $15.00

Superconscious Meditation - Kundalini & Understanding the Whole Mind
Dr. Daniel R. Condron ISBN 0944386-21-0 $13.00

First Opinion: Wholistic Health Care in the 21st Century
Dr. Barbara Condron ISBN 0944386-18-0 $15.00

The Dreamer's Dictionary-Dr. Barbara Condron ISBN 0944386-16-4 $15.00

The Work of the Soul
Dr. Barbara Condron, ed. ISBN 0944386-17-2 $13.00

Uncommon Knowledge: Past Life & Health Readings
Dr. Barbara Condron, ed. ISBN 0944386-19-9 $13.00

The Universal Language of Mind – The Book of Matthew Interpreted
Dr. Daniel R. Condron ISBN 0944386-15-6 $13.00

Permanent Healing
Dr. Daniel R. Condron ISBN 0944386-12-1 $13.00

Dreams of the Soul - The Yogi Sutras of Patanjali
Dr. Daniel R. Condron ISBN 0944386-11-3 $9.95

Kundalini Rising: Mastering Your Creative Energies
Dr. Barbara Condron ISBN 0944386-13-X $13.00

To order write:

School of Metaphysics
World Headquarters
163 Moon Valley Road
Windyville, Missouri 65783 U.S.A.

Enclose a check or money order payable in U.S. funds to SOM with any order. Please include $4.00 for postage and handling of books, $8 for international orders.

A complete catalogue of all book titles, audio lectures and courses, and videos is available upon request.

Visit us on the Internet at *http://www.som.org*
e-mail: som@som.org

About the School of Metaphysics

We invite you to become a special part of our efforts to aid in enhancing and quickening the process of spiritual growth and mental evolution of the people of the world. The School of Metaphysics, a not-for-profit educational and service organization, has been in existence for three decades. During that time, we have taught tens of thousands directly through our course of study in applied metaphysics. We have elevated the awareness of millions through the many services we offer. If you would like to pursue the study of mind and the transformation of Self to a higher level of being and consciousness, you are invited to write to us at the School of Metaphysics World Headquarters in Windyville, Missouri 65783.

*The heart of the School of Metaphysic*s is a four-tiered course of study in mastering consciousness. Lessons introduce you to the Universal Laws and Truths which guide spiritual and physical evolution. Consciousness is explored and developed through mental and spiritual disciplines which enhance your physical life and enrich your soul progression. For every concept there is a means to employ it through developing your own potential. Level One includes concentration, visualization (focused imagery), meditation, and control of life force and creative energies, all foundations for exploring the multidimensional Self.

*Experts in the Universal Language of Min*d, we teach how to remember and understand the inner communication received through dreams. We are the sponsors of the National Dream Hotline®, an annual educational service offered the last weekend in April. Study centers are located throughout the Midwestern United States. If there is not a center near you, you can receive the first series of lessons through correspondence with a teacher at our headquarters.

For those desiring spiritual renewal, weekends at our Moon Valley Ranch offer calmness and clarity. Spiritual Focus Weekends center around a theme – kundalini, genius, meditation, influence – or explore marriage, parenting, or your purpose in life. Each includes an intuitive report designed for the session and given in your presence. Mentored by College instructors and Psi counselors, these weekends are experiences in multidimensional awareness.

The Universal Hour of Peace was initiated by the School of Metaphysics at noon Universal Time (GMT) on October 24, 1995 in conjunction with the 50th anniversary of the United Nations. We believe that peace on earth is an idea whose time has come. To realize this dream, we invite you to join with others throughout the world by dedicating your thoughts and actions to peace through reading the Universal Peace Covenant as ONE VOICE at midnight December 31st. Living peaceably begins by thinking peacefully. Please contact us about how you can participate.

There is the opportunity to aid in the growth and fulfillment of our work. Donations supporting the expansion of the School of Metaphysics' efforts are a valuable way for you to aid humanity. As a not-for-profit publishing house, SOM Publishing is dedicated to the continuing publication of research findings that promote peace, understanding and good will for all of Mankind. It is dependent upon the kindness and generosity of sponsors to do so. Authors donate their work and receive no royalties. We have many excellent manuscripts awaiting a benefactor.

One hundred percent of the donations made to the School of Metaphysics are used to expand our services. Donations are being received for Project Octagon, the first educational building on the College of Metaphysics campus. The campus is located in the beautiful Ozark Mountains of Missouri. This proposed multipurpose structure will include an auditorium, classrooms, library and study areas, a cafeteria, and potential living quarters for up to 100 people. We expect to finance this structure through corporate grants and personal endowments. Donations to the School of Metaphysics are tax-exempt under 501(c)(3) of the Internal Revenue Code. We appreciate any contribution you are free to make. With the help of people like you, our dream of a place where anyone desiring Self awareness can receive wholistic education will become a reality.

We send you our Circle of Love.

The Universal Peace Covenant

Peace is the breath of our spirit. It wells up from within the depths of our being to refresh, to heal, to inspire.

Peace is our birthright. Its eternal presence exists within us as a memory of where we have come from and as a vision of where we yearn to go.

Our world is in the midst of change. For millennia, we have contemplated, reasoned, and practiced the idea of peace. Yet the capacity to sustain peace eludes us. To transcend the limits of our own thinking we must acknowledge that peace is more than the cessation of conflict. For peace to move across the face of the earth we must realize, as the great philosophers and leaders before us, that all people desire peace. We hereby acknowledge this truth that is universal. Now humanity must desire those things that make for peace.

We affirm that peace is an idea whose time has come. We call upon humanity to stand united, responding to the need for peace. We call upon each individual to create and foster a personal vision for peace. We call upon each family to generate and nurture peace within the home. We call upon each nation to encourage and support peace among its citizens. We call upon each leader, be they in the private home, house of worship or place of labor, to be a living example of peace for only in this way can we expect peace to move across the face of the earth.

World Peace begins within ourselves. Arising from the spirit peace seeks expression through the mind, heart, and body of each individual. Government and laws cannot heal the heart. We must transcend whatever separates us. Through giving love and respect, dignity and comfort, we come to know peace. We learn to love our neighbors as we love ourselves bringing peace into the world. We hereby commit ourselves to this noble endeavor.

Peace is first a state of mind. Peace affords the greatest opportunity for growth and learning which leads to personal happiness. Self-direction promotes inner peace and therefore leads to outer peace. We vow to heal ourselves through forgiveness, gratitude, and prayer. We commit to causing each and every day to be a fulfillment of our potential, both human and divine.

Peace is active, the motion of silence, of faith, of accord, of service. It is not made in documents but in the minds and hearts of men and women. Peace is built through communication. The open exchange of ideas is necessary for discovery, for well-being, for growth, for progress whether within one person or among many. We vow to speak with sagacity, listen with equanimity, both free of prejudice, thus we will come to know that peace is liberty in tranquillity.

Peace is achieved by those who fulfill their part of a greater plan. Peace and security are attained by those societies where the individuals work closely to serve the common good of the whole. Peaceful coexistence between nations is the reflection of man's inner tranquillity magnified. Enlightened service to our fellowman brings peace to the one serving, and to the one receiving. We vow to live in peace by embracing truths that apply to us all.

Living peaceably begins by thinking peacefully. We stand on the threshold of peace-filled understanding. We come together, all of humanity, young and old of all cultures from all nations. We vow to stand together as citizens of the Earth knowing that every question has an answer, every issue a resolution. As we stand, united in common purpose, we hereby commit ourselves in thought and action so we might know the power of peace in our lifetimes.

Peace be with us all ways. May Peace Prevail On Earth.

created by teachers in the School of Metaphysics 1996-7